"This book is groundbreaking. Local governments, whether urban or rural, play a critical role in delivering public services, essential to the realization of economic, social, and cultural rights. By aligning their economic policies with human rights, local governments can significantly contribute to transforming economies for the benefit of people and the planet."

Nada Youssef A. Al Nashif, *UN Deputy High Commissioner for Human Rights*

"A compelling and timely book that discusses whether the principle of 'leave no one behind' can be realized by applying a human rights–based approach to the economic paradigms, particularly in cities. What roles do politics and administration as well as actors from business and civil society play? It is about community infrastructures for water, food, and housing which should not be seen as commodities, but as resources available to all."

Shams Asadi, *Human Rights Commissioner, Vienna, Austria*

"This volume addresses a wide spectrum of economic issues related to human rights at the local level, exploring both familiar and less-examined topics. It is essential reading for anyone seeking to broaden their understanding of human rights while working to advance justice, equality, and sustainable development."

SHIN Gyonggu, *Chair, World Human Rights Cities Forum Global Steering Committee; Executive Director, Gwangju International Center, South Korea*

"An imaginative collection that will reinvigorate thinking on how economies can serve people and nature rather than the other way around and the role of human rights in that vital endeavour. The ideas, models, and case studies from around the world are locally conceived and operationalised, offering numerous ways of thinking and realising bottom-up change that could yet spur greater economic democracy. This is a novel and welcome work that will contribute to our collective efforts to begin anew."

Margot Salomon, *Associate Professor of International Law and Human Rights, London School of Economics and Political Science, UK*

"The sharply rising economic inequalities of income and wealth, as a result of neoliberal global economic policies, have undermined the social fabric and democratic coherence of our societies and led to the current polarization and radicalization. The editors and authors of this book counter this trend by arguing for human rights–based economies to be implemented at the local level of human rights cities."

Manfred Nowak, *Professor of International Law and Human Rights, University of Vienna, Austria, and Secretary General of the Global Campus of Human Rights, Venice, Italy*

Human Rights Economies and Subnational Governance

This book examines the understudied area of subnational human rights and the human rights economy.

Against the context of increasing economic and political power of local level governments – both cities and subnational regions – this interdisciplinary volume provides a crucial examination of economic policies that are grounded in human rights principles and obligations while being implemented in the places people live. Policies which promote economic justice and prosperity present many opportunities and challenges, and this book proposes ways in which local economic policies can respect, protect, and fulfil human rights, with positive multiplier effects at the national and global levels.

This book will be of keen interest to scholars, students, and practitioners in human rights, economics, law, development, and urban studies; as well as professionals and policymakers involved in local economic development planning and the implementation of human rights norms.

Savitri Bisnath is Senior Director of Global Policy at the Institute of Race, Power and Political Economy at the New School, USA.

Morten Kjaerum is Adjunct Professor at the University of Aalborg, Denmark, and Affiliated Scholar at the Raoul Wallenberg Institute (RWI), Sweden.

Martha F. Davis is Distinguished Professor of Law and Co-director of the Center on Global Law & Justice at Northeastern University, USA. She is an affiliated scholar at the Raoul Wallenberg Institute, Sweden.

Routledge Studies in Human Rights

The Routledge Studies in Human Rights series publishes high-quality and cross-disciplinary scholarship on topics of key importance in human rights today. In a world where human rights are both celebrated and contested, this series is committed to creating stronger links between disciplines and exploring new methodological and theoretical approaches in human rights research. Aimed towards both scholars and human rights professionals, the series strives to provide both critical analysis and policy-oriented research in an accessible form. The series welcomes work on specific human rights issues as well as on cross-cutting themes and institutional perspectives.

Series Editors: Mark Gibney, UNC Asheville, USA, Bonny Ibhawoh, McMaster University, Canada, and Rossana Rocha Reis, University of São Paulo, Brazil.

Human Rights and Climate Change
The Law on Loss and Damage
Linnéa Nordlander

States, Human Rights, and Distant Strangers
The Normative Justification of Extraterritorial Obligations in Human Rights Law
Angela Müller

Childism, Intersectionality and the Rights of the Child
The Myth of a Happy Childhood
Rebecca Adami

Transnational Asylum
Toward a Principled Framework
Nikolas Feith Tan

Human Rights Economies and Subnational Governance
Theory and Practice
Edited by Savitri Bisnath, Morten Kjaerum and Martha F. Davis

Human Rights Economies and Subnational Governance

Theory and Practice

Edited by Savitri Bisnath, Morten Kjaerum and Martha F. Davis

Routledge
Taylor & Francis Group
LONDON AND NEW YORK

First published 2026
by Routledge
4 Park Square, Milton Park, Abingdon, Oxon OX14 4RN

and by Routledge
605 Third Avenue, New York, NY 10158

Routledge is an imprint of the Taylor & Francis Group, an informa business

British Library Cataloguing-in-Publication Data
A catalogue record for this book is available from the British Library

ISBN: 978-1-032-75599-1 (hbk)
ISBN: 978-1-032-75620-2 (pbk)
ISBN: 978-1-003-47484-5 (ebk)

DOI: 10.4324/9781003474845

Typeset in Times New Roman
by SPi Technologies India Pvt Ltd (Straive)

This book is dedicated to all those who on a daily basis promote and protect human rights by building local economic systems for a more equal, just, and peaceful society with shared prosperity for all.

Contents

List of Illustrations

Figures

Table

Contributors

Maria Ron Balsera is the Executive Director at the Center for Economic and Social Rights. She completed her PhD in Education and Human Development at Bielefeld University in 2014, on a Marie Curie Fellowship. She also holds an MSc in Human Rights from the London School of Economics.

Ester Barinaga is Professor at Lund University School of Economics and Management, Sweden. She specializes in social innovations aiming to make cities more inclusive.

Savitri Bisnath is a feminist political economist and the Senior Director of Global Policy at the Institute of Race, Power and Political Economy at the New School. She was formerly Senior Economist at the United Nations Office of the High Commissioner for Human Rights and has a PhD from Cornell University.

Martha F. Davis is Distinguished Professor of Law at Northeastern University, where she co-directs the Center on Global Law & Justice, site of the International Justice Online Resource Hub. She is an affiliated professor with the Raoul Wallenberg Institute of Human Rights. Her scholarship focuses on local human rights implementation.

Giulio Ferrini is a chartered engineer with cross-sector experience spanning the private, public, and not-for-profit domains. He leads the Built Environment programme at the Institute for Human Rights and Business, where he focuses on advancing social and environmental responsibility in urban development and infrastructure.

Indraraj Gunasekara is an Attorney-at-Law, currently finalizing his MSc in the Sociology of Law at Lund University. His work includes litigation, legal research, and advocacy, with transnational experience, including a research internship at the Raoul Wallenberg Institute of Human Rights and Humanitarian Law, focusing on law, rights, and governance.

LaDawn Haglund is Associate Professor of Climate Justice at John Jay College, City University of New York. Her research analyses the social and political dimensions of sustainability and environmental governance, with a focus on frontline communities facing threats from climate change. She received her PhD in sociology from NYU in 2005.

Todd Howland is Visiting Professor, Environmental Justice Clinic, Vermont Law and Graduate School, USA. He is Senior Fellow, Institute for Race, Power and Political Economy, New School for Social Research, USA, and a former official, United Nations Office of the High Commissioner for Human Rights.

Claudia Ituarte-Lima is an international public lawyer with over 20 years of expertise in human rights, climate change, and biodiversity. Holding an MPhil from Cambridge and a PhD from UCL, she works as Thematic Lead and Senior Researcher at the Raoul Wallenberg Institute (RWI) and as Director of the Global Network for Human Rights and the Environment.

Mihir Kanade is the Head of the Department of International Law of the United Nations-mandated University for Peace (UPEACE) and Director of its Human Rights Centre. Dr Kanade currently serves as an independent expert of the United Nations Human Rights Council as part of its Expert Mechanism on the Right to Development. He chaired the UN drafting group of international experts to prepare a legally binding instrument on the Right to Development.

Morten Kjaerum is Adjunct Professor at the University of Aalborg, Denmark, and an affiliated scholar at RWI, Sweden. He was Director of the Danish Institute for Human Rights (1991–2008), the EU Agency for Fundamental Rights (2008–2015), and RWI (2015–2024), and a member of the UN Committee on the Elimination of Racial Discrimination from 2002 to 2008.

Sara Miellet is a researcher at the Utrecht University of Applied Sciences. At Utrecht University and the Netherlands Institute of Human Rights, she conducted a PhD study on the local politics of human rights and co-edited a book titled *The Urban Politics of Human Rights* (2022).

John Morrison has been CEO of the Institute for Human Rights and Business since its inception in 2009. He holds a number of formal advisor roles for governments, businesses, and intergovernmental organizations. His published books include *The Social License: How to Keep Your Organisation Legitimate* (2014) and *The Just Transition: A Systems-Thinking Approach to Climate Action* (2024).

Markus Möstl is Senior Legal Researcher at the International Centre for the Promotion of Human Rights at the Local and Regional Levels under the auspices of UNESCO in Graz, Austria, and Member of the Federal Commission for the Enforcement of Penalties and Measures (Austrian National Preventive Mechanism).

Zvimekria Clive Mukushwa is an independent researcher based in Zimbabwe. He holds a PhD in Local Government Studies from Midlands State University, Gweru, Zimbabwe.

Martin Mulwa is a heterodox economist specializing in macroeconomic and budget analysis with a human rights focus. His research covers public policy, gender, poverty, and labour markets. He holds a master's degree in economics from the University of Nairobi.

Edson Paul Mutema is Senior Lecturer and Chairperson, Department of Governance and Public Management, Midlands State University, Gweru, Zimbabwe. His research interests cover corruption studies, participatory budgeting, human rights in local governance, and local governance. He holds a Doctor of Philosophy degree in Local Governance Studies from Midlands State University, Zimbabwe.

Gerd Oberleitner is Professor of International Law and the Law of International Organisations, UNESCO Chair in Human Rights and Human Security, and Director of the European Training and Research Centre for Human Rights and Democracy at the Law Faculty, University of Graz.

David Radcliffe is the Director of State and Local Policy at the New School's Institute on Race, Power and Political Economy in New York. He previously served in the Office of Connecticut State Treasurer and with the Federal Reserve Bank of Boston.

Klaus Starl is the Director of the International Centre for the Promotion of Human Rights at Local and Regional Levels under the auspices of UNESCO in Graz, Austria. For over three decades, Starl has worked as a consultant and trainer for local and regional authorities, as well as for European and International Organisations.

Maria José Veramendi Villa is a Human Rights Officer at the Economic, Social and Cultural Rights Section in OHCHR Geneva.

Pradeep Wagle is the Chief of the Economic, Social and Cultural Rights Section in OHCHR Geneva.

Michael Windfuhr is Deputy Director of the German Institute for Human Rights, the national human rights institution of Germany. He is a member of the UN-Committee on Economic, Social and Cultural Rights, with a focus on the right to work, labour rights, social security, and the right to adequate standard of living.

Amos Zevure is Lecturer in the Department of Peace and Security Studies, Midlands State University, Zimbabwe.

Foreword

Human rights are not abstract global ideals. Respect for, or lack of respect for, those rights impacts the lives of people every day and shapes our communities and neighbourhoods. It is in cities around the world that these rights are most tangible and the places where they can be claimed, defended, and realized.

In recent years, we have witnessed a growing recognition of the essential role local and regional governments play in advancing human rights. The intertwined crises of our time – from rising inequalities, health and climate emergencies to democratic erosion – have made abundantly clear the need for a decisive push of the international municipal movement, fostering the membership to embrace human rights and explore the links with local service provision.

The idea of the Human Rights City, once a bold vision, is today an expanding global practice. Across continents, local governments are embracing principles of dignity, inclusion, transparency, and accountability, while also innovating how services are delivered, how participation is fostered, and how budgets are aligned with social justice.

At UCLG, we have long argued that the future of human rights is local, and this important book comes at a pivotal moment. It provides an opportunity to reflect on how far we've come, and how much further we still must go. The contributions collected here speak to a shared ambition: to rethink local governance and economic systems in ways that are accountable to international human rights standards and responsive to local needs. It also highlights a critical gap: while we are seeing innovation and commitment on the ground, we still lack a cohesive framework to define what constitutes a Human Rights City or how human rights–based economies can be systematically implemented.

The absence of a comprehensive framework should not be mistaken for a lack of progress. Rather, it speaks to the need for dialogue, mutual learning, and solidarity. The Local Social Covenant – a multilevel, multistakeholder platform that amplifies our collective voice – is the vehicle to support the creation of a multilateral space from the bottom up, where civil society and local governments can shape a roadmap for a renewed social contract based on the priorities of communities.

This book also holds special significance for our Committee on Social Inclusion, Participatory Democracy, and Human Rights. From advancing the Charter-Agenda on Human Rights in the City to supporting the global campaign "10, 100, 1000 Human Rights Cities and Territories by 2030," local and regional governments have shown that they are not just implementers – they are pioneers. This book reinforces that belief and calls on us to deepen our collaboration – among governments, civil society, and international partners – to build a more just and sustainable future from the ground up, and a human rights economy that serves everyone, everywhere.

Let this book be both a milestone and a reference for the work ahead. Let it also be a tribute to all of those working every day at local level to improve the lives of their communities.

Emilia Saiz Carrancedo
UCLG Secretary General

Acknowledgements

The editors are grateful to the many individuals who provided feedback, research, and other critical support for this book.

The following individuals at Northeastern University School of Law (NUSL) provided excellent research and editorial assistance, without which the project would not have been possible: Ashley Agonstinelli, Heather Ducharme, William Maione, and Zachary Varrichhione. Craig Eastland provided exceptional reference support. William Fegan and other members of the NUSL faculty support staff provided indispensable administrative assistance.

We also extend our gratitude to the following authors and publishers who kindly granted us permission to reprint copyrighted material:

For Figure 4.1, Institute for Human Rights and Business (2019), Dignity by Design, https://www.dignitybydesign.org/, reprinted with permission of Sam Simmons of Institute for Human Rights and Business.

For Figure 11.1, S.R.A. Arnstein, A Ladder of Citizen Participation, *Journal of the American Planning Association*. 1969, Vol. 35 No. 4, 216–224. DOI: 10.1080/01944366908977225, used with permission of the *Journal of the American Planning Association*, permission conveyed through Copyright Clearance Center, Inc.

For Figure 13.1, Social Trade Organization 2016, reprinted with the permission of Jaap Vink of the Social Trade Organization.

For excerpts from the following materials, reprinted and acknowledged in accordance with the United Nations copyright permission policy:

- United Nations. 2021. "Operationalizing the right to development in achieving the Sustainable Development Goals." Thematic Study of the Expert Mechanism on the Right to Development. doi:A/HRC/48/63.
- United Nations. 2023. "Draft International Covenant on the Right to Development, Report by the Chair-Rapporteur of the Working Group on the Right to Development, Zamir Akram, A/HRC/54/50."
- United Nations. 2023. "Draft international covenant on the right to development, with commentaries, A/HRC/54/50/Add.1."
- United Nations. 2023. "Draft international covenant on the right to development: consideration of comments and textual proposals, A/HRC/54/50/Add.2."

Introduction

Towards Local Human Rights Economies

Savitri Bisnath, Morten Kjaerum, and Martha F. Davis

Introduction

The concepts of Human Rights Cities and human rights-based economies have developed rapidly over the past decade across all continents. Yet much work remains to be done to fully conceptualize both phenomena. Clearer criteria for what it means to be a Human Rights City –potentially serving as the basis for formal labelling or accreditation – have been under discussion for some time. Similarly, while human rights-based economic models and budgeting practices are increasingly being explored, a comprehensive framework has not been established.

With this book, we aim to contribute to the ongoing conceptual and practical development of human rights-based economic policies and practices at the local level, recognizing that such efforts may strengthen both the Human Rights City profile and our broader understanding of the human rights economy. This volume is exploratory in nature, and we look forward to seeing future academic work build upon these initial steps, offering deeper insights into the realities across different continents. Given the growing global and local inequalities alongside the declining respect for human rights and democratic principles, we believe that this work is both timely and urgent.

Within this context, it is important to discuss questions such as: What is the purpose of an economy and economic policies? Across different schools of thought on the subject of the economy – e.g., capitalist, welfare economics, feminist economics – there is general agreement that the economy and associated economic policies should serve to improve the well-being of people. They should enable people to look after themselves and thrive, and contribute to their communities and the larger society. Achieving these goals requires evidence-based macroeconomic and microeconomic policies that create enabling environments for people to realize their potential.

Different economic systems deploy distinct approaches, including through fiscal and monetary policies, to achieve the general objective of societal well-being. The neoclassical mode of production (and in particular neoliberalism) prioritizes private ownership, personal responsibility, a small administrative state, and 'free trade' to meet its objective, with workers, consumers, and

DOI: 10.4324/9781003474845-1

producers positioned in neutral terms. While capitalism promotes the view that people must "pull themselves up by their bootstraps", welfare states, exemplified by the Nordic countries, have utilized redistributive policies and labour protections in line with human rights to better facilitate the well-being of their citizens and the economic security of their countries.

Economic tools, including the budget and infant industry protection, have been used by countries to develop the structure of their economies in areas such as agriculture, manufacturing, electronics, and services, including financial, information, and telecommunication services. Within this context, economic activities at the local level are essential for economic prosperity and societal well-being. Local-level governance – economic, social, and political – is critical to the achievement of well-being, inclusive economies, and shared prosperity.

In situations of uneven development, marginalization, and multiple and intersecting forms of discrimination, evidence-based local-level governance policies, programmes, and processes informed by human rights obligations and principles can enhance well-being. In addition, they can facilitate the progressive realization of human rights, particularly economic and social rights. Such policies include the budget, transparent governance processes, and participatory processes, all of which contribute to increased accountability and trust in institutions and facilitate democratic governance. From an economic point of view, they also facilitate efficiency and erode corruption.

A political economy analysis of the economic realities of the end of the 20th century and the beginning of the 21st century reveals that the effects of economic globalization are uneven and unequal within and across countries and regions. This is in part because they are constitutive of context-specific socio-economic realities, levels of development, and the positions of individual countries – in terms of production, distribution, and consumption – within the world system (Benería and Bisnath, 2004). Current economic uncertainties and tensions and the polycrisis underline that there is no necessary relationship between open and competitive markets and the achievement of well-being, sustainable development, shared prosperity, equality, justice, and peace. In other words, economic growth as defined by gross domestic product is necessary but insufficient. The economic reality of the last decades illustrates that inequality and uneven development can increase in the presence of economic growth. In addition, and as feminist economists have both argued and illuminated, globalization, the market, and economic theories, policies, and their applications are informed by power relations as well as racialized, patriarchal values and norms, with differential effects on low-, middle-, and high-income countries and the lives of women and men therein.

In this book, we highlight the many ways in which human rights-enhancing economic policies, programmes, investment decisions, and business models at the local level can tackle root causes of poverty, inequality, and uneven development and redress structural barriers to inclusive economies and shared prosperity. It is urgent that human rights-enhancing economic policies centre people, the places in which they live, and the planet in decisions about production, distribution, and consumption of goods and services. Such policies can result in human rights economies that achieve the objectives of well-being and shared prosperity for all.

Chapters in this volume argue that human rights obligations and principles such as participation, transparency, and accountability should transform economic thinking and policies and challenge neoliberal approaches of the international financial architecture. Practitioners and international institutions have begun to loosely refer to this area of work at the nexus of human rights and economics as the quest to advance a "human rights economy". As economists Giovanni Dosi and Nobel Prize winner Joseph Stiglitz (2021) note, we need a radical departure with radically different foundations:

> The economy has to be analyzed as a complex evolving system. [...] Inequality is an endemic property of the system and it affects its short- and long-term performance. Its drivers and the policies to curb it ought to be under the spotlight. [...] Markets do not work in a vacuum. The functioning of a market economy depends on the laws, rules, norms, and institutional structures under which it operates, all determined by power relations; and the outcomes it produces affect the distribution of power itself.

This volume aims to contribute to emerging discussions about the role of human rights obligations and principles in economic policy-making and to reimagine current economic systems for a world where everyone is able to live dignified lives and countries are able to co-exist in peace and shared prosperity.

Part 1: Human Rights Economy

The first part of this volume situates the human rights economy in relation to other economic theories and the right to development. Further, this part positions human rights economy in relation to sub-national structures at the regional and municipal level.

In the opening chapter, "Towards Localized Economic Policies for People and the Planet", Savitri Bisnath highlights the growing consensus among economists and policy makers that the current economic model, based on neoliberal economic assumptions and increasing protectionism, is failing to deliver economic prosperity for all and resulting in worldwide uncertainty and potential instability. In recent decades, consumption and production models and patterns are contributing to increasing inequities and the climate crisis. Bisnath argues that the root and structural causes of economic inequality within and between countries are grounded in global, regional, and national economic and political systems, wherein the groups most left behind experience multiple, persistent, and intersecting forms of human rights violations. These realities challenge us to forge new ideas and measurements, and a new course of action grounded in human rights with people and the planet at the centre. There is an urgent need for economic policies that better facilitate inclusive economies and sustainable development, and ensure that human rights are respected, protected, and fulfilled.

Building on the analyses of feminist economists, Bisnath argues that asymmetric power relations often influence political and economic processes as well as spatial realities and the built environment. The chapter outlines key elements of localized human rights economies and makes suggestions for operationalizing the human rights economy with its context-specific iterations at the local level. Bisnath makes the case for localized human rights-enhancing economic policies, investments, and programmes that can contribute to increased equality, inclusion, and prosperity. The human rights economic conceptual framework presented in this chapter provides a plausible road ahead for countries looking to operationalize the human rights economy with its positive multiplier effects for societies and countries.

In "Right to Development and Local Economies", Mihir Kanade notes that local economies are deeply entrenched in a multiplex network such that opportunities and challenges to thrive emanate from all levels, including the international and national. From the normative lens of the human right to development, Kanade explores the correlation between local economies that both enhance human rights and improve human well-being and sustainable development. Kanade argues that constructing human rights economies at the sub-national levels can greatly contribute to the enhancement of the right to development and the human rights of individuals and communities. He argues that the effective operationalization of the right to development programmes can contribute to the building of local economies that mainstream and enhance all human rights.

This chapter presents the right to development as an empowering normative framework for the design of societies grounded in rights and highlights the importance of implementing the human rights principle to participate in, contribute to, and enjoy self-determined and sustainable development. Kanade notes that the right to development rejects an image of local economies in watertight compartments that operate in isolation from each other and recognizes that the local is very much connected to the national and international order. The chapter underlines the recognition that States are obligated, not only within their respective jurisdictions but also extraterritorially and collectively, to foster an enabling international and national environment for local economies to thrive. The chapter concludes by noting that the objective of establishing local economies that mainstream and enhance human rights can benefit greatly from the conceptual framework of the human rights economy.

Sara Miellet's chapter, "Scaling the Human Rights Economy: Sub-national Engagements", seeks to complement institution- and actor-centred approaches and argues for an understanding that considers the sub-national as an arena through which the human rights economy can be developed in conversation with existing approaches and practices. The chapter explores some of the ways in which the human rights economy approach can strengthen local and regional authorities' and civil society's engagement with human rights and vice versa. It explores the potential of a human rights economy approach for local and regional engagements with human rights, including human rights cities. Miellet draws on research conducted in Dutch and German contexts, with a focus on migration politics as an example.

The examples presented in the chapter highlight concrete ways in which social movements have been intensifying 'accountability politics' and scrutinizing hitherto unknown municipal activities, such as municipal shareholding. Miellet argues that the human rights economy concept provides a framework which makes sense of the interconnections between different sub-national struggles for rights. It also provides local actors with another avenue to address longstanding concerns and critiques by drawing on human rights principles such as accountability and by bringing into focus often obscured dimensions of local and regional authorities such as municipal management of finances. Rather than dismissing municipal human rights commitments as symbolic politics, activists and political actors using human rights sought to move beyond critiques to focus pragmatically on the role of the municipality as a shareholder and the ways in which financial policies can be harmonized with local human rights commitments.

In the chapter "Human Rights Economies and the Role of Local Government Public Budgets", Todd Howland and Martin Mulwa focus on public budgets as one of the most powerful economic tools to meet the needs of individuals and communities, especially marginalized communities living in conditions of poverty. They argue that to ensure any human right, whether it is the right to health care or education, or civil and political rights, financial resources are necessary. However, in many countries, public budgets do not reflect human rights standards and obligations, and the budget planning and execution processes do not always apply human rights principles such as participation, transparency, and accountability. This chapter discusses the ways in which human rights principles and obligations can be applied in the budget-making process, with the aim of progressively achieving the full realization of rights in line with the leave no one behind principle and the promotion of equality and non-discrimination.

Through budgeting, the State establishes its priorities and commits to concrete actions which may improve or limit the enjoyment of certain rights. The authors note that when human rights obligations and principles are embedded in the process and content of public budgets at the local and national levels, a pathway is provided that ensures that fiscal policies serve the needs of people, particularly those living in conditions of poverty and facing multiple forms of discrimination. A budget that is transparent and grounded in a State's human rights obligations and implemented and monitored with multi-stakeholder participation is essential for the realization of all human rights, the promotion of accountability, and the deepening of trust between the State and its people. Equally, local budgets that reflect adequate investments in essential public goods and services are important for realizing an adequate standard of living and redressing uneven development. At the sub-national level, governments can play a central role in enhancing human rights economies because they have stronger incentives to provide services consistent with local needs and preferences within the framework of their human rights obligations. The authors provide a Kenyan case study as a compelling example of the role of local budgets in better facilitating human rights and inclusive economies with shared prosperity.

Part 2: Local–National–International Nexus

Part 2 collects chapters addressing arenas of human rights that extend across longstanding jurisdictional boundaries between the local, national, and global. In these areas – taxation, climate, water governance, the built environment, and spatial planning – local communities are often on the front lines, the first to experience the effects of government missteps, unintended consequences, and lack of coordination between levels of government. As a whole, these chapters argue for greater recognition of the unique voice of local communities in shaping human rights-responsive policies in these arenas. They firmly assert the need to include local leadership in developing approaches designed to avoid or address negative economic impacts that impinge on fundamental human rights.

In "What Human Rights and the 5Rs Can Provide for the Reform of the Tax Architecture at the Global, National, and Local Levels", Maria Ron Balsera employs the prism of human rights to argue that tax reform at every level of government should be guided by the 5Rs of taxation: revenue, redistribution, re-pricing, representation, and reparations. As she points out, local tax architecture can play a critical role in achieving important local goals that have national and global resonance, including addressing wealth disparities, environmental concerns, and social issues. Globally, the current tax landscape is marked by corruption, inconsistencies, and a lack of transparency. These loopholes make it possible for multinational corporations and wealthy individuals to avoid contributing their fair share of taxes to support common projects and the public good. Balsera argues that international tax cooperation should be aligned with human rights in addressing a development agenda and that tax systems must be transparent, accountable, and participatory. Some of these elements are already realized at the local level, which can serve as a potential base for incubating more progressive approaches to tax justice. As the international community weighs alternative approaches to the current tax architecture, including the possibility of a UN Tax Convention, Balsera argues that the role of local taxation should be part of the dialogue.

Indraraj Gunasekara and Claudia Ituarte-Lima tackle the formidable challenge of climate change in their chapter titled "Biosphere Defenders Operationalising the Prevention Principle in Climate Adaptation through Territorial Planning". As they note, most prescriptions for integrating human rights into climate change analyses and policies have focused on the national level. As a result, the role of sub-national actors as biosphere defenders is under-explored and under-appreciated. The authors argue that greater focus on sub-national developments and opportunities in the environmental arena is critical to the development of more regenerative economic models to replace the exploitation-centred models that inform the global economy. To drive this point home, Gunasekara and Ituarte-Lima explore several detailed case studies of indigenous biosphere defenders using traditional knowledge, individually and collectively, to adapt to climate changes in ways that promote biodiversity and sustainability in the long term.

Multi-level regulation and responding to environmental challenges are also themes of LaDawn Haglund's contribution, "Water Governance and Human Rights Economies". Recognizing the crucial importance of water and sanitation, and acknowledging the pressures placed on water access by climate change and commodification of this fundamental human right, Haglund examines the transformative potential of the human rights economies framework for this sector. While national and global policies are important elements of water governance, water and sanitation are in many respects quintessentially local, creating unique opportunities for community participation and accountability, potentially yielding rights-responsive governance structures. Examining a series of "moments" where policy interventions might be available and effective, Haglund concludes that there exists a real possibility of achieving human rights economies that deliver equitable and sustainable water governance. But though it is not beyond imagining, such systemic incorporation of human rights frames would require cultural, structural, and power-based shifts.

The final two chapters in this part turn to the spatial dynamics and demands of local human rights economies. In the first of these contributions, John Morrison and Giulio Ferrini ask, "Can human rights find a space in a just transition for the built environment?" They argue that cities are in a position to take a leadership role in ensuring that necessary actions to address climate change do not ignore concerns of social equity, i.e., cities can take leadership in the Just Transition to a more sustainable, low carbon economy. Achieving a Just Transition will require a particular focus on the built environment in urban centres, which account for a significant percentage of greenhouse gas emissions worldwide. To operationalize this agenda and balance the twin needs for climate action and social justice, the authors explore four foundational imperatives for urban centres drawn from international human rights framing documents: risk and adverse impact prevention, equal access to opportunities and benefits, accountability to and agency of affected groups, and transformational systems change.

In "Human Rights and Spatial Planning: Addressing the Increasing Tensions over Access to Land and Resources", Michael Windfuhr also turns to international law guidelines to develop a framework for local decision making as pressures increase regarding land use, particularly in urban areas. Climate change, agricultural policy, urban growth, and other factors have all contributed to growing conflicts over land use. Human rights guidelines are developing to address some of these issues, drawing on instruments such as the

International Covenant on Economic, Social, and Cultural Rights. However, Windfuhr identifies several important gaps, particularly in the arena of procedural protections when conflicts arise over issues such as land tenure. Given this, Windfuhr argues that the idea of human rights-based spatial planning should be expanded and used as a tool to deal with the increasing conflictuality of land use demands. Implemented at the local level, such a human rights approach can allow affected individuals and communities to be heard and provide accountability for complex land use decisions.

Part 3: Subnational Implementation of Human Rights Economy

The final part of the book critically examines current knowledge and practice regarding human rights-based budgeting and participatory budgeting. The authors offer in-depth analysis of the realities encountered at the local level, highlighting the complexity of implementing such policies even in contexts shaped by well-intentioned devolution and development strategies. A significant challenge identified is the prevalence of corruption, which annually diverts substantial resources from local budgets – funds that ought to be allocated to realizing human rights such as food, education, health, and other essential services, particularly for individuals and groups in vulnerable situations.

The concluding chapters of this section – and of the book – present practical case studies demonstrating how innovative economic instruments can be deployed to advance specific human rights objectives. In particular, they examine the application of social currencies and baby bonds as tools for promoting equity and inclusion. Taken together with the preceding analyses, these chapters aim to contribute to ongoing scholarly and policy debates, encouraging further innovation in addressing the growing inequalities and the erosion of respect for human rights and democratic values.

In their chapter "Towards the Realisation of a Human Rights Economy through Human Rights Budgeting at Local Level", Markus Möstl, Gerd Oberleitner, and Klaus Starl explore the role of local budgets in advancing a human rights economy. They argue that local governments, being closest to citizens, have a unique responsibility to allocate resources in ways that fulfil human rights obligations. However, their research indicates that current budget practices rarely reflect human rights standards systematically. Human rights budgeting – or a human rights-based approach to budgeting – would require principles like equality, transparency, and accountability to guide resource allocation and spending in a more systematic manner. Through mapping of 34 local government practices worldwide, the study finds no standardized model exists; instead, practices are diverse, selective, and often focus more on processes than outcomes. The authors conclude that while important elements for a local human rights economy exist, they are scattered and undeveloped. To advance, local governments need concrete tools, structural integration of human rights principles, and a commitment to transparency and public participation. The chapter highlights an urgent need for interdisciplinary research to build practical models for implementing human rights budgeting at the local level, aiming to bridge the gap between economic governance and the fulfilment of human rights.

The following contribution, "Devolution and the Right to Budgetary Participation: Insights from Subnational Governments in Midlands Province, Zimbabwe", written by Edson Paul Mutema, Zvimekria Clive Mukushwa, and Amos Zevure, examines how Zimbabwe's devolution policy and participatory budgeting processes aim to empower citizen participation in local governance under the National Development Strategy. The authors argue that, despite constitutional provisions encouraging citizen involvement, real participation remains minimal due to resource constraints, elite domination, poor communication, and lack of inclusivity. Using Arnstein's Ladder of Citizen Participation as a framework, the study finds that most citizen involvement in budgeting falls into tokenistic categories like consultation and placation, with little actual influence over final budget decisions. Through qualitative research, the chapter reveals major gaps, including poor dissemination of budget information, lack of civic education, exclusion of vulnerable groups, and political and economic barriers that demotivate public participation. The findings show that participatory budgeting often serves more as a formality than a meaningful exercise of citizen power.

The chapter concludes that for genuine citizen participation to take root, local governments must improve transparency, actively include marginalized groups, strengthen accountability, and create incentives to motivate broader citizen engagement. Without addressing these systemic gaps, the ideals of devolution and inclusive development risk remaining largely unfulfilled. This chapter read in conjunction with the chapter of Todd Howland and Martin Mulwa in Part 1 illustrates that participatory budgeting in itself does not guarantee the promotion of human rights, and why it needs to be human rights-based.

Corruption has the potential to render the human rights economy approach meaningless. In the chapter "The Role of Local Governments in Upholding Human Rights and Promoting Economic Justice: Addressing Corruption and Illicit Financial Flows", Pradeep Wagle and Maria José Veramendi Villa explore the profound and multidimensional impacts of corruption on the enjoyment of human rights, with a focus on its consequences at the local level. Using the definition from Transparency International – "the abuse of entrusted power for private gain" – they distinguish between grand and petty corruption and examine how both undermine access to human rights like healthcare, education, and political participation. Grand corruption siphons off public funds, compromising State capacity, while petty corruption obstructs individuals' access to public services, disproportionately affecting marginalized groups. The authors argue that corruption erodes public trust, impedes sustainable development, and entrenches inequality, particularly among vulnerable populations such as ethnic minorities, women, and the poor. Local governments, often the front line in public service delivery, are especially susceptible to corruption due to proximity, lack of oversight, and limited accountability. However, they are also well-positioned to combat it through participatory governance, transparency, and robust anti-corruption frameworks. The chapter concludes that addressing corruption at the local level is essential to realizing economic, social, and cultural rights.

The book closes with two chapters offering very specific tools to be added to the regular municipal tool box, namely local or social currencies and baby bonds. In the first contribution, "Municipal Monies as Policy Tools to Advance Human Rights Economies", Ester Barinaga explores how local currencies, like Mumbuca in Maricá, Brazil, and Vilawatt in Viladecans, Spain, are reshaping local economies by addressing social and environmental challenges. In Maricá, Mumbuca was created to support vulnerable families and stimulate the local economy by keeping money circulating within the city. In Viladecans, Vilawatt incentivizes energy efficiency while helping low-income households retrofit their homes and reduce energy poverty.

Barinaga argues that these municipal currencies complement national currencies rather than replace them, preventing capital flight and boosting local trade. She critiques traditional monetary systems for failing to address local needs and highlights how local currencies can make money a tool for advancing human rights, democracy, and sustainable development. The chapter concludes that municipal currencies challenge the notion of money as a neutral medium and instead present it as a socio-political infrastructure that can be reimagined to serve collective goals. By tailoring currencies to local priorities like human rights, municipalities are reclaiming monetary power, fostering economic democracy, and offering scalable models for more just and resilient communities. These experiments demonstrate how money can be redesigned to prioritize community well-being and environmental stewardship, quietly reshaping how societies organize economic life.

In the final chapter, "The Racial Wealth Gap and Localised Solutions for Promoting Equality and Justice", David Radcliffe examines the racial wealth gap in the United States as a persistent legacy of systemic racism, tracing its roots to historical policies like the Homestead Act, Social Security exclusions, the G.I. Bill, and urban renewal projects. Radcliffe argues that wealth – not just income – is crucial for economic security, yet Black and Latino families have disproportionately low wealth due to centuries of discriminatory policies. The author highlights that addressing income alone is insufficient; true equity requires intentional wealth-building interventions. One major policy solution discussed is Baby Bonds, which provide public seed capital to children from low-wealth families to fund education, homeownership, or entrepreneurship. The success of the state of Connecticut's Baby Bonds programme has inspired similar efforts in over 20 states. Radcliffe argues that Baby Bonds, alongside broader policies like health equity, job guarantees, and investments in public goods, are necessary to dismantle structural barriers to wealth. Concluding, the chapter stresses that the racial wealth gap is a result of deliberate policy choices, and with intentional, equity-driven reforms like Baby Bonds, the United States can build a more inclusive, prosperous society where economic rights are realized for all.

References

Benería, Lourdes, and Savitri Bisnath. *Global Tensions: Challenges and Opportunities in the World Economy*. New York: Routledge, 2004.

Dosi, Giovanni, and Joseph E. Stiglitz. "Introduction to the First Annual Special Issue on Macro Economics and Development." *Industrial and Corporate Change* 30, no. 2 (April 2021): 269–271. https://doi.org/10.1093/icc/dtab011

Part 1

Human Rights Economy

1 Towards Localized Economic Policies for People and the Planet

Savitri Bisnath

Introduction

The United Nations (UN) Secretary General (United Nations, 2020) stated in his Mandela Lecture that the current moment calls into question many of our accepted economic concepts and models that inform decisions and policies. The current realities challenge us to forge new ideas, measurements, and a new course of action grounded in human rights with people and the planet at the centre to ensure that there is shared prosperity, inclusive economies, sustainable development, and that human rights are respected, protected, and fulfilled. Economic growth, in and of itself, is not a tide that lifts all boats, and the market, despite conventional thinking, is incapable of solving all problems, addressing all challenges, and filling all gaps. The United Nations (2024) underlined this in the *Pact for the Future*. Action 53 notes: "[w]e reaffirm the need to urgently develop measures of progress on sustainable development that complement or go beyond gross domestic product. These measures should reflect progress on the economic, social and environmental dimensions of sustainable development" (United Nations, 2024).

The global economy and regional, national, and local economies have evolved over time. The majority of UN member states operate within a mixed economic model. Economies operate through a combination of a market economy with varying degrees of government/state interventions – regulatory and/or financial – for national security and well-being (through social security systems). This mixed economic model reveals and relies on the complementary roles of the public and private sectors. Within this model and across countries uneven development and pockets of poverty exist.

This chapter engages within the framework of a mixed economic model and focuses on economic policies at the local level with the aim of better facilitating inclusive economies that serve people; enable a safe, healthy, and sustainable environment; fulfil, protect, and respect human rights; and promote justice and more inclusive economies. The first section explores the limits of neoliberal policies, the second section outlines key elements of localized human rights economies, and the third section makes suggestions for operationalizing the human rights economy/human rights economies at the local level.

DOI: 10.4324/9781003474845-3

The Limits of Neoliberal Policies

Neoliberalism has promoted the ideas of the invisible hand and trickle-down economics and a small state as sufficient to ensure growth, development, and prosperity. Milton Friedman, a prominent economist in the 20th century, continues to influence 21st century economic and development policies and planning. Friedman (1962, 1970) promoted the following mainstream thinking in the field of economics that contributed to uneven development and increased inequality: (i) the private sector and its objective of profit maximization;[1] and (ii) the notion that markets would restore communities in distress.

However, increasing inequalities within and between low-, middle-, and high-income countries and poverty within countries are evidence of the failures of this economic model. There is data-driven consensus that the neoliberal economic model is failing to deliver economic prosperity for all. Over the last decades, this dominant economic thinking, with the assistance of the International Monetary Fund (IMF, 2022) and the World Bank, promoted deregulation and privatization and insisted that a restricted and small public sector is necessary to enable the private sector to thrive. However, the current realities, informed by the challenges of the pandemic, highlight that the public sector plays a crucial role, especially in those areas that are not seen as profitable, such as health and education. In addition, the consumption and production models and patterns promoted by this economic approach are contributing to the climate crisis.

Widening fiscal deficits across countries, increasing inflationary pressures, and high debt-to-gross domestic product (GDP) ratios (Barrett, 2022) are all exacerbating deprivation and signalling a scarcity of resources in low- and middle-income countries. According to the United Nations (2017), "austerity became African leaders' default coping mechanism for periods of economic stress". In 2019, the African Commission on Human and People's Rights expressed concerns about the trend among bilateral donors and international institutions of "putting pressure on States Parties to privatize or facilitate access to private actors in their health and education sectors". In addition, high food prices are squeezing households' incomes and resulting in increased hunger, with low-income families skipping meals. This coping strategy has multiplier effects on their nutrition, health, and education.

The effects of globalization are uneven and unequal within and across countries and regions and are partially constitutive of context-specific socio-economic realities, levels of development, and the positions of individual countries – in terms of production, distribution, and consumption – within the world system. In addition, the stratification within countries resulting from discrimination is deepening poverty and inequality within specific communities, for example, people of African descent and indigenous groups. The socio-economic realities underline that there is no necessary relationship between open and competitive markets and the achievement of sustainable development, equality, justice, or peace. According to the United Nations (2022), 811 million people face hunger, and without decisive action, the number of people living in extreme poverty is expected to reach 600 million, or 7 per cent of the world's population, by 2030.

Neoliberalism also prioritizes GDP as the metric of economic growth. GDP counts air pollution, cigarette advertising, destruction of forests, and weapons of mass destruction, while work conducted in the informal and care economies is left out, and uneven development and local level disparities are obscured. Users of GDP often conflate economic growth with well-being. According to the Report by the Commission on the Measurement of Economic Performance and Social Progress (Stiglitz, Sen, and Fitoussi, 2009), GDP mainly measures market production, though it has often been treated as if it were a measure of economic well-being. Conflating the two can lead to misleading indications about how well-off people are, resulting in ineffective and counter-productive policy decisions.

The conflation of GDP with well-being often results in policy decisions that fail to value shared prosperity and equality – with implications for local governance and the attainment of human rights. Economist Simon Kuznets (1962), the creator of GDP, noted "[d]istinctions must be kept in mind between quantity and quality of growth, between its costs and return, and between the short and the long term. Goals for more growth should specify more growth of what and for what". Merging well-being and GDP can also lead to misleading assumptions about States' respect for and fulfilment of economic and social rights. The latter is in part demonstrated through budget allocations and expenditures, as well as labour market regulations to facilitate decent work.

According to the United Nations (2018a), before COVID-19, countries experienced increasing concentrations of wealth, most often resulting in the disproportionate political influence of elites in economic policymaking through which they are positioned to benefit. At the same time, the policy space to adopt redistributive economic and social policies, such as progressive taxation and social protection, to redress and/or mitigate inequalities and poverty was severely reduced. Worldwide, fiscal privileges of elites persist in the shape of exemptions, evasion, and low rates of income and wealth taxes, while much of the tax burden is indirect, tied to consumption and carried by low-income individuals and households. In terms of spatial implications, this unbalanced and corrupting influence results in uneven development, with some neighbourhoods and locations having better essential infrastructure and access to quality services and others lacking access to quality and affordable services, living with crumbling infrastructure, and with the increased presence of security forces due to perceptions about criminality.

In addition, the climate crisis is compounding poverty and inequalities. Floods and droughts are resulting in displacement and loss of livelihoods, with implications for the right to food, water, education, adequate housing, an adequate standard of living, etc. It is also clear that wealthy communities and countries are better able to withstand disasters, while communities and countries lacking in financial resources have lower levels of resilience and are often unable to plan for, or implement, necessary adaptation measures.

Widening fiscal deficits, increasing inflationary pressures, and high debt-to-GDP ratios are exacerbating deprivation and resulting in debt distress in many low- and middle-income countries. Currently most low- and middle-income countries allocate a significant share of their national budgets to debt servicing. Neoliberal policies reinforce economic restructuring prescriptions that often result in the shrinking of national and provincial budgets for the progressive realization of economic and social rights, and the attainment of a clean, healthy, and sustainable environment and sustainable development.

A key element of neoliberalism is the imposition of austerity budgets. Austerity budgets per the IMF prioritize fiscal consolidation at the local level and often result in either a lack of, or insufficient, allocations and expenditures for social spending and the essential infrastructure necessary for the progressive realization of economic and social rights as well as equitable and sustainable development. For societies implementing austerity measures, the less income a person has, the more diminished their access to services, such as health care, due to the privatization of public services. In low- and middle-income countries, approximately 60–80 per cent of the population are working in the informal sector. Informal sector workers lack social protections as well as the right to organize. The realities of increasing inequalities and poverty; the legacies of austerity and structural adjustment policies; the current effects of austerity policies;[2] and the impacts of the pandemic, containment measures, and supply chain disruptions serve to compound and intensify poverty and inequalities, especially in marginalized communities.

As Dosi and Stiglitz (2021) noted in relation to economics:

> We need a radical departure with radically different foundations. The economy has to be analyzed as a complex evolving system. Inequality is an endemic property of the system and it affects its short- and long-term performance. Its drivers and the policies to curb it ought to be under the spotlight. Markets do not work in a vacuum. The functioning of a market economy depends on the laws, rules, norms, and institutional structures under which it operates, all determined by power relations; and the outcomes it produces affect the distribution of power itself.

Towards Localized Human Rights Economies[3]

> Recognizing that, in accordance with the Universal Declaration of Human Rights, the ideal of free human beings enjoying freedom from fear and want can only be achieved if conditions are created whereby everyone may enjoy his economic, social and cultural rights, as well as his civil and political rights.
>
> (International Covenant on Economic Social and Cultural Rights)

The focus of this chapter is on the "local". I problematize the "local" to move beyond its traditional definition: within the context of the global economy, the local can refer to a country and within the context of a national economy the local can refer to a particular place or region. This chapter is intentional about the countries (low- and middle-income) and places/regions within countries that experience multiple and persistent forms of marginalization and vulnerability, and wherein specific people and communities experience multiple, persistent, and intersecting forms of discrimination and marginalization.

The architecture of inequality within and between Nation-States is propagated through actors, institutions, policies, and practices. Understanding economic inequality within countries from a human rights perspective requires context-specific analysis that takes into consideration the economic and political histories of the country in question, including the contemporary effects of colonialism on the structure of the economy, the country's position within the global economy, and uneven development and marginalization of specific groups, for example, Afro-descendants, specific castes, and indigenous people. Although countries in the Global South have gained political independence, many of the economic structures, processes, and mechanisms, including for monetary policy, that enabled colonialism have left enduring effects on the realities of, and the processes that result in, discrimination, inequality, poverty, and uneven development.

The root and structural causes of economic inequality within and between countries are grounded in global, regional, national, and local economic and political systems, wherein the communities most left behind experience multiple, persistent, and intersecting forms of discrimination and are often historically marginalized. Asymmetric power relations often influence political and economic processes and lack of remedy for human rights violations. There is growing consensus that economic growth alone is insufficient to enable specific communities to catch up/pull themselves up by their bootstraps.

Inequality of opportunities and outcomes is partly influenced by the ways in which specific individuals and communities are positioned by race/ethnicity, gender, income, parents' education, place of birth, occupation, sexual orientation and gender identity, and wealth. They also serve to justify inequalities in property rights, standards of living, access to assets, networks of influence and power, and citizenship status. In addition, economic inequalities are evidenced by the large and persistent disparities that exist in ownership and control of economic wealth, access to resources and markets, and the exercise of political power (Khouri, 2019). The culture of privilege also crystallizes in social relations due to the rigidity of intergenerational social mobility (United Nations, 2018b).

Shared prosperity and increased equality require a more integrated, systems-wide, and intentional approach to human rights-enabling economic policies. Feminist economists posit that we need a definition of economics "that considers humans in relation to the world". They argue that we need to focus economics on the provisioning of human life and on the commodities and processes necessary for human survival (Nelson, 1993). Identity Group Stratification Economics (Darity, Hamilton, and Stewart, 2015) notes that intergroup inequalities result from processes of structure, investment, and treatment by which privileged groups maintain relative status. Intergroup inequalities are the result of strategic behaviours on the part of dominant groups "to attain and maintain relative positions in a social hierarchy".

This framing highlights the links between power, racial and gender discrimination, and economic outcomes, as well as the reality that social hierarchy will persist in the absence of public interventions. The Identity Group Stratification approach shows that group-based disparities exist and are sustained because identity itself carries material and non-material returns (Chelwa, Maboshe, and Hamilton, 2024). It posits Identity Group Stratification Economics and Feminist Economics as important theoretical underpinnings for understanding and addressing racial and gender discrimination in economic policies.

A human rights economy is one that centres all people; the planet; and civil, cultural, economic, political, and social rights as appropriate and necessary, in economic, social, and environmental policies, plans, programmes, projects, processes, and decision-making (Bisnath, 2023). It recognizes the indivisibility of human rights and highlights ESC rights as essential for the realization of an adequate standard of living and sustainable development. As a result, fiscal and monetary policies and tools, including the budget, and microeconomic policies would be put in service to promote, fulfil, and respect human rights for all, including ensuring a clean, healthy, and sustainable environment; reducing inequalities and poverty; facilitating the attainment of sustainable development; and prioritizing the generation of sustainable revenue. Human rights-enhancing economic policies at the local level would necessarily adapt economic policies to context-specific realities, opportunities, and challenges in ways that would promote human flourishing.

A human rights conceptual framework for analysing the economy is embedded in the recognition that the market is a social construction, that production and reproduction are intrinsically linked, constituted, and reconstituted through relations of power, and that countries and rights holders often enter and participate in global, regional, national, and local markets on differential terms. Siloed analyses tend to erode the multiple factors that contribute to discrimination, marginalization, inequality, and poverty, and marginalize and compartmentalize human rights solutions. This conceptual framework enables the space for an acknowledgement that: (i) discriminatory policies exist, including in such areas as education, employment, trade, and investments; and (ii) intentional economic policies, programmes, projects, and decisions informed by human rights principles and obligations are necessary to facilitate inclusive economies, sustainable development, and shared prosperity for all.

Human rights principles and obligations can provide guardrails and ring fencing for local and national economic policies, such as public budgets, and promote participation, transparency, and accountability to better facilitate trust, peace, and justice, as well as reduce elite capture and corruption. They can also result in baselines for progress. In times of crisis, they offer solutions to keep everyone afloat, including through the minimum core obligation.[4] All international, regional, and national sources of human rights, such as General

Comments developed by the Committee on Economic, Social and Cultural Rights, specific country recommendations,[5] regional standards and guidelines, and national constitutional law are relevant to inform analyses and forge solutions.

Economic policies, programmes, projects, and decision-making that are informed by human rights principles and obligations will intentionally address and redress root causes and structural barriers to equality, justice, and sustainability. To construct human rights economies at the local level, intentionality about the stated outcomes of inclusive economies and shared prosperity at the interconnected spheres of governance and economic planning are crucial.

To better understand the material realities of a local economy and linkages with particular economic policies and practices it is necessary to pose specific questions:

i In what sectors/subsectors is growth taking place (structure of the economy)?
ii What is the performance capacity of existing public services?
iii Who benefits from wealth creation and accumulation, and decent jobs (winners)?
iv Where is economic growth stagnant, and which communities are left behind (uneven development and losers)?
v Is the middle class growing over time, why/why not (sources of growing inequality and poverty push factors)?
vi Who makes/made up the middle class (demographic, education, employment, and location)? What are the costs of adequate food and housing, essential medicines, water, and fuel relative to the minimum wage/medium household income (trade and industrial policies, decent work, and social spending)?
vii What are the sources and level of national revenue (structure of the economy and trade, industrial and tax policies)?
viii What is the purchasing power parity (PPP), value of currency, debt level?
ix What are the austerity measures in place, and is there fiscal space for social spending?
x What are the impacts of climate change on livelihoods and food, etc.?

How do we go beyond reforms of privatizing and liberalizing markets, reducing trade barriers, and cutting social spending through austerity measures, to centring the people and communities at the bottom, who often experience multiple, persistent, and intersectional forms of discrimination? What questions do we ask, what categories of analysis do we deploy? The answers to these questions must be contextualized within the political and human rights histories and current realities of the country in question to enable analyses that highlight human rights violations, signal early warning, and from which recommendations can emerge about prevention, the attainment of human rights, and well-being.

In summary, to construct human rights-enhancing economic policies at the local level it is necessary to:

i Conduct context-specific assessments that include the local socio-economic (structure of the local economy and linkages with national, regional, and global supply chains and budget allocations and expenditures) and demographic landscapes, human development measurements, quantitative and qualitative information on the human rights situations, employment, underemployment and unemployment figures, the formal, informal, and care and support economies, etc.;
ii Engage in discussions with relevant stakeholders while being intentional about including the local communities, especially groups who experience multiple, persistent, and intersecting forms of discrimination about the design and implementation of economic policies that promote their well-being;
iii Design and implement human rights-enhancing economic policies, including fiscal policies, that are aimed at the progressive realization of economic and social rights and the satisfaction of the minimum core obligations at the start;
iv Design and implement monitoring and evaluation processes and procedures that include the attainment of economic and social rights and the rights to development and a clean, healthy, and sustainable environment; and
v Foster substantive collaboration with all relevant stakeholders, the public and private sectors, academia, and civil society for inclusive, just, and sustainable outcomes.

In addition, it is necessary to use economic data points that go beyond aggregate growth to include gross national income and PPP; underemployment; the shares of workers in the formal and informal sectors; care and support work; inequality by income, wealth, and race; gender and regional disparities; etc. Such actions are consistent with the follow-up commitments in the United Nations Pact for the Future which calls for multi-stakeholder engagement in the development of measurements to complement GDP (United Nations, 2024).

A key step is to identify sources of revenue, which would include resources from different sectors and linkages with tax policies, decent work, environmental sustainability, industrial policies, as well as the processes that shrink fiscal space, including debt servicing, corruption, unfair tax policies, and illicit financial flows. Human rights impact assessments of potential trade and development agreements and projects would be a necessary element of the ex-ante due diligence process informing investment decisions. For local-level economic planning, the process is as important as the content of what is being decided. Ensuring the substantive participation of local authorities and communities has the potential to increase transparency and accountability.

Fiscal Policy[6] – A Key Macroeconomic Tool for Localizing Economies Grounded in Rights

Development and anti-poverty strategies have historically focused on the national level. However, and as noted by the UN Secretary General (United Nations Economic Commission for Asia and the Pacific, 2020), many challenges currently require global frameworks and global approaches linked to human rights principles and obligations informed by evidence-based analysis and with context-specific actions. While human rights principles and obligations are universal and global, human rights solutions must necessarily be context specific and evidence based.

Governments manage their economies through fiscal and monetary policies. Fiscal policies cover governments' spending, taxation, and borrowing and are related to the management of the national budget. A government's budget is one of the most important economic policy tools to facilitate the fulfilment of human rights. It is the key policy document reflecting governments' priorities as well as how resources are allocated among them. To ensure any human right, be it the right to due process in an independent judicial system or the right to quality health care or education services, financial resources are necessary to invest in human resources, medicines, equipment, essential infrastructure, training, as well as to develop and strengthen state capacity.

Long-standing investments in health and other public services are in part the legacies of the taxation and budgetary conditionalities attached to loans to low- and middle-income countries from the International Financial Institutions, as well as the budget decisions of many governments. Regressive taxes, such as value-added taxes, are often a burden disproportionately assumed by low-income communities (given the proportion of their incomes spent on basic commodities), while progressive income taxes and wealth taxes have redistributive functions. Loan conditionalities have been informed by the policy (structural adjustment programmes and austerity policies) priorities of economic liberalization for trade promotion and the privatization of public services, including health. Budgets for the security agenda with militarization have steadily increased, while the health and social protection budgets have shrunk, at the same time as the private sector increasingly began to replace the State in those sectors that were once seen as essential for the public good. This has in turn contributed to increasing inequalities. Illicit capital flows and corruption have also eroded fiscal space for social spending which is essential for the realization of ESC rights and attainment of sustainable development.

In many countries, local and national budget documents do not reflect human rights standards and obligations in their financial content. Local budgets also reflect bias informed by uneven development and historical marginalization. Additionally, budget processes at the national and local levels most often do not apply human rights principles such as participation, transparency, and accountability. Public participation in the budget process necessarily requires fiscal transparency, facilitates accountability, and builds trust and social cohesion. To be meaningful at the local level, ensuring that documents are in local languages and that meetings are held at times that ensure community involvement are key elements of participation. When rights holders are able to follow the money, the level of corruption goes down, trust in government goes up, sustainable development is better facilitated, and shared prosperity and inclusion are enhanced.

Similarly, when national and local budgets integrate States' human rights obligations and recommendations, including from the Universal Periodic Review, they can be powerful levers for the progressive realization of ESC rights and sustainable development. Increased spending in social sectors, with a focus on accessibility, affordability, and quality of services as well as non-discrimination, will strengthen countries' capacities to withstand shocks and facilitate inclusive economies and societies. It will also result in more sustainable and equitable development outcomes. This approach, within a framework of fiscal transparency and accountability, and the substantive participation of rights holders, is also key to guiding States' investment decisions for the well-being of people and the planet.

National and provincial budgets are also accountability tools; redistributive fiscal policies such as the adoption and implementation of progressive taxation and efficient tax administration to tackle tax evasion and avoidance are key within the current economic realities. Economic analysis from a human rights lens and advocacy with all stakeholders, including finance ministries, are important herein.

The International Covenant on Economic, Social and Cultural Rights (United Nations, 1966) notes that the minimum core obligation[7] is considered to be of immediate effect to meet the *minimum essential levels of each of the rights* – in many ways it's a guarantee of well-being. If a State fails to meet this because it does not have the resources, it must demonstrate that it has made every effort to use all available resources to satisfy, as a matter of priority, the core obligations.

Even if a State has inadequate resources at its disposal, the Government must still introduce low-cost and targeted programmes to assist those most in need so that its limited resources are used efficiently and effectively. However, social spending often fails to reflect the evidence-based needs of populations.

Context-specific policies, plans, programmes, projects, and processes that are designed and administered through a human rights lens are necessary to ensure that every member of society is able to live in dignity. Within this context, different stakeholders have specific roles and responsibilities, including duty bearers, international financial institutions, the private sector, and rights holders. Such policies and programmes would provide necessary scaffolding for medium- and longer-term recovery. When they are in place, people and communities who are marginalized can be sheltered from the negative impacts of economic shocks and related crises.

Reform of the debt and financial architecture is also necessary as many governments are having to make the difficult decision of either investing in the health, social protection, and other public services that are critical for human rights or servicing the debt. There is an urgent need to revise global tax rules – a complex web of tax and bilateral treaties combined with soft law, diplomatic forums, and transparency clauses – to combat illicit financial flows in line with human rights law and standards, including extraterritorial obligations, and enable low- and middle-income countries to increase sustainable revenues.

The following are some of the potential benefits of investing in local economies that centre people and the planet:

i The respect for, and protection and fulfilment of, human rights will be enhanced and inclusive sustainable development will be facilitated through, in part, a focus on uneven development and marginalized communities.
ii Policies that either establish a minimum wage within the framework of decent work or protect the rights of all workers, including those in the informal sector, to join a union will serve to address issues of economic insecurity, unequal power relations, corporate capture, and uneven development.
iii Sustainable domestic revenue generation will be prioritized and maximized, including through progressive taxation and the curtailing of corruption and illicit financial flows.
iv Budget decisions and increased and more effective public investments related to ESC rights and sustainable development will reduce inequalities within and between countries.
v Human rights-enhancing industrial and trade policies would promote consumption and production patterns, investment decisions, and business models that facilitate the creation of a clean, healthy, and sustainable environment and an adequate standard of living[8] for all.
vi Within the context of human rights economies, Nation-States would not be sanctioned by market forces, international financial institutions, or credit rating agencies for choosing to centre the needs and rights of people and the planet in their budget decisions.
vii Space for social dialogue, scrutiny, and participation at the local level will be facilitated.

Sustained and intentional investments in all people (human capital) will also contribute to productivity, growth, prosperity, and inclusivity, and have positive multiplier effects on families, communities, the private sector, and the society at large.

Moving Forward

The orthodoxy of globalization is being eroded as the world experiences increasing fragmentation. The Global Trends 2040 Report (National Intelligence Council, 2021) noted that in the next two decades: "No single state is likely to dominate all regions or domains, and a broader range of actors will compete to advance their ideologies, goals, and interests". A one-size-fits-all approach has failed to address the root causes and structural impediments to ensuring that no one is left behind and will continue to do so in this changing reality. How do we move from business as usual to promote human rights and ensure human flourishing and shared prosperity? Violations of human rights result from and through political and economic decisions, policies, plans, programmes, projects, and processes.

Within the context of the current poly crisis, a multi-pronged, unified, coherent, integrated, and building block approach grounded in human rights for all is urgently needed. To succeed, this approach must have the substantive participation of all stakeholders – from women's rights organizations to Afro-descendants and indigenous peoples' movements, and climate advocates. All stakeholders are necessary to create a world in which all can live free from fear and want. Duty bearers, rights holders, civil society organizations, academics, and the private sector all have important and specific roles to play, not only because the integrity of the multilateral system is at stake, but also because the lives of people and the health of the planet are in the balance.

Quality of life in part depends on people's health, their access to food, social security and quality education, their participation in decent jobs, as well as the health, safety, and sustainability of the natural environment. These elements speak to the importance of human rights and sustainable development. Economic theory and practice are social constructions, and as a result, we have the space to rethink our current economic model, and GDP as the main indictor of national well-being. Economies grounded in human rights can have stabilizing effects on societies and the world community, with sustainable development and increased equality, prosperity, and peace.

Given that the conceptualization and implementation of localizing human rights economies are emerging, the following considerations are necessary as the work progresses:

i Centring fiscal and monetary policies and processes are necessary for the attainment of rights and justice for all communities to flourish. This requires intentionality about the availability, affordability, accessibility, and quality of public services and essential infrastructure as well as linkages with national and sectoral industrial policies.
ii Understanding that global challenges, including the processes of climate change, economic fragmentation, and friend shoring, have uneven effects between and within countries and may intensify inequalities and poverty experienced by communities who experience multiple, persistent, and intersecting forms of discrimination.
iii Being mindful to develop local-level economic initiatives that are rights enhancing beyond the superficial to ensure and facilitate a systems change approach.
iv Ensuring that localized human rights initiatives focused on economic and social rights substantively include local and regional authorities and impacted communities to ensure a holistic approach.
v Appreciate that facilitating human rights economies at the local level will contribute to an enhanced understanding of the opportunities, gaps, and challenges therein and aid the overall well-being of societies, boosting stability and security.

Notes

1 Friedman (1970), "there is one and only one social responsibility of business—to use its resources and engage in activities designed to increase its profits so long as it stays within the rules of the game, which is to say, engages in open and free competition without deception or fraud".
2 See Ray, Gallagher, and Krin, (2020).
3 This chapter refers to the human rights economy and human rights economies because no two economies are exactly the same, and there are context-specific articulations at the regional, national, subnational, and local levels. The concept of the human rights economy benefits from the contributions of OHCHR Surge Economists Jihen Chandoul, Maria Jose Eva, Martin Mulwa, and Priya Lukka.
4 For details, see OHCHR: https://www.ohchr.org/en/human-rights/economic-social-cultural-rights.
5 Treaty bodies oversee the normative development of the rights contained in the core international human rights instruments and monitor their implementation. The seven treaty bodies are: the Human Rights Committee; the Committee on Economic, Social and Cultural Rights; the Committee on the Elimination of Racial Discrimination; the Committee on the Elimination of Discrimination Against Women; Committee Against Torture; the Committee on the Rights of the Child; and the Committee on Migrant Workers.
6 Building on the mainstream definition, a human rights description of fiscal space includes resources generated through domestic mobilisation, unconditional/concessional loans, and development aid to ensure that the necessary resources are available to respect, protect, and fulfil human rights as well as provide remedy for human rights violations.
7 For details, see OHCHR's Frequently asked Questions on Economic, Social and Cultural Rights (United Nations Office of the High Commissioner for Human Rights, n.d.).
8 See Article 25 of the United Nations Universal Declaration of Human Rights and Article 11 of the United Nations International Covenant on Economic, Social and Cultural Rights.

Bibliography

African Commission on Human and People's Rights. 2019. *Resolution on States' Obligation to Regulate Private Actors Involved in the Provision of Health and Education Services – ACHPR/Res. 420 (LXIV) 2019*. https://achpr.au.int/index.php/en/adopted-resolutions/420-resolution-states-obligation-regulate-private-actors-involved-pro

Barrett, Philip. 2022. "How Food and Energy Are Driving the Global Inflation Surge." *IMF Blog*, September 12. https://www.imf.org/en/Blogs/Articles/2022/09/09/cotw-how-food-and-energy-are-driving-the-global-inflation-surge

Bisnath, Savitri. 2023. *Towards a Human Rights Economy: A Conceptual Framework*. Policy Paper for the Surge Initiative. Geneva: United Nations Office of the High Commissioner for Human Rights, December.

Chelwa, Grieve, Mashekwa Maboshe, and Darrick Hamilton. 2024. "The Racial Wealth Gap in South Africa and the United States." *Review of Political Economy* 36 (2): 423–440..

Darity, William A., Darrick Hamilton, and J. B. Stewart. 2015. "A Tour de Force in Understanding Intergroup Inequality: An Introduction to Stratification Economics." *The Review of Black Political Economy* 42 (1–2): 16.

Dosi, Giovanni, and Joseph E. Stiglitz. 2021. "Introduction to the First Annual Special Issue on Macro Economics and Development." *Industrial and Corporate Change* 30 (2) (April): 269–271. https://doi.org/10.1093/icc/dtab011

Friedman, Milton. 1962. *Capitalism and Freedom*. Chicago: University of Chicago Press.
Friedman, Milton. 1970. "A Friedman Doctrine: The Social Responsibility of Business Is to Increase Its Profits." *The New York Times Magazine*, September 13. https://www.nytimes.com/1970/09/13/archives/a-friedman-doctrine-the-social-responsibility-of-business-is-to.html
International Monetary Fund. 2022. "Public Debt and Real GDP: Revisiting the Impact." In Constance de Soyres, Reina Kawai, and Mengxue Wang. Working Paper, Finance Department, April. https://share.google/1POEd2xDY32CIIRyI
Khouri, Rami. 2019. "Poverty, Inequality and the Structural Threat to the Arab Region." In *POMEPS Studies 34: Shifting Global Politics and the Middle East*. Cambridge, MA: Harvard University Belfer Center for Science and International Affairs. https://www.belfercenter.org/publication/poverty-inequality-and-structural-threat-arab-region
Kuznets, Simon. 1962. "About Rethinking the System of National Accounting." In *The New Republic*, edited by Herbert David Croly, 147. Republic Publishing Company, the University of California.
National Intelligence Council. 2021. *Global Trends 2040 Report: A More Contested World*. https://www.dni.gov/files/ODNI/documents/assessments/GlobalTrends_2040.pdf
Nelson, Julie. 1993. "The Study of Choice or the Study of Provisioning? Gender and the Definition of Economics." In *Beyond Economic Man: Feminist Theory and Economics*, edited by Marianne Ferber and Julie Nelson. Chicago: University of Chicago Press.
Ray, Rebecca, Kevin P. Gallagher, and William Kring. 2020. "IMF Austerity Since the Global Financial Crisis: New Data, Same Trend, and Similar Determinants." Working Paper, Boston University Global Development Center. https://www.bu.edu/gdp/files/2020/11/IMF-Austerity-Since-the-Global-Financial-Crisis-WP.pdf
Stiglitz, Joseph E., Amartya Sen, and Jean-Paul Fitoussi. 2009. *Report by the Commission on the Measurement of Economic Performance and Social Progress*. https://ec.europa.eu/eurostat/documents/8131721/8131772/Stiglitz-Sen-Fitoussi-Commission-report.pdf
United Nations. 1948. *Universal Declaration of Human Rights*. https://www.youthforhumanrights.org/what-are-human-rights/universal-declaration-of-human-rights/introduction.html
United Nations. 1966. *International Covenant on Economic, Social and Cultural Rights*. https://www.ohchr.org/en/instruments-mechanisms/instruments/international-covenant-economic-social-and-cultural-rights
United Nations. 2017. "Closing Africa's Wealth Gap." *UN Africa Renewal*. https://www.un.org/africarenewal/magazine/december-2017-march-2018/closing-africa%E2%80%99s-wealth-gap#:~:text=%E2%80%9CUnder%20the%20influence%20of%20Western,a%20freelance%20researcher%20and%20historian
United Nations Economic and Social Commission for Asia and the Pacific. 2018a. *Inequality in Asia and the Pacific in the Era of the 2030 Agenda for Sustainable Development*. Bangkok: United Nations.
United Nations Economic and Social Commission for Asia and the Pacific. 2018b. *The Inefficiency of Inequality*. Santiago de Chile: United Nations.
United Nations Economic and Social Commission for Asia and the Pacific. 2020. *Secretary-General's Nelson Mandela Lecture: Tackling the Inequality Pandemic: A New Social Contract for a New Era*. New York: United Nations.
United Nations Economic and Social Commission for Asia and the Pacific. 2022. "Commission for Social Development Begins 2022 Session amid Robust Calls for Overcoming Food Insecurity, Poverty Laid Bare by COVID-19." https://press.un.org/en/2022/soc4898.doc.htm

United Nations Economic and Social Commission for Asia and the Pacific. 2024. "Summit of the Future Outcome Documents: Pact for the Future, Global Digital Compact and Declaration on Future Generations." September. https://www.un.org/sites/un2.un.org/files/sotf-pact_for_the_future_adopted.pdf

United Nations Office of the High Commissioner for Human Rights. n.d. *Frequently Asked Questions on Economic, Social and Cultural Rights*. Fact Sheet 33. https://www.ohchr.org/sites/default/files/Documents/Issues/ESCR/FAQ_on_ESCR-en.pdf

2 Right to Development and Local Economies

Mihir Kanade

Introduction

The positive correlation between local economies that enhance human rights on the one hand, and the improvement of human well-being and sustainable development within such economies on the other, has been explored in several chapters of this book. This chapter explores this relationship from the normative lens of the human right to development (RTD). It is axiomatic that building human rights economies at the subnational levels can greatly contribute to the enhancement of the RTD as well as other human rights of individuals and peoples within local communities and at the national and global levels. At the same time, this relationship is not unidirectional. This chapter concerns itself with the relationship in the other direction. It contends that effective operationalization of the RTD can also help build local economies that mainstream and enhance all human rights. It presents the RTD as an empowering normative framework for such an endeavour because, within it, development itself is seen as a human right that entitles all individuals and peoples engaged in local economies to the three guarantees of the right to participate in, contribute to, and enjoy self-determined and sustainable development. The RTD also rejects an imagination of local economies in watertight compartments that operate in isolation from each other and recognizes as well that the local is very much connected to the national and international order. This framework therefore places great importance to a critical examination of the capacities of local economies to flourish within the context of obstacles that may emanate from a restrictive national or international environment. The RTD framework further obliges States to eliminate such obstacles including through the discharge of their duty to cooperate. Indeed, it recognizes obligations for States not only within their respective jurisdictions, but also extraterritorially and collectively to foster an enabling international and national environment for local economies to thrive.

The RTD and the Concept of a Human Rights Economy: Commonalities and Differences

The relatively new concept of Human Rights Economy on the one hand, and the much older norm of the RTD on the other, share several commonalities

DOI: 10.4324/9781003474845-4

since they both assert an approach to building local economies that are based on human rights and also seek to enhance human rights. Advancement of human rights is thus both the means and the end for achieving both. There are, however, pertinent differences between the two. It is important to highlight these commonalities and differences to appreciate the value-added by the normative framework of the RTD to efforts at promoting the concept of human rights economy and to ensure its successful implementation. This chapter contends that operationalizing the RTD is indispensable if local economies that enhance human rights are to be successfully constructed.

The principal legal instrument elaborating the RTD is the Declaration on the Right to Development (DRTD) adopted by the United Nations General Assembly in 1986 (United Nations 1986). The DRTD describes development as a

> comprehensive economic, social, cultural and political process, which aims at the constant improvement of the well-being of the entire population and of all individuals on the basis of their active, free and meaningful participation in development and in the fair distribution of benefits resulting therefrom.
>
> (United Nations 1986, Preambular Paragraph 2)

By presenting development as a comprehensive social, cultural, political, and economic process that aims at the constant improvement of human well-being, this description signified a rejection of a purely econometric understanding of the development process and its outcomes (Kanade 2018a, 2018b). In the context of local economies, this essentially means that the appropriate metric for evaluation is not one based on economic indicators alone, but one that considers the social, cultural, and political dimensions as well in addition to the contribution of the local economy to enhancing human well-being and rights.

The DRTD marked a paradigm shift in both human rights and development theory by stipulating that self-determined development is to be understood as a human right of all persons and peoples and not merely as charity bestowed upon them by States, individually or collectively. Specifically, the DRTD in its article 1(1) stipulates that

> the right to development is an inalienable human right by virtue of which every human person and all peoples are entitled to participate in, contribute to, and enjoy economic, social, cultural and political development, in which all human rights and fundamental freedoms can be fully realized.

It firmly recognized that rights-holders are the central subjects of development and should be the active participants in and beneficiaries of the RTD (United Nations 1986, article 2(1)). The aforementioned description of development, which economists such as Amartya Sen subsequently endorsed (Sen 1999), and the recognition of development as a right, provides a useful pathway for governments, including subnational, since the very establishment of a local economy that mainstreams and enhances human rights and well-being is "development". The DRTD also clearly articulates the duty-bearers, and at the least, includes States, individually and collectively. More broadly, duty-bearers include any local, national, regional, or international actor that may impair or nullify the realization of the RTD. As shall be elaborated presently, this expands the scope of duty-bearers from subnational or national governments (more appropriately, the "State", in international law) (United Nations 2001, article 4),[1] to regional and international organizations as well as international development cooperation partners (bilateral or multilateral), since each can have direct impacts on local economies and the possibilities of realizing human rights.

There is a general belief that the RTD does not enjoy universal recognition and is divisive along the Global North/South lines. While there is truth to this in terms of the precise nature, scope, and content of the duties entailed under the DRTD and the means for operationalizing the RTD, the norm itself enjoys widespread recognition among States. The DRTD was adopted with an overwhelming majority of 146 countries voting in its favour, eight abstaining and only one voting against (United Nations 2016).[2] However, the RTD has since been reiterated and reaffirmed unanimously by all States in over 25 key instruments, including in the 1992 Rio Declaration (United Nations 1992, Principle 3), the 1993 Vienna Declaration and Programme of Action (United Nations 1993, Paragraph 11), the 2030 Agenda for Sustainable Development (United Nations 2015b, Paragraphs 10–12), and the 2015 Paris Climate Agreement (United Nations 2015a, Preambular paragraph 11). It has also been reaffirmed in several regional human rights instruments (United Nations 2023b, Preambular paragraphs 10 and 11). At the time of writing this chapter, a Draft International Covenant on the Right to Development has been forwarded by the Human Rights Council to the General Assembly for its consideration, negotiation, and subsequent adoption (United Nations 2023b, Paragraph 17).

The essential normative features of the RTD have been summed up by this author in a study developed on behalf of the United Nations Excerpt Mechanism on the RTD as follows (United Nations 2021a, Paragraph 12):

a The RTD is an inalienable self-standing human right. Development is not merely a privilege enjoyed by human beings and peoples, nor are they mere subjects of charity [article 1(1)];
b Rights-holders are guaranteed three entitlements: to participate in, contribute to, and enjoy economic, social, cultural, and political development [article 1(1)];
c The RTD also implies the full realization of the right of peoples to self-determination [article 1(2)];
d Operationalizing the RTD entails respecting, protecting, and fulfilling all other human rights – civil, cultural, economic, political, and social. This signifies that given the very nature of development as a human right, it cannot be realized when there are violations of other human rights;

e The RTD requires a focus not only on outcomes that are to be realized from a development plan or agenda (the "what" question), but also on the process by which those outcomes are achieved (the "how" question). Both the processes and outcomes of development must be consistent with and based on all other human rights;
f Human beings are individually (that is, all human persons) and collectively (that is, all peoples) the rights-holders of the RTD. Every State is entitled, as an agent of all persons and peoples subject to its jurisdiction, to demand respect for the RTD from other States and international organizations;
g The Declaration entails duties for all States to respect, protect, and fulfil the RTD at the following three levels (United Nations 2010):

   i Internally, that is, States acting individually as they formulate national development policies and programmes affecting persons within their jurisdiction;
   ii Extraterritorially, that is, States acting individually as they adopt and implement policies that affect persons not strictly within their jurisdiction; and
   iii Collectively, that is, States acting collectively in global and regional partnerships.

h The Declaration obliges States, individually and collectively, to eliminate existing obstacles to the realization of the RTD, refrain from adopting policies that undermine its realization, and positively create conditions favourable for its realization;
i The Declaration reaffirms the duty of international cooperation for States and obliges them to carry out that duty to realize the RTD for all [articles 3(1), 3(3), 4(1), 4(2), and 6].

On the other hand, Human Rights Economy has been conceived of by the Office of the United Nations High Commissioner for Human Rights and has been presented to member States of the Human Rights Council. By the end of 2024, the concept has, however, not yet been endorsed by the Council. In July 2023, in a resolution titled the "Contribution of Development to the Enjoyment of all Human Rights", the Council included a recital in the preamble as follows:

> *Noting* the concept of human rights economy proposed by the Office of the United Nations High Commissioner for Human Rights as a tool of an approach based on full respect for human rights to reduce inequalities and realize the 2030 Agenda, which seeks to redress root causes and the structural barriers to equality, justice and sustainability, placing emphasis on inclusive participation and social dialogue, including the delivery of better results for people and the planet, grounded in economic, civil, political, social, cultural and environmental rights.
>
> (United Nations 2023a, Preambular Paragraph 23)

It is well-known that "noting" in the language of United Nations resolutions signifies that there is not yet a full acceptance among Member States of what follows in the recital. While the concept is still in its nascent stages in terms of its precise nature, scope, and content, it clearly promises to offer a specific conceptual framework for the recreation of an economic landscape at all levels that consciously mainstreams human rights and contributes to reduction of inequalities and realization of sustainable development. While the language reflects the typical crypticity redolent of Council resolutions where consensus is absent, it is evident that Human Rights Economy has been proposed by the Office, or at least understood by States, as a "tool of" "an approach based on full respect for human rights" – what is commonly referred to as the Human Rights-Based Approach (HRBA). HRBA is a conceptual framework "for the process of human development that is normatively based on international human rights standards and operationally directed to promoting and protecting human rights" (United Nations n.d.-a). Several States, especially from the Global South, remain deeply sceptical of the conceptual framework of HRBA, which was adopted by the United Nations Development Group in 2003 (United Nations 2003). This provides indications for the hesitation to endorse the concept.

While the Global North has generally supported HRBA, it has vehemently been opposed by many from the developing world, which has resulted in the concept never being endorsed in any intergovernmental instrument (United Nations 2023c, 20–21). Instead, as the title of the Council's resolution noted above indicates, the alternative concept of "Contribution of development to human rights" (or sometimes "development-based approach to human rights") has been advanced. The problem with both these approaches is that they compartmentalize human rights and development into separate boxes, such that one is presented as a precondition for the other, rather than framing development itself as a human right. It can be assumed that the same political considerations may, unfortunately, dent a consensual acceptance of Human Rights Economy since it is perceived as a tool of HRBA. However, it is also important to state that this unfortunate situation need not be the case. In theory, the international human rights norms, standards, and principles of HRBA frameworks ought to be strongly rooted in the RTD, in which case, there is no necessary incompatibility (United Nations 2021a). The same can be said about Human Rights Economy, and it is, in fact, important that the normative framework of the RTD underpins this concept if it hopes to gain a buy-in from the developing world.

Clearly, many of the principles enshrined in the RTD are also reflected in Human Rights Economy. While they are complementary and mutually reinforcing, it is important to not confuse the two. The RTD is a self-standing human right whereas Human Rights Economy is a concept and strategy. In other words, while Human Rights Economy provides a *conceptual* framework for linking human rights with the economy both as the end and the means, the RTD establishes a *normative* framework whereby development, through the establishment of an economy that mainstreams its principles and enhances all other human rights, is itself to be considered a human right.

To ensure that the establishment of a local economy that mainstreams and enhances all human rights is itself seen as a right and not merely a practice of good national or subnational governance, it is important that the RTD is operationalized as the legal basis and normative framework of Human Rights Economy.

RTD Principles, Human Rights Economy, and Local Economies

This section analyses the key principles of the RTD in the context of building local economies that mainstream and enhance all human rights. The following analysis also incorporates relevant illustrations, good and bad, from around the world to support the contention that a Human Rights Economy, including at the local level, can only be established when it is normatively anchored in the RTD.

Development as a Human Right

Development is an inalienable right of all individuals and peoples and not merely a privilege. The RTD can be violated when any of its three guaranteed entitlements viz. the right to participate in, contribute to, and enjoy economic, social, cultural, and political development are violated. For local economies to flourish, it is fundamental that the individuals and peoples therein have the right to participate in such economies in an active, free, and meaningful manner. It is equally important that this entitlement is ensured in all aspects that affect them as a matter of human rights rather than as guiding principles of good governance. For instance, laws, policies, or practices aimed at supporting local economies must ensure free, prior, and informed consultation (and consent in case of indigenous peoples) from the very outset, of those that are seen as beneficiaries or those that may be affected. In the case of *Saramaka People v. Suriname*, the Inter-American Court of Human Rights held that the State, including at the subnational level, had violated the rights of the tribal community by not ensuring their right to effective participation in development projects affecting them due to the lack of free, prior, and informed consultation and consent (Inter-American Court of Human Rights 2007). On the other hand, there is credible research demonstrating a positive correlation between citizen participation, including civil society participation, and welfare-enhancing subnational governance of local economies (Coyoli and Gara 2025).

The right to contribute to their own development and thus to their local economies can be violated, *inter alia*, when local infrastructure projects deny local employment, or when local companies, even where available and capable, are excluded. For instance, national and subnational governments have often been accused of succumbing to the conditionality of employing predominantly Chinese workers to the exclusion of local workers in construction projects under China's Belt and Road Initiative (Chandran 2018). Protests by local communities challenging the denial of their ability to contribute to their own economy do however appear to have led to some policy changes for localizing employment (Kley 2021). An award-winning positive example is the municipality of Buenos Aires in Argentina which has created a programme called *Manos a la Obra* to ensure that dwellings in selected neighbourhoods are safe, accessible, and adequate (Buenos Aires City 2023, 23–24). Residents carry out the improvement works with their own hands, while the subnational government is responsible for monitoring the work and for the progressive provision of materials (Buenos Aires City 2023).

The right to enjoy development can be violated if human rights or the environment is negatively impacted, or specific individuals and peoples within local communities are denied the benefits due to discrimination. Indeed, the DRTD insists on "fair distribution of benefits" resulting from the development process as an essential component of the RTD. Examples of violations abound. In Mpumalanga, South Africa, for instance, while coal mining contracts issued by the government have enhanced economic growth and energy production, the benefits have largely been captured by mining companies and are concentrated in urban areas, whereas the local communities in the mining regions have faced pollution, health hazards, and loss of agriculture (Kamolane-Kgadima and Kathi 2024).

Authors of Development and Setting of Development Priorities

As rights-holders, human beings and peoples define what development means to them in their local contexts and thus self-determine their development priorities. The role of subnational governments is to guarantee that local economies are shaped by and built on the development priorities of the rights-holders and to facilitate support from national governments and international actors towards this objective. In doing so, particular attention must be paid to the rights of marginalized and vulnerable persons and groups, including disadvantaged women, persons with disabilities, children, indigenous peoples, peasants, and others working in rural areas.

Consensually agreed global development agendas such as the 2030 Agenda significantly shape development goals for national and local economies. It is, however, of utmost importance that such agendas are localized by subnational governments based on the priorities identified by rights-holders. This process includes identifying the obstacles that local economies face in realizing these priorities and which emanate from the national or international levels. Doing so is crucial because, as elaborated presently, subnational governments do have the duty to seek national and international cooperation in case they are unable to overcome such obstacles on their own. In this respect, a number of subnational governments have localized SDG targets and indicators to contextualize their development priorities and have submitted good practices and lessons learnt through Voluntary Local Reviews at the United Nations (United Nations n.d.-b).

Attention to Both the Processes and Outcomes of Development

A distinct value-added of the normative framework of the RTD in building human rights-enhancing local economies is that it requires a focus not only on the outcomes that are sought to be achieved through development, but also on the processes by which those outcomes are achieved. As development is a human right that is indivisible from and interrelated and interdependent with all other human rights, development in the context of local economies must be normatively anchored in a system of human rights and corresponding obligations established by international law. Accordingly, the promotion of, respect for, and enjoyment of certain human rights cannot justify the denial of other human rights. For instance, severe water shortages can negatively impact local economies. In such a scenario, assisting a local community suffering from drought through installing water pipelines may bring a positive outcome (water to the community), but if the lands of poor farmers are forcibly acquired for laying such pipelines without their free, prior, and informed consultation or without adequate compensation and/or rehabilitation, the process by which those outcomes are achieved is flawed and violates the core principles of the RTD. A much-researched illustration comes from the Brazilian Amazons where the regime of President Bolsonaro (2019–2022) promoted agribusiness through large-scale logging. While it could be argued that this led to enhancement of the local economy in some respects, especially in the State of Acre, the rights of local communities, including environmental and health, were seriously violated in the process. Recent efforts to ensure the participation of local communities in addressing both the process and outcome aspects have demonstrated positive results (Wit and Mourato 2022).

The Duty to Cooperate and the Three Levels of State Obligations

The duty of States to cooperate with each other for development is a fundamental principle of the RTD that is of utmost importance to local economies. International cooperation for development as an obligation on States is firmly embedded in international law. This obligation is recognized, *inter alia*, in the Charter of the United Nations; the Universal Declaration of Human Rights; the Vienna Declaration and Programme of Action; the International Covenant on Economic, Social and Cultural Rights; the Convention on the Rights of the Child; the Convention on the Rights of Persons with Disabilities; and the DRTD (United Nations 2024a, Paragraphs 9–11). The "Declaration on Principles of International Law concerning Friendly Relations and Co-operation among States in accordance with the Charter of the United Nations" of 1970, consensually adopted by the General Assembly, elaborates on the various dimensions of the duty of States to cooperate, and especially on matters related to development (United Nations 2024b). As highlighted in article 13 of the Draft International Covenant on the RTD titled "the duty to cooperate", it is an indispensable element of the normative framework of the RTD.

The duty to cooperate permeates all dimensions of national and international law, policy and practice, and engages the responsibility of States to eliminate existing obstacles to development, not create new obstacles, and positively foster policies that promote the realization of the RTD for all. That duty is not limited to collective actions taken by States at international organizations or in other global or regional partnerships, but also necessarily includes the obligation to refrain from adopting national policies that impair or nullify the RTD of those not strictly within their jurisdiction. It is a recognition of the fact that obstacles to development can emanate not only from national circumstances but also from actions by other States or through international or regional organizations (United Nations 2021a).

It is for this reason that the DRTD entails the three levels of duties for all States to respect, protect, and fulfil the RTD viz. internally, extraterritorially, and collectively.

In this respect, the RTD breaks away from the traditional focus of State obligations which is heavily inward-looking. It does recognize that each State retains the primary responsibility for ensuring that the RTD of persons within its jurisdiction, including stakeholders in local economies, is realized through appropriate national policies and programmes. As noted above, this includes ensuring that the rights-holders are guaranteed the right to participate in, contribute to, and enjoy development through local economies in a non-discriminatory manner.

However, it also recognizes that development cannot be realized in that State unless other States also discharge their duty not to impede such realization in the former through their own conduct. For instance, unilateral coercive measures that are not in accordance with international law imposed by some countries against Venezuela have had significant harmful impacts, devastating local economies in the country (United Nations 2021b). On the other hand, there is also a positive obligation on all States who are able to bilaterally or otherwise cooperate with another State (including its subnational governments) to help overcome development obstacles, and upon receipt of a request, to consider it in good faith and respond in a manner consistent with their extraterritorial obligation to realize the RTD. A good example is India's support to Antigua and Barbuda for the reconstruction of a multispecialty hospital and a post office ravaged by Hurricanes Irma and Maria in 2017, pursuant to the latter's specific request based on its self-determined priorities (United Nations 2024a). The extraterritorial obligation of States also extends to regulating conduct of corporations domiciled in their territories but operating in other States with respect to impacts on the RTD and other human rights. Indeed, article 11 of the Draft Covenant titled "Obligation to protect" seeks to codify obligations of both home states and host states in this regard and stipulates that:

> States Parties shall adopt and enforce all necessary, appropriate and reasonable measures, including administrative, legislative, investigative, judicial, diplomatic and others, to ensure that natural or legal persons,

> peoples, groups or any other State or agents that the State is in a position to regulate do not nullify or impair the enjoyment and exercise of the right to development within or outside their territories when:
>
> a Such conduct occurs, partially or fully, on the territory of the State Party;
> b The natural or legal person has the nationality of the State Party;
> c The State Party has the requisite legal duty under either domestic or international law to supervise, regulate or otherwise exercise oversight, through, inter alia, requiring human rights due diligence, of the conduct of the legal person engaging in business activities, including those of a transnational character.
>
> (United Nations 2023b)

Several cases described in this chapter demonstrate that foreign corporations can have negative impacts on local economies. The RTD thus provides an appropriate framework for regulating corporate conduct by both host and home countries to prevent and mitigate harm and ensure positive contribution to a human rights economy.

The RTD framework further recognizes that for development as a human right to reach every individual and all peoples everywhere, it must be treated as a common concern of humankind (United Nations 2023c, Preambular Paragraph 25), and as such, States must act collectively in global and regional partnerships. Such partnerships have the potential to assist States in overcoming their capability deficits through appropriate assistance, such as Special and Differential Treatment for developing and least-developed countries at the World Trade Organization, or through Special Drawing Rights or debt relief at the International Monetary Fund. Such cooperation is often essential for local economies.

At the same time, through international organizations that act as convening forums for such partnerships, especially in areas of finance and trade, States can also create significant barriers for local economies to thrive or even survive. Several trade rules adopted at the WTO have since its inception been described as a "veritable nightmare" for human rights of those in developing countries and a threat to the RTD, including of local communities (Kanade 2018c). The UN Special Rapporteur on the Right to Food has called for its Agreement on Agriculture to be wound down due to its detrimental impacts on local economies and self-sufficiency and food security therein (United Nations 2020). The long-prevailing concerns about adverse impacts of the Agreement on Trade Related Aspects of Intellectual Property Rights on public health (Hestermeyer 2007) were brought in full view also during the COVID-19 pandemic when strict rules on patenting seriously impeded access to vaccines and therapeutics in most of the developing countries, leading to over 130 countries demanding that developed countries agree to temporary waivers at the WTO (Yu 2024). Clearly, local economies suffered significantly due to the lack of access to vaccines and long lockdowns, thereby undermining the RTD (United Nations 2021a). It is important to point out that while States have collective obligations, international organizations, as independent legal persons under international law, also have obligations not to violate the RTD and human rights. The implications of this obligation for local economies are discussed separately.

The Duty to Seek National and International Cooperation

When subnational governments find themselves unable to realize their development priorities for the local economy on their own due to technological, financial, or other capacity deficits, or where obstacles emanate from international conditions, they must discharge their duty to seek international cooperation. This is especially so when national resources are also inadequate. Depending on the constitutional structure, coordination with national governments may become essential to align with national development cooperation policy frameworks and to channel requests for international cooperation through national governments. The duty of a government – subnational or national – is not affected by its right to reject any cooperation that undermines local development priorities. However, the burden to justify the rejection lies on the government concerned. Additionally, that government has an obligation to ensure that assistance provided is used appropriately (United Nations 2021b, 9).

The Duty to Conduct Human Rights Impact Assessments

Impact assessments are the only way to ensure that the rights to actively, freely, and meaningfully participate in, contribute to, and enjoy development on a non-discriminatory basis are not denied while building local economies. Additionally, since development as a right must be consistent with all other human rights, assessment of the actual and potential impacts on all human rights is indispensable. It is imperative, therefore, that subnational or national governments conduct prior and ongoing assessments of the actual and potential risks and cumulative impacts of their projects and programmes on the RTD and other human rights.

While this is also an aspect of HRBA and, perhaps Human Rights Economy, the normative framework of the RTD requires that such impact assessments are conducted not only by national and subnational governments as part of their obligations internally, but also by external cooperation providers and international organizations. A well-documented critique of HRBA is its lopsided deployment in praxis which requires impact assessments to be conducted by recipients of international cooperation but not also by the providers (United Nations 2021b). Thus, while national or subnational governments receiving cooperation to build a highway in support of a local economy may be mandated by the provider to conduct impact assessment to ensure that rights of indigenous peoples or farmers are not violated during the land acquisition or construction process, there is no such insistence on assessments to be conducted of the impacts of conditionalities that may be imposed by the provider of such cooperation (Kanade 2018c). This applies both to bilateral and multilateral cooperation providers. Providers of Official Development Assistance often determine the sectors to which assistance will be provided, insist on construction being carried out by their companies, and shape assistance as loans rather than grants. These practices clearly undermine the RTD since the cooperation is not aligned with development priorities of local economies, local companies are excluded from participation and contribution, and the assistance is debt-enhancing rather than debt-relieving. As noted previously, in some cases, conditionalities even include that the construction would be carried out by workers of the cooperation-providing country, thereby denying local employment to the rights-holders (Chandran 2018). At the multilateral level, the analysis above has demonstrated that there are often severe negative impacts on local economies as a result of conditionalities imposed by IFIs or standards adopted at the WTO, and yet, there are no impact assessments conducted therefor (United Nations 2024b). It is the responsibility of both national and subnational governments as well as of cooperation providers to individually and jointly ensure, through impact assessments, that international cooperation for enhancing local economies does not undermine the RTD and other human rights. As the Draft Covenant indicates, impact assessments are a key obligation of States (United Nations 2023b, article 21).

Data Gathering, Monitoring, and Evaluation

Local economies cannot be founded on or enhance human rights in the absence of data gathering, monitoring, and evaluation of laws, policies, and practices for development. The normative framework of the RTD, which requires appropriately disaggregated data, helps channel and focus the objectives of such exercises towards an analysis of compliance with localized development targets, and elimination of obstacles thereto, as well as to verify a fair distribution of benefits of development within local economies. Voluntary Local Reviews play a crucial role in this regard and several subnational governments have demonstrated good practices (Institute for Global Environmental Strategies 2024).

Duties of Legal Persons

As noted previously, legal persons such as business corporations and international organizations can create deep inroads into the ability of local economies to enhance human rights. The normative framework of the RTD recognizes the obligation to respect human rights, that is, the "do no harm" principle, on not just States but everyone who is capable of violating rights.

Thus, article 9 of the DRTD stipulates that

> Nothing in the present Declaration shall be construed as being contrary to the purposes and principles of the United Nations, or as implying that any State, group or person has a right to engage in any activity or to perform any act aimed at the violation of the rights set forth in the Universal Declaration of Human Rights and in the International Covenants on Human Rights.

This article in fact reflects article 30 of the Universal Declaration and common article 5(1) of the International Covenant on Civil and Political Rights and the International Covenant on Economic, Social and Cultural Rights.[3] In terms of the RTD, the duty to respect human rights is not limited to States and applies to all actors, including legal persons such as business corporations and international organizations. While debates are ongoing within the United Nations' "Open-ended Intergovernmental Working Group on Transnational Corporations and other Business Enterprises with Respect to Human Rights" on a legally binding instrument, the Draft International Covenant on the RTD already stipulates in its article 7 that:

> Nothing in the present Covenant may be interpreted as implying for any natural or legal person, people, group or State any right to engage in any activity or perform any act aimed at the destruction, nullification or impairment of any of the rights and freedoms set forth herein or at their limitation to a greater extent than is provided for in the Covenant. To that end, States Parties agree that all natural and legal persons, peoples, groups and States have the general duty under international law to refrain from participating in the violation of the right to development.[4]

International organizations enjoy independent legal personality under international law separate from the States that constitute them. As noted previously, conduct of such organizations can have detrimental impacts on local economies. A well-known example is the "Cochabamba Water Wars" where massive protests arose in 2000 in Cochabamba, Bolivia, in response to conditionalities imposed by the IMF and the World Bank requiring the municipality to privatize its water supplies, leading to significant hikes in rates for municipal customers (Hines 2022). Although demands were not articulated in the language of the RTD, it is obvious that the protests were centred around the fact that the rights-holders were neither consulted nor were their development priorities reflected in the harmful decision to privatize (Ledo 2012). Similar protests arose in many municipalities in Kenya pursuant to conditionalities imposed by the IMF during the COVID-19 pandemic requiring the government to severely cut down social spending on health and education and increase in taxes on citizens (Bhattacharya 2024).

In this context, article 9 of the Draft Covenant stipulates that

> Without prejudice to the general duty contained in article 7, States Parties agree that international organizations also have the obligation to refrain from conduct that aids, assists, directs, controls or coerces, with knowledge of the circumstances of the act, a State or another international organization to breach any obligation that the State or the latter organization may have with regard to the right to development.[5]

The RTD framework thus establishes checks not only on States when they act collectively in such organizations but also separately on the latter (United Nations 2011). This norm seeks to ensure that international organizations like the IMF or the World Bank do not require national and subnational governments to adopt policies that may undermine the RTD of those engaged in local economies.

Conclusion

The preceding analysis makes it clear that local economies are deeply entrenched in a multiplex network such that opportunities and challenges to thrive emanate from all levels, including the international and national. The ability of subnational governments to shape local economies is heavily dependent on the availability of an enabling or limiting national and international environment. The objective of establishing local economies that mainstream and enhance human rights can benefit greatly from the conceptual framework of Human Rights Economy. However, this conceptual framework can deliver success only if it is itself based on the normative framework of the RTD. Numerous advantages of operationalizing the RTD in building local economies have been discussed in this chapter. The RTD itself emerged as a norm in response to the realization that obstacles to development arise not only from national incapacities but also from an international order that may limit the governance space needed by national and subnational governments to enhance human rights. Its normative framework, with equal attention paid to internal, extraterritorial, and collective obligations of States to respect, protect, and fulfil the RTD, is indispensable if local economies are to enhance human rights. It is also important that the concept of Human Rights Economy progresses in such a way that does not frame development and human rights as separate imperatives. Seen through the RTD lens, the very establishment of local economies that enhance human rights is "development", which itself is a right of all individuals and peoples with corresponding obligations on States, international organizations, and other legal persons.

Notes

1 In international law, obligations undertaken by States apply to all its organs, including subnational governments. Article 4 of the Draft Articles on the Responsibility of States for Internationally Wrongful Acts, titled "Conduct of organs of a State" stipulates that

> The conduct of any State organ shall be considered an act of that State under international law, whether the organ exercises legislative, executive, judicial or any other functions, whatever position it holds in the organization of the State, and whatever its character as an organ of the central Government or of a territorial unit of the State.

2 Denmark, Finland, the Federal Republic of Germany, Iceland, Israel, Japan, Sweden, and the United Kingdom abstained while the United States of America voted against.
3 Article 30 of the Universal Declaration of Human Rights stipulates that

> Nothing in this Declaration may be interpreted as implying for any State, group or person any right to engage in any activity or to perform any act aimed at the destruction of any of the rights and freedoms set forth herein.

Similarly, common article 5(1) of the two current Covenants stipulates that

> nothing in the present Covenant may be interpreted as implying for any State, group or person any right to engage in any activity or perform any act aimed at the destruction of any of the rights and freedoms recognized herein or at their limitation to a greater extent than is provided for in the present Covenant.

4 See United Nations (2023d) for an extensive legal commentary analysing the international law position on this article.
5 This article is based directly on articles 14–16 of the Draft Articles on the Responsibility of International Organizations adopted by the International Law Commission.

Bibliography

Bhattacharya, Subhendu. 2024. "Economic Turmoil in Debt Distressed Kenya During Post Pandemic Years." *International Journal of Multidisciplinary Research and Publications* 7 (3): 84–89.

Buenos Aires City. 2023. *Voluntary Local Review 2023*. United Nations, 23–24. https://sdgs.un.org/topics/voluntary-local-reviews

Chandran, Nyshka. 2018. "China Can Make Its Belt and Road Project More Successful If It Taps Locals, Experts Say." *CNBC*, September 14. https://www.cnbc.com/2018/09/14/china-must-do-more-to-tap-locals-in-belt-and-road-initiative-panel.html

Coyoli, Julia, and Candalaria Gara. 2025. "Subnational Democracy, Protest, and Welfare." *World Development* 188 (Article 106784). ISSN 0305-750X, https://doi.org/10.1016/j.worlddev.2024.106784. (https://www.sciencedirect.com/science/article/pii/S0305750X24002547)

Hestermeyer, Holger. 2007. *Human Rights and the WTO: The Case of Patents and Access to Medicines*. Oxford: Oxford University Press.

Hines, Sarah. 2022. *Water for All: Community, Property, and Revolution in Modern Bolivia*. Oakland: University of California Press.

Institute for Global Environmental Strategies. 2024. "State of the Voluntary Local Reviews 2024: Strengthening the Local Implementation of the 2030 Agenda." Kamiyamaguchi, Japan. https://www.iges.or.jp/en/publication_documents/pub/researchreport/en/13753/State+of+the+Voluntary+Local+Reviews+2024%2C+Strengthening+the+Local+Implementation+of+the+2030+Agenda.pdf

Inter-American Court of Human Rights. 2007. "Saramaka People v. Suriname, Judgement on Preliminary Objections, Merits, Reparations, and Costs." *Paras*: 134–137. https://www.corteidh.or.cr/docs/casos/articulos/seriec_172_ing.pdf

Kamolane-Kgadima, Busisiwe, and Thandeka Kathi. 2024. "The Mpumalanga Highveld Air Pollution Crisis: A South African Reparations Framework for Environmental State–Corporate Harm." *International Journal for Crime, Justice and Social Democracy* 13 (1): 1–13.

Kanade, Mihir. 2018a. *Operationalizing the Right to Development for Implementation of the Sustainable Development Goals*. Geneva: United Nations. https://www.ohchr.org/en/training-materials-online-course-right-development-and-sustainable-development-goals

Kanade, Mihir. 2018b. "Operationalizing the Right to Development for Implementation of the Sustainable Development Goals." *Compendium of Articles from an Online Course on the Right to Development and the Sustainable Development Goals*. https://www.ohchr.org/en/training-materials-online-course-right-development-and-sustainable-development-goals

Kanade, Mihir. 2018c. *The Multilateral Trading System and Human Rights: A Governance Space Theory on Linkages*. New York: Routledge.

Kley, Dirk van der. 2021. "Do Belt and Road Projects Provide Local Benefits?" *Lowy Institute*. https://www.lowyinstitute.org/the-interpreter/do-belt-road-projects-provide-local-benefits

Ledo, Carmen. 2012. *Inequality and Access to Water in the Cities of Cochabamba and La Paz–El Alto*. Research Paper. Geneva: United Nations Research Institute for Social Development. https://www.unrisd.org/en/library/publications/inequality-and-access-to-water-in-the-cities-of-cochabamba-and-la-paz-el-alto

Sen, Amartya. 1999. *Development as Freedom*. Oxford: Oxford University Press.

United Nations. 1986. "Declaration on the Right to Development, Adopted by General Assembly Resolution 41/128 of 4 December 1986."

United Nations. 1992. "Report of the United Nations Conference on Environment and Development, Rio de Janeiro, Brazil, 3–14 June 1992 (A/CONF.151/26 Vol. I), annex 1." Principle 3. https://www.un.org/en/development/desa/population/migration/generalassembly/docs/globalcompact/A_CONF.151_26_Vol.I_Declaration.pdf

United Nations. 1993. "Vienna Declaration and Programme of Action, A/CONF.157/24 (Part I)." Paragraph 11. https://docs.un.org/en/A/CONF.157/24

United Nations. 2001. "Draft Articles on the Responsibility of States for Internationally Wrongful Acts." Annex to General Assembly Resolution 56/83 of 12 December 2001, and corrected by document A/56/49(Vol. I)/Corr.4, article 4. https://legal.un.org/ilc/texts/instruments/english/draft_articles/9_6_2001.pdf

United Nations. 2003. "The Human Rights-Based Approaches to Development Cooperation: Towards a Common Understanding Among UN Agencies." Prepared by the United Nations Development Group. https://unsdg.un.org/resources/human-rights-based-approach-development-cooperation-towards-common-understanding-among-un

United Nations. 2010. "Report of the High Level Task Force on the Right to Development, A/HRC/15/WG.2/TF/2/Add.2, annex, para. 1." https://docs.un.org/en/A/HRC/15/WG.2/TF/2/Add.2https://docs.un.org/en/A/HRC/15/WG.2/TF/2/Add.2

United Nations. 2011. "Draft Articles on the Responsibility of International Organizations, adopted by the International Law Commission at its sixty-third session, Yearbook of the International Law Commission, 2011, vol. II, Part Two." https://legal.un.org/ilc/texts/instruments/english/draft_articles/9_11_2011.pdf

United Nations. 2015a. "Paris Agreement to the United Nations Framework Convention on Climate Change, United Nations Treaty Series, vol. 3156." Preambular paragraph 11. https://treaties.un.org/pages/viewdetails.aspx?src=treaty&mtdsg_no=xxvii-7-d&chapter=27&clang=_en

United Nations. 2015b. "Transforming Our World: The 2030 Agenda for Sustainable Development, Resolution A/RES/70/1." Paragraphs 10–12. https://docs.un.org/en/A/RES/70/1

United Nations. 2016. "Frequently Asked Questions on the Right to Development, Fact Sheet Number 37." 19. https://www.ohchr.org/sites/default/files/Documents/Publications/FSheet37_RtD_EN.pdf

United Nations. 2020. "The Right to Food in the Context of International Trade Law and Policy." *Interim Report of the Special Rapporteur on the Right to Food*. https://docs.un.org/en/A/75/219

United Nations. 2021a. "Operationalizing the Right to Development in Achieving the Sustainable Development Goals." *Thematic Study of the Expert Mechanism on the Right to Development*. https://docs.un.org/en/A/HRC/48/63

United Nations. 2021b. "Visit to the Bolivarian Republic of Venezuela – Report of the Special Rapporteur on the Negative Impact of Unilateral Coercive Measures on the Enjoyment of Human Rights, Alena Douhan, A/HRC/48/59/Add.2." https://docs.un.org/en/A/HRC/48/59/Add.2

United Nations. 2023a. "Contribution of Development to the Enjoyment of All Human Rights, Resolution of the Human Rights Council on 14 July 2023, A/HRC/RES/53/28." https://docs.un.org/en/A/HRC/RES/53/28

United Nations. 2023b. "Draft International Covenant on the Right to Development, Report by the Chair-Rapporteur of the Working Group on the Right to Development, Zamir Akram, A/HRC/54/50." https://docs.un.org/en/A/HRC/54/50

United Nations. 2023c. "Draft International Covenant on the Right to Development, with Commentaries, A/HRC/54/50/Add.1." https://docs.un.org/en/A/HRC/54/50/Add.1

United Nations. 2023d. "Draft International Covenant on the Right to Development: Consideration of Comments and Textual Proposals, A/HRC/54/50/Add.2." https://docs.un.org/en/A/HRC/54/50/Add.2

United Nations. 2024a. "Good Practices in Operationalizing the Right to Development in South-South Cooperation." https://www.ohchr.org/sites/default/files/documents/issues/development/study-good-practices-operationalizing-rtd-ssc.pdf

United Nations. 2024b. "Operationalizing the Right to Development in International Development Cooperation, A/HRC/EMRTD/10/CRP.1."

United Nations. n.d.-a "Human Rights-Based Approach." https://unsdg.un.org/2030-agenda/universal-values/human-rights-based-approach

United Nations. n.d.-b "SDG Localization and Voluntary Local Reviews." https://sdgs.un.org/topics/voluntary-local-reviews

Wit, Fronika de, and João Mourato. 2022. "Governing the Diverse Forest: Polycentric Climate Governance in the Amazon." *World Development* 157 (Article 105955). ISSN 0305-750X, https://doi.org/10.1016/j.worlddev.2022.105955. (https://www.sciencedirect.com/science/article/pii/S0305750X22001450)

Yu, Peter. 2024. "The COVID-19 TRIPS Waiver and the WTO Ministerial Decision." In *Intellectual Property Rights in Times of Crisis*, edited by Jens Schovsbo, 1–24. Cheltenham: Edward Elgar Publishing Limited.

3 Scaling the Human Rights Economy

Sub-national Engagements

Sara Miellet

Introduction

Discussions on the human rights economy (HRE) concept often highlight *global* dimensions, focusing on a reform of the global financial architecture and critical policy areas in need of radical transformation, including fiscal, tax, trade, investment, labour and public policies (Donald et al. 2020). Rights-based approaches to the economic system have been grounded in analyses of government budgets, policies aimed at promoting social and economic rights and economic and regulatory institutions needed to enable rights-based economies (Leite & Kohonen 2024).

Taking stock of this genealogy, HRE advocates have called for a "space for wider audiences and participants [...] to share stories, perspectives, strategies and ideas in order to own the concept and approach of the HRE" and to enable "a dialogue about what HRE means in different contexts" (Sanghera 2024). This inquiry is inspired by this call and seeks to complement institution and policy-centred approaches. It considers the sub-national as an arena through which the HRE can be developed in conversation with existing approaches and practices. This chapter addresses the question of how a HRE approach can strengthen local and regional authorities' and civil society's engagements with human rights and vice versa.

In developing this approach, I draw on earlier efforts to examine the 'urbanisation of human rights'. This line of work considers the urban not simply as an empty container, but rather approaches cities and localities as critical arenas for social and democratic contestations against social injustices (Oomen & Durmuş 2019, Oomen et al., 2022). While these works highlight the urban politics of human rights, they also show "distinctions between urban, suburban, and regional no longer hold neatly" (Angel-Cabo & Sotomayor 2021). A focus on sub-national engagements broadly understood acknowledges the need to address an urban bias in research on local human rights governance and politics (Miellet 2019; Goodhart 2019). As this chapter highlights, to broaden the scope beyond cities is not just a conceptual choice. It is also inspired by examples of regions and rural communities already engaged in discussions on the need for and potential of human rights economies.

DOI: 10.4324/9781003474845-5

To develop this approach, this chapter consists of four sections. First, I clarify my understanding of the concept 'human rights economy'. Then I move on to position the HRE concept vis-à-vis broader discussions on urban and local engagements with human rights. The third section seeks to advance the debate with the help of empirical evidence by grounding the approach in an empirical analysis of local and regional governments' (LRGs) sub-national engagements with human rights, focusing on self-designated 'Human Rights Cities' (HRCs). The final section suggests how a HRE approach can deepen and sustain such sub-national engagements with human rights.

HRE and Sub-national Governance

The HRE has been described as a concept in need of operationalisation, a solution hiding in plain sight and an exciting new normative orientation. In line with Leite and Kohonen, I consider the HRE as a normative orientation, plural in nature, consisting of a set of economic alternatives with social propositions and heterogeneous framings, an "umbrella term that aims to enable plural alternative economic models that promote the realisation of human rights" (Leite & Kohonen 2024, 40).

As a pluriform approach, the HRE has grown out of decades of disillusionment with neoliberal economies policies and is rooted in evidence that the current economy model does not work for all people or the planet (de Schutter 2024a, 2024b; Hamilton & Bisnath 2024). It speaks to critiques of neoliberal macroeconomic policies and a growing interest in alternative economic models that improve the conditions of living for all.

Some of these visions of alternative economic models are far from new: debates about a feminist economy, for instance, have proliferated since its first inception in the 1970s. The feminist economy, just like a HRE, is essentially a pluralistic project, based on the idea that "improving the conditions of living for all requires dismantling of institutional structures and policies that reproduce or exacerbate gender and intersecting inequalities and addressing the climate crisis" (Berik & Kongar 2021, 3).

Many of these alternative models are not couched in the language of rights, but their aims and ambitions align with human rights principles and objectives (see, for instance, Balakrishnan & Heintz 2021). What advocates of alternative economic models have in common is that they focus on structural (economic) violence, root causes of inequalities and seek to bring about regenerative politics and fundamental changes to our economic system so that it promotes economic justice and human rights for all.

Often, alternative economic models highlight how neoliberal economic policies undermine the progressive realisation of economic, social and cultural rights. In such accounts, human rights are usually not framed as instrumental, in the sense of offering economic guardrails, or examined for their potential to transform economic systems. As Leite and Kohonen note, "rarely have human rights been seen as a fundamental axis and principled approach to (re)shaping neoliberalism" (Leite & Kohonen 2024, 42).

Efforts to examine emerging possibilities of the human rights paradigm to transform global (neoliberal) capitalism usually begin by addressing longstanding concerns and critiques. As human rights lawyer Philip Alston, in his capacity as the former UN Special Rapporteur for Extreme Poverty and Human Rights, pointed out, major human rights organisations have been reluctant to factor questions of distribution and resources into their advocacy, leaving the deep structures that perpetuate such inequalities left untouched (Whyte 2017). Others have pointed fingers at human rights expert bodies, arguing that "if ideas of human rights are to be used to challenge neoliberalism, it seems likely they will come from across a range of sites, and surely not only from elite institutions and organizations" (Nash 2019).

However, calls for a HRE have also been coming from those very bastions of the international human rights regime. The plea of the United Nations Office of the High Commissioner for Human Rights (OHCHR) for a shift to human rights economies and the efforts of the Centre for Economic and Social Rights to develop a vision on a rights-based economy suggest the tide may slowly be turning.

Policy and academic debates on the HRE show the context of its emergence, the concept's potential and the need for its operationalisation. Terms like 'operationalisation' suggest novelty or that it is an emerging concept, a reading that aligns with accounts of HRE advocates who frame it as a "fresh approach that welds together human rights with economic policymaking" (Sanghera 2024, 21). Whether we consider it entirely novel or not, it is useful to understand how the HRE approach intersects with broader debates and existing approaches and practices. Here, I follow the example of others, who have drawn on other visions of alternative economies with the intention to "include and make space for these visions to flourish; to crowd them in, not crowd them out" (Donald et al. 2020, 7).

In the following section, I argue that studies on the 'urban' and 'local' turn in human rights governance contain useful insights to further frame the contours of the HRE approach. In the introduction, I already hinted at an urban bias in research on human rights and local governance. Besides this tendency to focus on cities, I suggest the HRE approach, given its normative orientation, should take note of three other pitfalls that can creep up in the process of translating concepts to the sub-national scale: the proximity bias, the progressive bias and the pro-innovation bias.

The Proximity Bias

> As the closest level of government to their communities, local and regional authorities (LRGs) have the deepest understanding of their needs and priorities. They also have the greatest spatial, organizational and social proximity to them, which allows them to better address local challenges and promote greater participation and social inclusion.
>
> (United Cities and Local Governments 2022)

The above quote captures an often-stated sentiment in discussions on sub-national governance. Whether we are dealing with migration, climate action or the housing crisis, the local scale and cities are often framed as ideal governance spaces to realise social justice aspirations. Research on human rights at the local or urban scale is no exception; here too, we can find sceptics and optimists fiercely debating the extent of LRGs' ability to commit to the progressive realisation of human rights.

It also highlights an often-assumed virtue of LRGs, namely their proximity to local communities. The reasoning being that social proximity better positions local and regional authorities to understand community needs and to address complex challenges. This assumption of proximity also undergirds the principle of subsidiarity, a structural principle of international human rights law which affirms the primacy of institutions closest to the individual in the implementation of human rights. Historically, studies on the subsidiarity principle have focused on the relationship between domestic institutions and supranational institutions, paying less attention to the role of regional and local governance in protecting human rights. In the wake of the local turn in human rights, socio-legal scholars have analysed HRCs, in which local authorities and other actors explicitly engage with human rights principles, as manifestations of the principle of subsidiarity (Boulos & La Barbera 2023).

That said, human rights scholars have also cast doubts on the assumption of proximity and directed the gaze from the principle to study the complexities of practices that constitute local governance. In their study of the implementation of Madrid's City Council Plan, Boulos and La Barbera argue that local authorities

> may inadvertently hamper the universality of human rights by designating civil servants as the new guardians of subsidiarity, when the latter have no access to ongoing dialogues between international, regional and state institutions on the interpretation of international human rights norms. (2023, 677)

There are other reasons to study how proximity plays out in practice. As Marius Pieterse notes, "local government is more often than not the space where public power fragments and disperses, to be shared with or surrendered to a variety of non-state actors" (2022, 1220). Similarly, Angel-Cabo and Sotomayor suggest that "any engagement with the urban will require attention to the fuzzy, fragmented, sprawling and reterritorialised reality of contemporary urban regions" (2021, 265).

Building on these arguments, I argue that the development of the HRE approach would benefit from developing a critical perspective on this proximity thesis by engaging deeper with empirically grounded and practice-oriented reflections, such as those on the fragmentation of public powers. Such an approach aligns with the understanding of human rights economies, as "necessarily context specific, evidence based and intentional in their focus on contributing to the promotion of adequate standard of living for all" (Hamilton & Bisnath 2024, 12). In other words, it requires placing the emphasis on how local community needs are identified and how (social) proximity is shaped in practice by multi-level governance arrangements across different contexts.

The Progressive Bias

Research on local governance, social justice and human rights also points towards a closely related tendency: conflating local or regional autonomy with greater democracy or justice (Purcell 2006). This tendency of some researchers, policymakers and activists to assume that local and regional authorities are inherently better or more democratic levels of government has been challenged by different scholars because it relies on a generalisation "across a diversity of political, social and economic contexts" (Russell 2019). One of the well-known critics of this 'local trap' is Mark Purcell, who cautions that

> as we discover, narrate and invent new ideas about democracy and citizenship in cities, it is critical to avoid what I call the local trap, in which the local scale is assumed to be inherently more democratic than other scales. (2006, 1921)

There are traces of this thinking in human rights research, where scholars and activists have critically examined the local and urban scale with the hopes of overcoming critiques of human rights, such as the enforcement gap (De Feyter et al. 2011; Durmuş 2021). Some studies reflect a growing faith in localisation as a pathway to human rights protection and in the city as a privileged space for the realisation of rights. Here, as elsewhere, however, romanticised understandings of the urban, the local and of rescaling of rights have been nuanced or challenged (Sabchev, Miellet & Durmuş 2021). Irrespective of whether one considers cities and municipalities to be well positioned to protect and fulfil human rights, they have an obligation to do so (Dragicevic & Porter 2020).

So how can these insights on this 'progressive bias' inform our understanding of the HRE and sub-national governance? Here, I focus on one possible response, informed by the normative concept of an 'enabling state' that has been developed by advocates of the HRE approach (de Schutter & De Deurdwaerdere 2021). They consider an enabling state to be essential for human rights economies to flourish, a necessary catalyst, by virtue of its "enabling capacities of financing, legislation and regulation" (Leite & Kohonen 2024). In a similar vein, Mariana Mazzucato has raised the question of "how the role of government can be envisioned in a way [...] allowing for pro-actively creating an economy towards collective goals" (Mazzucato 2024, 9). A regularly cited promising practice in relation to the HRE is the "Fairer Scotland Duty" (de Schutter 2021). This regulatory measure, imposed since 2018 on several public bodies in Scotland, places a duty on them to actively consider how they can reduce inequalities of outcome caused by socio-economic disadvantage when making strategic decisions, such as where to locate a school or hospital (de Schutter 2021).

Drawing on this criticism of a 'progressive bias', I argue that it is important to complement this normative perspective and ideal type of an enabling state with empirical research on the full spectrum of local and regional engagements with HRE approaches. A broad view examines both the 'enabling' and the 'disabling' capacities of LRGs and considers the 'enabling state' as well the possibility of an 'evasive' or 'erratic state'. This means looking beyond the promising practices of LRGs that have put elements of HRE approaches, such as alternative measures of social, environmental and economic progress into practice, to (also) examine instances in which HRE approaches fail to take root. Such an elaborated typology of LRGs' engagement with the HRE would also serve another goal. It would show that LRGs, irrespective of whether they explicitly engage with HRE approaches, are relevant stakeholders, simply because of their enabling and disabling capacities.

The Pro-innovation Bias

Accounts that present the local, the urban or the sub-national scale as an ideal governance space often present it as 'new frontier'. This emphasis on novelty has been subject to increasing scrutiny. In relation to local migration law and governance, for instance, historians have criticised how the framing of cities as new battlegrounds of migration policies glosses over historical examples of city-states controlling migration. This insistence on novelty also speaks to another challenge, or rather tendency, known as 'neophilia': a focus on the new and exciting, rather than the effective and boring (Lee 2023).

Studies on global governance also show that research agendas can suffer from a 'pro-innovation bias' when they fixate on successful innovations, thus excluding from the literature the study of phenomena like "imitation, resistance, discontinuance, disinnovation, failures, withdrawal and de-adoption" (Godin & Vinck 2017). Such cautionary remarks can remind us of the importance of questions that otherwise may seem self-evident, such as what constitutes new in a given context, why a new framework is proposed and how the emphasis on novelty relates to other characteristics of approaches.

The HRE is said to have its roots in heterodox economic models that promote the realisation of human rights (Hamilton & Bisnath 2024). But what exactly the approach builds on needs to be more clearly spelled out. Is it drawing on successful innovations within each of these models, or does it also offer insight into their imitations, discontinuances, differences and failures? This question, abstract as it may sound, holds immediate relevance to the sub-national scale where new concepts and agendas are after all translated and operationalised.

Studies on alternative economic models, such as inclusive growth, show how local and regional actors navigate a diverse and often confusing policy space (Crisp et al., 2024). They suggest policymakers may perceive the top-down introduction of a new approach as a strategy to "skirt challenging questions of practice" and as desire of others to "move on to the next big shiny policy agenda" rather than "to build on existing approaches and work through some of the challenging aspects of operationalisation" (Waite & Roy 2022, 1997). This line of research shows what happens when these kinds of questions are not addressed. The point here is not to formulate standardised answers to such questions, but rather to enable sub-national actors to formulate localised understandings of the potential and novelty of HRE approaches.

This discussion on these three pitfalls in research on sub-national governance can be read as a cautionary tale, but it should not be mistaken for an attempt to dishearten or discourage advocates of a HRE approach. On the contrary, these insights are intended as stepping stones in the process of operationalising the HRE concept.

Grounding the HRE in Empirical Evidence from Cities and Regions

This chapter also seeks to further empirically ground debates on the HRE and sub-national governance. To anchor this part of my inquiry, I formulated two questions that examine LRGs' role in strengthening the link between human rights and economic policies. First, I analyse what scholarship on HRCs can tell us about how human rights cities and regions have sought to strengthen the link between human rights and economic policies. Second, I briefly explore literature on local and regional authorities' involvement in two alternative economic models, the social and solidarity economy (SSE) and the post-growth economy.

HRCs and Human Rights Economies?

Since 2021, global actors such as the World Organisation of Local and Regional Governments (UCLG) have increasingly called for a new generation of human rights as key standards for a renewed social contract that safeguards basic notions of human dignity, caring and solidarity. While their focus has been on a people-centred generation of new rights, the emphasis on dignity, caring and solidarity also suggests an effort to strengthen the link between human rights and the economy. The concept of a HRE has, moreover, started to feature in transnational city networks dealing with human rights. For instance, in 2023, during the World Human Rights City Forum (WHRCF), there was a panel dedicated to the topic Poverty Eradication through a Human Rights Economy (WHRCF 2023). During the panel, participants highlighted the critical role of LRGs in driving the systemic changes needed to reshape economies and sought to better understand the obstacles that LRGs face in implementing the HRE.

The WHRCF is part of a broader phenomenon in which local and regional actors, including LRGs, explicitly engage with human rights in local policy design and implementation. Rather than a unified consortium of cities or a movement, the 'Human Rights City' (HRC) movement refers to a broad and diverse spectrum of local initiatives, city and civil society networks committed to localising human rights.

The number of human rights cities and communities has grown since the first emergence of the movement in Argentina in the late 1990s, when the city of Rosario local NGOs and the mayor signed a proclamation expressing their commitment to building a human rights community and promoting respect for human rights, equity and peace, thereby declaring Rosario the first HRC in the movement (Oomen 2016). Historically, the NGO People's Movement for Human Rights Learning, the WHRCF and the UCLG have been important drivers of this phenomenon. The WHRCF is an annual forum coordinated by the South Korean city of Gwangju. There are also national initiatives, such as the US-based network, the National Human Rights City Alliance. In various smaller hamlets and towns not represented in these networks, local actors have also explicitly drawn on human rights in local policies (Miellet 2019).

Some of these networks have produced local human rights charters, such as the European Charter for Safeguarding Human Rights in the City (2001) and the Global Charter for Human Rights in the City (2011). The latter is the main global framework produced by local authorities to date, aimed at addressing human rights from a local perspective, and was adopted by UCLG in 2011. The Global Charter does not explicitly acknowledge the potential of a human rights approach to economic policy and appears to have been drafted with a view on realising rights *in* the city rather than rethinking economic policies at the sub-national scale based on human rights principles. In 2021, UCLG announced a participatory process dedicated to "updating and expanding the global-local vision on human rights offered by the Charter-Agenda with new approaches and territorial experiences". At the time of this writing, this process had not yet been concluded, but there were already indications that the HRE concept has been taken on board in the process of updating the Global Charter.[1]

So far, this discussion of the HRC movement has focused on the role of LRGs. As stated in the introduction, this chapter considers the sub-national as an important arena for the development and implementation of the HRE. In adopting this approach, I am drawing on and developing the observation of Fernandez-Wulff and Yap that the

> increased recognition of sub-national processes in human rights has primarily concerned itself with state actors, paying attention to actors inside local governments and to the institutionalisation of human rights within them, rather than with the power to promote a particular vision of justice that community-based groups and social movements can exert on these processes, which may in fact be the determining factor in the success or failure of their strategies.
>
> (2020)

In my research on human rights policies, practices and discourses in Dutch and German self-designated HRCs, I found that an explicit commitment on the part of the local government can create a strategic window of opportunity for other local actors to hold the local government accountable to deliver on its own human rights ambitions (Miellet 2022). In other words, I observed what socio-legal scholars have described as the 'paradox of empty promises' in the context of transnational movements unfolding within cities (Hafner-Burton & Tsutsui 2005). In cities such as Utrecht and Nuremberg, these negotiations between local governments, civil society and social movements resembled a sort of 'accountability politics', in which grassroots and civil society organisations pressed or encouraged the local government to commit to local human rights ambitions and subsequently and successfully used these documents, charters and declarations as standards for the municipal council to measure itself by, or to be measured by others in the city.[2]

The focus of those research projects was on the role of human rights in local responses to forced migration. However, in the literature on social movements and human rights politics in cities, we can find other illustrations of this point. In his work on the Brighton Homeless Bill of Rights, for instance, David Thomas describes how the grassroots Brighton and Hove Housing Coalition in the United Kingdom sought to complement everyday activism on the streets by constructing dissensus at the level of local democracy and bureaucracy (Thomas 2022). In this case, the grassroots coalition used the legal discourse of rights as a tool of resistance, not (only) as legally enforceable rights, but "as an aspiration and a standard for the council to measure itself by – rather rights as a vehicle for political argument" (Thomas 2022, 995).

Sub-national Engagements with the SSE and Post-growth Economy Perspectives

These examples from Utrecht, Nuremberg and Brighton show why it is important to consider HRCs both as actors in transnational settings and as arenas within which various actors and groups mobilise for rights or rights-based approaches. In these cities, human rights or human rights principles have been explicitly invoked by local actors in documents, such as local human rights agendas to develop rights-based responses to complex and intersecting challenges. Such cities, as we know from empirical research, appear to be the exception than the rule (Sabchev, Miellet & Durmuş 2021; Saul & Lambert 2024). For this reason, the next section broadens the scope by examining examples from cities and regions in which local actors have been pioneering other alternative economic models that align with human rights principles and concerns. In other words, it examines alternative pathways for grounding the HRE.

Take the social and solidarity economy (SSE), which is one of the alternative economic models officially recognised at the local, national and global levels.[3] Like the HRE, UN officials often frame it as crucial for the sub-national implementation of SDGs and the 2030 Agenda for Sustainable Development. SSE and HRE are value-centred approaches that acknowledge the primacy of people and social purpose over capital, consistent with care for people and planet, equality and fairness, interdependence, self-governance, transparency and accountability.[4] In a 2024 report, the Special Rapporteur on extreme poverty and human rights, Olivier De Schutter (2024b), outlines five priorities to move from a profit-driven economy to a HRE, the first of which is stimulating the social and solidarity economy.[5] Meanwhile, scholars have examined common features of alternative economic models, analysing whether alternative economies, such as the SSE, have human rights concerns in their concepts, theories, models and/or practices (Yi 2024, 252). These comparative inquiries of SSEs and HREs have focused on macro-economic dimensions, rather than practices at the sub-national scale.

Since 2014, local and regional authorities across the world have adopted plans to boost the SSE. Some well-known examples are Cordoba in Argentina, Barcelona in Spain and the South Korean city of Seoul. Other LRGs have drawn on general guidelines, such as the United Nations Research Institute for Social Development guidelines for local governments on policies for SSE. How exactly LRGs can build on this engagement with the SSE as they turn their focus towards human rights economies is yet to be fully understood. As Yi notes, although the SSE does not mention human rights as a cornerstone, it does align with HRE principles (2024, 252). Moreover, the SSE approach also aligns with several proposed HRE practices.

Advocates of both approaches have, for instance, set their hopes on participatory budgeting, post-growth trajectories to sustainable development and alternative measures of environmental and economic progress. In a 2023 speech, the UN High Commissioner for Human Rights, Volker Türk, referred to the HRE as a "participative project".[6] An important component is "participative, inclusive, transparent and accountable budget processes that allow the public and civil society to 'follow the money' - bolstering trust in government, and ensuring that policies will be more effective and advance people's rights".[7] Participatory budgeting has been central to many alternative economic approaches, another reason to examine how rights-based practices, such as participatory (rights-based) budgeting in the context of the HRE, could build on these earlier efforts of LRG to develop alternative economic models.

At the same time, a HRE approach offers a new perspective on the limits of, and challenges involved in, participatory budgeting. Following decades of experimenting with and using participatory budgeting, it has become an established and powerful avenue for citizen participation, but with limited capacity to address structural issues, such as minimum wage or housing policies. An often-heard argument is that participatory budgeting cannot contribute to more radical reforms if only a small percentage of LRGs' annual investments budgets are allocated to participatory projects (Sintomer et al. 2008). A HRE approach might offer new pathways to address these limitations and to scale-up participatory budgeting as part of a broader sub-national reorientation to develop a HRE.

Human rights professionals have also built on critiques of "growthism" and stressed the importance of post-growth trajectories to human rights economies. At the OHCHR, the Special Rapporteur on Extreme Poverty and Human

Rights, Olivier De Schutter, has become an advocate for post-growth trajectories to human rights economies (de Schutter 2024a). The United Nations (2024) Pact for the Future, the Global Digital Compact and Declaration on Future Generations also state a commitment to develop a framework on measures of progress on sustainable development to complement and go beyond gross domestic product.[8]

Attempts to translate post-growth thinking into practice have been made across European cities in particular, where local governments and residents are seeking to "realign their priorities away from Gross Domestic Product (GDP) growth and towards the pursuit of social and ecological well-being" (Rogers et al. 2024, 124). Besides local experiments, city networks, such as the C-40 Cities Climate Leadership Group (2024), have developed implementation guidelines, outlining how cities can use alternative measures of social, environmental and economic progress.[9] This framework does not explicitly refer to human rights: it enables cities to design local climate plans and post-growth trajectories with an equity lens. Another example is the multi-stakeholder Postgrowth Cities Coalition, which has drafted its own principles for urban justice within planetary boundaries.[10]

These networks and approaches, despite the commonalities on the level of policy mechanisms and practices (such as participatory budgeting), rarely refer to human rights. A more curious omission in some networks, however, are economic policies. While networks such as the Wellbeing Economic Alliance foreground economic policies, the Postgrowth Cities Coalition focuses on urban infrastructures and services to address the twin challenge of social equality and ecological regeneration. In these cases, a HRE approach can shed light on how these challenges are linked and shaped by broader trends, such as financialisation (see, for instance, Farha & Schwan 2021).

It is this kind of thinking that underpins, for instance, recent efforts to develop human rights-based frameworks to support local governments to address "some of the ways in which financialisation, climate change, and housing intersect to the detriment of their climate targets and human rights obligations" (Perucca, Freeman & Farha 2023). Similarly, in their discussion of racial and gender inclusion through human rights-informed economic policies, Hamilton and Bisnath note that "within the context of the current poly crisis, an integrated, systems, and building block approach which is intentional about redressing racial and gender inequalities and discrimination is urgently necessary" (2024, 12). These perspectives suggest that human rights-based frameworks, such as the HRE, offer a useful framework to develop local rights-based responses to multiple, converging crises (Donald et al. 2020). This point will be illustrated further in the following, final section of this chapter.

The HRE as a Catalyst for Sub-national Engagements with Human Rights?

I conclude this inquiry by suggesting how a HRE perspective can deepen and sustain sub-national engagements with human rights. To make this argument,

I draw on empirical material developed between 2017 and 2023 in the scope of a research project on the relationship between human rights politics and forced migration governance in Dutch and German municipalities. Several cities in which I conducted fieldwork are so-called self-designated 'human rights cities'.

Local and regional governments (LRGs) have defined, translated and applied the HRC concept in different ways. Despite these differences, it is possible to discern some trends. As Jones (2022) notes, within the HRC movement, there appears to be a prioritisation of non-discrimination and issues related to civil and political rights over economic and social rights. We also see this reflected in the focus of some HRC networks. In Utrecht and Nuremberg, human rights-inspired policies were historically strongly oriented towards anti-discrimination and inclusion. My interlocutors, active within local human rights organisations in these cities, stressed that it is important for urban human rights agendas to reflect a broader range of human rights (issues) to sustain popular and political support for sub-national engagements with human rights. They also argued that local human rights agendas should centre on escalating crises, such as the cost-of-living crisis.

Shifting the primary focus from civil and political rights to economic rights, however, fails to consider the indivisibility of human rights. It also makes it difficult to understand how emerging challenges, such as financialisation, negatively impact various human rights. In relation to the right to housing, activists and academics alike have drawn on human rights principles to develop a human rights *approach* to address the financialisation of housing: the prioritisation of housing as a financial asset rather than as a place to live (Mazzucato & Farha 2024). Such interventions seek to place human rights firmly within larger trends of worldwide structural inequality, speculation, privatisation and financialisation (Fernandez-Wulff & Yap 2020, 426).

In my research, I observed how discussions about the financialisation of housing were taking off in Dutch and German cities, but that a broader rights-based approach to financialisation was often missing. In Utrecht, for instance, the financialisation of migrant labour was flagged by scholars, but policymakers and street-level bureaucrats have been slower in responding to exploitation in emerging sectors, such as the gig economy. Municipal officials have committed to progressive and rights-based responses to forced migration, and long-standing collaborations with civil society have yielded well-documented results in Utrecht, such as shelters and legal support for undocumented migrants. The shadow side of these success stories, however, is that the attention for best practices may eventually come to overshadow other questions, such as how, if at all, human rights principles have been translated into Utrecht's financial management and economic policies.

Drawing on this example, a HRE perspective provides a pathway to deepen sub-national engagements with human rights. It positions the local government's inclusionary measures for forced migrants vis-à-vis aforementioned broader trends, such as financialisation and privatisation. A HRE approach broadens the scope from individual rights and responsibilities of, in this case, migrants, to the structural conditions that shape their inclusion in the city or region, as well as push and pull factors related to migration. This aligns with efforts of migration scholars to 'demigranticise research' and to reorient the focus of investigation away from 'migrant populations' towards 'overall populations' (Dahinden 2016). A HRE approach can not only shed new light on these parallel trends, but it can also help to give further normative direction and legitimation.[11]

A HRE approach also speaks to another issue that has preoccupied HRC advocates, namely concerns about the risks of symbolic surpluses of sub-national engagements with human rights. "Sheer symbolism well beyond cities legal ambit, window-dressing and false promises" – these are some of the more sceptical responses of critics when municipal actors attempt to develop inclusionary rights-based policies for forced migrants, even if these policies have resulted in improved access to rights and enhanced human rights protection (Hirschl 2020).

In Utrecht and Nuremberg, I observed how the self-designation as a HRC created openings for local actors to gain more insight into and control over otherwise low-visibility discretionary practices and to contest the scope and use of discretion in migration governance. The open-ended nature of municipal human rights ambitions thus enabled local activists to shed light on municipal practices that had remained outside their purview in political debates on migration governance. Let me illustrate this with an example from Nuremberg.

In June 2019, the Bavarian State Office for Asylum and Repatriation announced its plans to use the regional airport for involuntary returns of refused asylum seekers to countries such as Afghanistan. Refugee rights organisations and opposition parties in Nuremberg's municipal council criticised the plans. Attempts to pressure the local government to exert influence over return policies proved unsuccessful, as the mayor stated the municipality has no legal mandate. Opposition parties, civil society and social movements pushed back, arguing that the municipality is involved, albeit indirectly, because the local government is a key shareholder of the airport. They urged the municipal executive to do justice to the city's self-designation as a HRC by leveraging its role as one of the airports' main shareholders to prevent the use of Nuremberg airport for involuntary returns of refused asylum seekers to such countries. This strategy was unsuccessful, although the municipal executive agreed to support the establishment of a civic human rights monitoring body at the airport.

However, in shifting the scope from human rights discourses and commitments in the municipal council to the municipality's financial activities, mobilisers in Nuremberg followed the example of others across German cities, such as Frankfurt and Cologne. Rather than dismissing the municipal human rights commitment altogether as symbolic politics, activists and political actors in the city sought to move beyond such critiques and to focus pragmatically on how the role of the municipality as a shareholder and its financial policies can be harmonised with its human rights commitment.

This story of the struggle over the city's airport may seem anecdotal but is part of a broader phenomenon in which social movements seem to be intensifying 'accountability politics' and scrutinising hitherto obscured municipal activities, such as municipal shareholding. It connects to ongoing discussions in Amsterdam and London where social movements and civil society organisations are putting pressure on their local governments to adopt an 'activist shareholder role' to stop plans for airport expansions and reduce CO_2 emissions.

It also speaks to ongoing efforts of climate activists in Rotterdam, Europe's largest port and responsible for 17% of the total CO_2 emissions in the Netherlands. In Rotterdam, climate action movements have begun to pressure the local government (the main shareholder of the Rotterdam Port Authority) to prioritise public interests and to "transform the Port of Rotterdam into an entity committed to climate justice and social good".[12] In Rotterdam, the campaign to "reclaim the harbour" not only pushes back against carbon emissions and environmental risks, but also addresses concerns about extractivism in neoliberal capitalism and working conditions, as reflected in the local demand, "Rotterdammers deserve a port that prioritizes their health and well-being, the job security of port workers, and the port's long-term economic viability in the face of a decarbonising world".[13]

Such tactics are not unique, but reflective of a broader turn towards prefigurative politics that "establishes the importance of combining economic, social and environmental issues as interrelated concerns to counter and expansive and multifaceted form of capitalism" (Cooper 2022). By asking *what if* the harbour is reclaimed by citizens or what *if* the harbour is made a site for transformative politics, climate activists in Rotterdam are employing prefigurative tactics and actions. An example is the fake press release written by climate activists in Rotterdam in 2025, purporting to be a genuine Port Authority statement that outlined an alternative future for the port and city. Prefiguration is often dismissed as a minor form of politics or criticised for being too performative. However, it can also contribute to transformative politics and institutional change by radically reimagining the environment in which actions are set, by "enacting some feature of an alternative world in the present as though it has already been achieved" (Yates 2015). In these examples, prefigurative practices also bring into focus fundamental questions about how financial activities and policies at the local and urban scale can be harmonised with LRGs' human rights obligations and commitments.

Conclusion

This chapter examined the sub-national scale, cities and regions, as arenas through which HRE approaches can be further developed. The added value of this understanding is, first, that it complements actor and policy-centred approaches to human rights economies. The second argument this chapter made is that scholarship on the urban and local turn in human rights can help in the process of operationalising the HRE concept. Drawing on governance studies, I argued that the research agenda on the HRE and sub-national governance should take note of three common pitfalls that creep up in debates on the local and urban scale: the proximity bias, progressive bias and pro-innovation bias.

Building on this, I suggested to further ground the HRE concept in empirical evidence, focusing on research on HRCs and LRGs' engagement with alternative approaches, such as social and solidarity and post-growth economies. In doing so, I highlighted how post-growth and SSE approaches are not only aligned with HRE principles but also with promising and proposed HRE practices. Based on an exploratory inquiry into common and converging practices, I outlined several ways in which the HRE can complement these alternative approaches to transformative change of the neoliberal economic system.

The fourth and final section of the chapter explored the potential of a HRE approach for local and regional engagements with human rights. Drawing on empirical research conducted in Dutch and German 'human rights cities', I discussed how a HRE perspective can deepen and sustain these sub-national engagements with human rights and why it is important for local actors to do so, even in established 'human rights cities' where HRC advocates have put international human rights standards to good use. The local politics of human rights, dynamics between social movements, civil society and local authorities have enabled citizens and residents to gain more insight and exert influence over strategic policy areas and municipal (economic) activities, such as municipal shareholding, that until then had remained beyond their purview.

Truth be told, these discussions about municipal shareholding have so far remained at the fringe of urban politics in cities such as Rotterdam, Amsterdam and Nuremberg. This brings us back to the potential of a HRE approach. I am not suggesting that a HRE approach will resolve longstanding debates about the symbolic surplus of LRGs' human rights initiatives. Or, for that matter, concerns about greenwashing in cities aspiring to become climate neutral. Rather, I am suggesting that the HRE can provide a framework to make sense of the interconnections between these different struggles for rights and efforts to push for transformative change. It can provide local actors with alternative avenues to address longstanding concerns through human rights principles (such as accountability) and by bringing into focus systemic, structural issues and forms of (economic) violence.

The HRE, however, is more than a diagnostic tool; its normative orientation can also help to link local struggles (such as in Rotterdam) to broader debates about global public goods and collaborative governance. As Mazzucato notes, such a perspective "acknowledges that no single actor, whether it be government, business, or civil society, should be positioned as more important or more able than another to create value" (Mazzucato 2024, 17), which brings us back to our starting point: that the current economic model does not work for all people or the planet.

Notes

1 Interview conducted for this study in August 2024 with a city official involved in the charter update process.
2 For a general discussion of accountability politics, see Keck, Margaret E., and Kathryn A. Sikkink. *Activists beyond borders: Advocacy networks in international politics* (Cornell university press, 2014).
3 See UNGA Resolution adopted by the General Assembly on 18 April 2023, Promoting the social and solidarity economy for sustainable development, A/RES/77/281.
4 See Resolution adopted by the General Assembly on 19 December 2024 and https://www.ilo.org/resource/news/definition-social-and-solidarity-economy-adopted-international-labour.
5 See UNGA report of the Special Rapporteur on extreme poverty and human rights, Olivier De Schutter, Eradicating poverty beyond growth, A/HRC/56/61, 1 May 2024.
6 Statement by UN Human Rights Chief on human rights economy, 20 April 2023.
7 Statement by UN Human Rights Chief on human rights economy, 20 April 2023.
8 See the United Nations Pact for the Future, Global Digital Compact and Declaration on Future Generations (2024), 34.
9 See C 40 Cities Climate Leadership Group (2024), *Beyond GDP: How your city can use alternative measures of social environmental and economic progress* (2024).
10 Postgrowth Cities Coalition, *Manifesto* (2024).
11 Such an approach also resonates with Mazzucato's discussion on human rights and global public good concepts (2024, 16).
12 Extinction Rebellion Netherlands, Herover de Haven, http://archive.today/CSrRX.
13 Extinction Rebellion Netherlands, Herover de Haven, http://archive.today/CSrRX.

Bibliography

Angel-Cabo, Natalia, and Luisa Sotomayor. 2021. "Seeing human rights like a city: the prospects and perils of the urban turn." In Martha F. Davis, Morten Kjaerum and Amanda Lyons (eds.), *Research Handbook on Human Rights and Poverty*, 264–278. Edward Elgar Publishing.

Balakrishnan, Radhika, and James Heintz. 2021. "Human rights and feminist economics." In Günseli Berik and Ebru Kongar (eds.), *The Routledge Handbook of Feminist Economics*, 81–89. Routledge.

Berik, Gunseli, and Ebru Kongar. 2021. "The social provisioning approach in feminist economics." In Ebru Kongar and Günseli Berik (eds.), *The Routledge Handbook of Feminist Economics*, 3–21. Routledge.

Boulos, Sonia, and Maria Caterina La Barbera. 2023. "Obstacles to and Opportunities for Protecting Human Rights at the City Level: The Case of Madrid City Council Human Rights Plan (2017–2019)." *The International Journal of Human Rights* 27 (4): 659–684. https://doi.org/10.1080/13642987.2022.2142213

C40 Cities Climate Leadership Group. 2024. *Beyond GDP: How Your City Can Use Alternative Measures of Social Environmental and Economic Progress*. https://www.c40knowledgehub.org/s/article/Beyond-GDP-How-your-city-can-use-alternative-measures-of-social-environmental-and-economic-progress?language=en_US

Cooper, Davina. 2022. "Afterword." In Lara Monticelli (ed.), *The Future is Now: An Introduction to Prefigurative Politics*, 230–241. Bristol University Press.

Crisp, Richard, David Waite, Anne Green, Ceri Hughes, Ruth Lupton, Danny MacKinnon, and Andy Pike. 2024. "'Beyond GDP' in Cities: Assessing Alternative Approaches to Urban Economic Development." *Urban Studies* 61 (7): 1209–1229. http://dx.doi.org/10.1080/14742837.2013.870883

Dahinden, Janine. 2016. “A Plea for the ‘de-migranticization’ of Research on Migration and Integration.” *Ethnic and Racial Studies* 39 (13): 2207–2225. https://doi.org/10.1080/01419870.2015.1124129

De Feyter, Koen, Stephan Parmentier, Christiane Timmerman, and George Ulrich (eds). 2011. *The Local Relevance of Human Rights*. Cambridge University Press.

de Schutter, Olivier. 2021. “A human rights-based approach to measuring poverty.” In Martha F. Davis, Morten Kjaerum and Amanda Lyons (eds.), *Research Handbook on Human Rights and Poverty*, 2–20. Edward Elgar Publishing.

de Schutter, Olivier. 2024a. “Towards a Rights-Based Economy: Post-growth economics and the future of welfare.” In Marianne Leite and Matti Kohonen (eds.), *Righting the Economy: Towards a People's Recovery from Economic and Environmental Crisis*. Agenda Publishing.

de Schutter, Olivier. 2024b. “Eradicating poverty beyond growth.” Report of the Special Rapporteur on extreme poverty and human rights for the United Nations Human Rights Council, Fifty-sixth session 18 June–12 July 2024, Agenda item 3. https://documents.un.org/doc/un.oc/gen/g24/069/70/pdf/g2406970.pdf

Donald, Kate, Ignacio Saiz, Sergio Chaparro, Allison Corkery, Marianna Leite, Nadia Saracini, and Matti Kohonen. 2020. *A Rights-Based Economy: Putting People and Planet First*. London & New York: Center for Economic and Social Rights and Christian Aid. https://www.cesr.org/sites/default/files/Rights%20Based%20Economy%20briefing.pdf

Dragicevic, Nevena, and Bruce Porter. 2020. *Human Rights Cities: The Power and Potential of Local Government to Advance Economic and Social Rights*. Discussion Paper. Maytree. https://maytree.com/wp-content/uploads/Human_Rights_Cities.pdf

Durmuş, Elif. 2021. “How Human Rights Cross-Pollinate and Take Root: Local Governments and Refugees in Turkey.” In: Claire Boost, Andrea Broderick, Fons Coomans and Roland Moerland (eds) *Myth or Lived Reality: On the (In) Effectiveness of Human Rights*, 123–157. The Hague: T.M.C. Asser Press. https://doi.org/10.1007/978-94-6265-447-1_6

Farha, Leilani, and Kaitlin Schwan. 2021. “The human right to housing in the age of financialization.” In Martha F. Davis, Morten Kjaerum and Amanda Lyons (eds.), *The Research Handbook on Human Rights and Poverty*, 385–400. Edgar Elgar Publishing. https://doi.org/10.4337/9781788977517

Fernandez-Wulff, Paula, and Christopher Yap. 2020. “The Urban Politics of Human Rights Practice.” *Journal of Human Rights Practice* 12 (2): 409–427. https://doi.org/10.1093/jhuman/huaa019

Godin, Benoît, and Dominique Vinck (eds.) 2017. *Critical Studies of Innovation: Alternative Approaches to the Pro-Innovation Bias*. Edward Elgar Publishing.

Goodhart, Michael. 2019. “Human rights cities: making the global local.” In Alison Brysk and Michael Stohl (eds.), *Contesting Human Rights: Norms, Institutions and Practice*, 142–158. Edward Elgar Publishing.

Hafner-Burton, Emilie M., and Kiyoteru Tsutsui. 2005. “Human Rights in a Globalizing World: The Paradox of Empty Promises.” *American Journal of Sociology* 110 (5): 1373–1411. https://doi.org/10.1086/428442

Hamilton, Darrick, and Savitri Bisnath. 2024. “Racial and Gender Inclusion though Economic Policies informed by Economic and Social Rights.” *Policy Brief T20 Brasil. Task Force 01 Fighting Inequalities, Poverty and Hunger*. TF01_ST07__Racial_and_Gender_166d8b3515116f.pdf

Hirschl, Ran. 2020. *City, State: Constitutionalism and the Megacity*. Oxford University Press.

Jones, Peris. 2022. “Economic and Social Rights and the City.” In Katherine G. Young and Malcolm Langford (eds.), *Oxford Handbook on Economic and Social Rights*. Oxford Handbooks Online.

Lee, Neil. 2023. “Inclusive Innovation in Cities: From Buzzword to Policy.” *Regional Studies* 1–12. https://doi.org/10.1080/00343404.2023.2168637

Leite, Marianne, and Matti Kohonen. 2024. "Introduction: what it means to 'right the economy' and why we need it now." In Marianne Leite and Matti Kohonen (eds.), *Righting the Economy: Towards a People's Recovery from Economic and Environmental Crisis*. Agenda Publishing.
Mazzucato, Mariana. 2024. "Governing the Economics of The Common Good: From Correcting Market Failures to Shaping Collective Goals." *Journal of Economic Policy Reform* 27 (1): 1–24. https://doi.org/10.1080/17487870.2023.2280969
Mazzucato, Mariana, and Leilani Farha. 2024. *The Right to Housing: A Mission-Oriented and Human Rights-Based Approach*. Working Paper Series. IIPP WP 2023-07. London, UK: UCL Institute for Innovation and Public Purpose.
Miellet, Sara. 2019. "Human Rights Encounters in Small Places: The Contestation of Human Rights Responsibilities in Three Dutch Municipalities." *The Journal of Legal Pluralism and Unofficial Law* 51 (2): 213–232. https://doi.org/10.1080/07329113.2019.1625699
Miellet, Sara. 2022. *Unmoored, Not Adrift: Local Perspectives on the Politics of Human Rights and Forced Migration*. PhD thesis, Utrecht University. https://dspace.library.uu.nl/bitstream/handle/1874/424385/phdmanuscriptmielletdigital%20copy%20-%206389d18f56b88.pdf?sequence=1&isAllowed=y
Nash, Kate. 2019. "The Cultural Politics of Human Rights and Neoliberalism." *Journal of Human Rights* 18 (5): 490–505. https://doi.org/10.1080/14754835.2019.1653174
Oomen, Barbara. 2016. "Introduction: The promise and challenges of human rights cities." In *Barbara Oomen*, Martha Davis and Michele Grigolo (eds.), *Global Urban Justice*: *The Rise of Human Right Cities*. Cambridge University Press.
Oomen, Barbara, and Elif Durmuş. 2019. "Cities and Plural Understandings of Human Rights: Agents, Actors, Arenas." *The Journal of Legal Pluralism and Unofficial Law* 51: 141–150. https://doi.org/10.1080/07329113.2019.1596731
Oomen, Barbara, Elif Durmuş, Sara Miellet, Janne E. Nijman, and Lisa Roodenburg. 2022. "General Introduction: Urban politics of human rights." In *Urban Politics of Human Rights*, 1–22. Routledge.
Perucca, Julieta, Sam Freeman, and Leilani Farha. 2023. "The True Cost of Financialization: Housing, Human Rights, and Climate Change." *Journal of City Climate Policy and Economy* 2: 20–36. https://doi.org/10.3138/jccpe-2023-0201
Pieterse, Marius. 2022. "Urbanizing Human Rights Law: Cities, Local Governance and Corporate Power." *German Law Journal* 23 (9): 1212–1225. https://doi.org/10.1017/glj.2022.77.
Purcell, Mark. 2006. "Urban Democracy and the Local Trap." *Urban Studies* 43 (11): 1921–1941. https://doi.org/10.1080/00420980600897826
Rogers, Ben, et al. 2024. "Prosperity Beyond Growth: An Emerging Agenda for European Cities." *Journal of City Climate Policy and Economy* 2 (2): 124–146. https://doi.org/10.3138/jccpe-2023-0001
Russell, Bertie. 2019. "Beyond the Local Trap: New Municipalism and the Rise of The Fearless Cities." *Antipode* 51 (3): 989–1010. https://doi.org/10.1111/anti.12520
Sabchev, Tihomir, Sara Miellet, and Elif Durmuş. 2021. "Human rights localisation and individual agency: From 'hobby of the few' to the few behind the hobby." In *Myth or Lived Reality: On the (In) Effectiveness of Human Rights*, 183–211. The Hague: TMC Asser Press.
Sanghera, Jyoti. 2024. "Human Rights Economy for People and the Planet: Framing the Contours of an Approach." In Marianne Leite and Matti Kohonen (eds.), *Righting the Economy: Towards a People's Recovery from Economic and Environmental Crisis*, xiii–xx. Agenda Publishing.
Saul, Matthew, and Elisabeth Lambert. 2024. "Subnational Authorities and Human Rights in Europe." *The International Journal of Human Rights* 28 (7): 1053–1059. https://doi.org/10.1080/13642987.2024.2372158

Sintomer, Yves, Carsten Herzberg, and Anja Röcke. 2008. "From Porto Alegre to Europe: Potentials and Limitations of Participatory Budgeting." *International Journal of Urban and Regional Research* 32 (1): 164–178. https://doi.org/10.1111/j.1468-2427.2008.00777.x

Thomas, David. 2022. "The Brighton Homeless Bill of Rights." *City* 26 (5–6): 983–997. https://doi.org/10.1080/13604813.2022.2126201

United Cities and Local Governments. 2022. *Pathways to Urban and Territorial Equality*. Gold VI report. https://gold.uclg.org/sites/default/files/field-document/211222_uclg-gold-vi_en_report_for_web.pdf

United Nations. 2024. *Pact for the Future, Global Digital Compact and Declaration on Future Generations*. https://www.un.org/sites/un2.un.org/files/sotf-pact_for_the_future_adopted.pdf

Waite, David, and Graeme Roy. 2022. "The Promises and Pitfalls of Operationalizing Inclusive Growth." *Regional Studies* 56 (11): 1989–2000. https://doi.org/10.1080/00343404.2022.2050201

Whyte, J. 2017. "Human Rights and The Collateral Damage of Neoliberalism." *Theory & Event* 20 (1): 137–151.

World Human Rights Cities Forum. 2023. *The 13th WHRCF Final Report*. https://en.whrcf.org/meetingdata/?q=YToyOntzOjEyOiJrZXl3b3JkX3R5cGUiO3M6MzoiYWxsIjtzOjQ6InBhZ2UiO2k6MjM7fQ%3D%3D&bmode=view&idx=50396620&t=board&category=5VB06FLQ80

Yates, Luke. 2015. "Rethinking Prefiguration: Alternatives, Micropolitics and Goals in Social Movements." *Social Movement Studies* 14 (1): 1–21. https://doi.org/10.1080/14742837.2013.870883

Yi, Icheong. 2024. "Social and solidarity economy as an alternative economy for the protection of human rights." In Marianne Leite and Matti Kohonen (eds.), *Righting the Economy: Towards a People's Recovery from Economic and Environmental Crisis*, 250–272. Agenda Publishing.

4 Human Rights Economies and Local Government Budgets

Todd Howland and Martin Mulwa

Introduction

Traditionally, human rights have had a marginal role in economic policymaking. The current socio-economic context makes it more urgent to link economic policymaking with human rights. According to the UN Office of the High Commissioner for Human Rights (OHCHR) (2023a), the human rights economy contributes to the establishment of a renewed social contract between Governments and people and re-prioritizes the well-being of people and the planet. This is realized when States design budgets and revenue generation strategies by prioritizing and investing in universal access to social services such as social protection, health, quality education, and other economic and social rights to curb the growing poverty and inequalities (Centre for Economic and Social Rights, 2020). Local Governments are an essential building block for constructing a human rights economy.

Public budgets are one of the most powerful economic tools to meet the needs of people, especially the poor and marginalized communities, and are critical in facilitating the fulfilment of human rights at the national, sub-national, and local levels. For instance, to ensure any human right, whether it is the right to healthcare or education, or civil and political rights, financial resources are necessary. However, in many countries, public budgets do not always reflect human rights standards and obligations in their content, and often budget processes are carried without applying human rights principles, such as participation and transparency. The open budget survey (OBS) (2023) (International Budget Partnership 2024) report finds the global average transparency score is only 45 out of 100, which is well short of a score of 61—the benchmark for indicating sufficient levels of budget information that is publicly available and can support informed public debate on the budget. This implies that Governments at national and local levels around the world are not providing adequate information to the public to facilitate effective participation. OBS (2023) also finds that meaningful public participation in the budget process is rare, with the global average score for public participation at only 15 out of 100.

DOI: 10.4324/9781003474845-6

What Is a Human Rights Budgeting Framework at the Local Level?

The human rights framework can and should be linked to all the components of a budget cycle. Budget processes differ across countries and between local Governments, but broadly speaking they have the following stages: budget formulation, budget approval, budget execution, and budget oversight. There are three key aspects (OHCHR, 2012) to human rights budgeting. First, it is essential to ensure that the budget-making process throughout the budget cycle conforms with the human rights cross-cutting principles of participation and transparency. Second, the extent to which the content conforms with the State's human rights obligations. Third, the extent to which budget allocations and expenditures are producing and enhancing the enjoyment of human rights for all (OHCHR, 2017).

The Budget Process—Transparency and Meaningful Participation

Budget transparency is the first critical step for local Government in respecting the rights to information and to effective participation in public affairs and has the potential to result in more rights-enhancing and evidence-based budgets. Often creating participation at the local level is easier to organize and eventually helps produce changes at both the local and national levels. Citizens should have access to budget-related information and the opportunity to actively engage in decisions regarding the budget's formulation, implementation, and evaluation. When these data are updated based on actual execution, rights holders can compare the government's initial estimates with real outcomes to advocate for needed reforms.

Budget Allocations and Expenditures

While few local Governments utilize their human rights obligations to guide budget allocations and expenditures, it is critical for local Governments to do so, and there are few principles that need to be integrated into the allocation and expenditure exercise. (1) Maximize available resources for the progressive realization of economic, social, and cultural rights (International Covenant on Economic, Social and Cultural Rights (ICESCR), 1966a).[1] (2) Ensure the minimum essential levels for the enjoyment of rights like food, housing, education, and health, and these rights should be prioritized in the budget (CESCR, 1990).[2] (3) Adhere to the Leave No One Behind principle, alongside the duty to promote equality and non-discrimination.

Budget Expenditures Producing Measurable Positive Change in Outcome

The third aspect for local Governments relates to the extent to which budget allocations and expenditure are producing and enhancing the enjoyment of rights for all in a non-discriminatory manner and how this information feeds back into the next budget cycle. Effective human rights budgeting relies on robust feedback mechanisms to assess the impact of fiscal policies on human rights outcomes. For instance, studies have found that crowdsourcing is an effective and efficient way of improving public service delivery and enhancing social contract between citizens and governments (Brabham, 2015; Clark et al., 2016). Feedback mechanisms provide essential data for evaluating the respect for and realization of human rights and allow local governments to make adjustments to achieve the desired rights-enhancing results.

Tools and Examples of the Three-Step Process

Participatory tools are increasingly offered to local Governments by the United Nations Population Fund (UNFPA, 2022) and the World Health Organisation (WHO, 2023) to transition from traditional sectoral budgeting to rights-centred frameworks. Some local Governments have successfully integrated feedback mechanisms into their governance models, such as Kerala's People's Plan Campaign in India and the participatory budgeting model in Porto Alegre, Brazil. These two examples demonstrate the critical importance to include feedback mechanisms in budgeting processes so that human rights compliance may be assessed and enhanced (World Bank, 2008; World Bank, 2003). The establishment of robust feedback loops empowers communities to work with local Governments in a continual process with the goal of maximizing available resources to measurably and progressively realize economic and social rights and thereby improve the lives of those living in the community. OHCHR has learned from this and taken a step further in capturing community feedback and accompanying local Governments to dynamically adjust budget priorities to better address the rights-based needs of their citizens (OHCHR, 2023c). This is particularly relevant in marginalized communities, where traditional sectoral analyses often overlook the specific human rights implications of budget allocations and expenditure (OHCHR & IBP, 2017).

Human rights budgeting at the local level operates as a dynamic framework where the three key aspects—participation and transparency in the process, alignment of budget allocations and expenditures with human rights obligations, and enhancing rights enjoyment through feedback mechanisms—function both independently and as part of a continuous and iterative process (see Figure 4.1). Each aspect has distinct roles: participation ensures that diverse voices, particularly from marginalized groups, influence budget decisions; alignment ensures resources are allocated and spent in ways that meet the State's human rights obligations; and outcomes measure the impacts of budget allocations and expenditures on improving access to essential services and reducing inequalities. Participatory processes at the local level inform budget content by highlighting unmet needs, particularly in vulnerable communities. Monitoring of the allocations by the community creates a new symbiotic relation of trust and enables the measurement of outcomes. These outcomes, in turn, provide critical feedback for refining future participatory

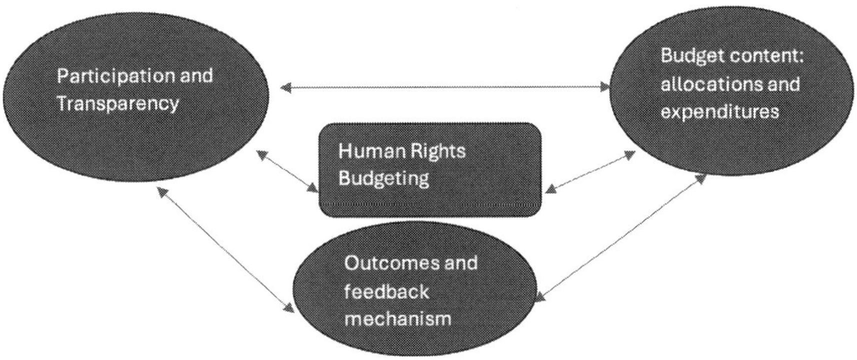

Figure 4.1 Diagram of the human rights budgeting as an iterative process.

Source: Created by the Authors.

processes and ensuring better alignment of budget allocations and expenditures with human rights obligations. This creates an iterative loop, where the principles, content, and outcomes continuously reinforce one another, fostering human rights-enhancing budgets that evolve and adapt across budget cycles.

Normative Framework of Human Rights and Budgets

This section briefly discusses the normative framework of human rights and public budgets to reinforce local authorities' familiarity with these obligations that apply at all levels of Government. First, we discuss the guiding principles for the budget process. Second, we present the guiding human rights obligations on the budget content. Third, we discuss the outcome and feedback mechanisms.

Transparency and Participation

For local Governments, during the budget process, it is critical to respect the rights to participate in the conduct of public affairs and access to information (International Covenant on Civil and Political Rights (ICCPR) art. 25, art. 19). First, Governments must ensure that rights holders have access to budget-related information[3] that can potentially result in effective participation in all stages of the budget process, from formulation and implementation to evaluation of the budget. For local Governments to respect these rights, there are eight key budget documents that should be made publicly available within specific timeframes, as per international standards (International Monetary Fund (IMF), 2019; Organisation for Economic Cooperation and Development (OECD) (2017). They are the pre-budget statement, no later than one month prior to the introduction of the budget proposal to the legislature; the budget proposal, while the legislature is considering it, and in no case should this be less than three months prior to the start of the fiscal year; the enacted budget, no later than three months after it is approved; citizen's budget after the budget is enacted; in-year reports, at least on a quarterly basis, within a quarter; the mid-year review, which should be released within six weeks of the end of the mid-year period; the year-end report, which should be released within six months of the end of the fiscal year; and an audit report, which should be produced at the year-end and this report should be published within 12 months.

The OHCHR guideline on the right to participate in public affairs recognizes the importance of fiscal transparency by indicating that: "Openness and transparency should be ensured at all stages of decision-making by public authorities, from initial planning to budgeting, implementation, monitoring and evaluation" (OHCHR, 2018). Transparency is essential for meaningful participation in the budget-making process.

Budget Content

The obligations guiding the budget content include the use of maximum available resources, the minimum core obligations, and equality and non-discrimination.

Use of Maximum Available Resources (MAR)

Local Governments are required to utilize the maximum of its available resources to progressively realize economic, social, and cultural rights (United Nations, 1966). This implies that when there is economic growth or growth in revenue, there is also an increased investment in these rights. At the sub-national level, local Governments have a duty to allocate their resources—revenues from local taxes, transfers from the national Government, and other sources—towards the progressive realization of healthcare, education, water, housing, etc., depending on the functions that are decentralized. To determine whether a Government at both national and sub-national levels is using the MAR for the progressive realization of economic and social rights, it is useful to consider the share of the budget allocated to economic and social rights-related areas (health, education, social protection, etc.) in relation to the level needed for everyone to enjoy these rights. To assess whether a Government is complying with its MAR obligation, it is also necessary to look at the composition of the funds (recurrent and capital expenditures) directed to economic and social rights-related areas. The Government revenue collection and expenditure must be efficient to avoid wasteful collection and expenditure. In addition, it is important for Government to unlock new sources of revenue and ensure that the burden does not fall disproportionately on those left behind, for example adopting fair and progressive taxation policies, addressing tax avoidance, illicit financial flows, and corruption (CESR, 2020 General Comment 3, para 9).[4] Government expenditure needs to result in a measurable improvement in the level of enjoyment of rights.

Minimum Core Obligations

The Committee on ESCR (CESCR) has discussed the meaning of minimum core obligations and concludes that the State Parties, including local Governments, have the obligation of providing minimum essential levels of each right. For example, the State should ensure no individual is deprived of essential food, primary healthcare, adequate shelter, and quality education to secure a minimum living standard (CESCR, 1990). Even in times of crisis, Governments should ringfence essential spending and implement counter-cyclical economic policies (CESCR, 2019)[5] to avoid 'retrogression' in economic and social rights. This implies that budget allocations and expenditures on economic and social rights-related areas should be given priority in the budget formulation and execution (CESCR, 2016; OHCHR, 2013).[6]

Equality and Non-discrimination

The obligation of equality and non-discrimination is cross-cutting and recognized in all international human rights treaties and applies at the local levels. This obligation requires that all policies and budgets promote equality, avoid both direct and indirect discrimination (CESCR, 2008),[7] and adopt special measures where necessary to address historical marginalization and discrimination, including along the lines of gender, race, ethnicity, disability, age, locations, and socio-economic status. This obligation is key as it moves beyond analysing economic policies and budgets in terms of their likely aggregate benefits, towards a more disaggregated approach, identifying the 'winners' and 'losers' of budget choices and economic reforms, to avoid or mitigate unequal impacts or entrench inequalities.

Outcomes and Feedback

The principle of progressive realization means local Governments not only need to invest more money in ESCR as the economy grows but also measurably improve the level of respect for those rights. However, simply spending does not guarantee measurable outcome and enjoyment of rights. Thus, feedback from rights holders is essential to knowing whether spending is producing the intended human rights improvement. Feedback from a human rights lens identifies and establishes the extent to which the laws, policies, institutions, and enforcement mechanisms facilitate necessary changes in budgets and the way money is spent for the realization of human rights.

Case Study: Local Governments in Kenya—Towards Human Rights Budgets

Kenya is a lower middle-income country with a per capita income of US $1,950 (World Bank, 2024). Kenya faces key development challenges, including high levels of poverty and inequality, youth unemployment, lack of fiscal transparency and accountability, climate change vulnerabilities, economic weakness to internal and external shocks, and high levels of debt vulnerabilities. Kenya was ranked 146 out of 193 countries in the United Nations Development Programme's Human Development Index (HDI)[8] (UNDP, 2024). Kenya came in at 75 out of 146 countries globally (and 13 out of 35 in sub-Saharan Africa) in the Global Gender Gap ranking[9] of gender equality (World Economic Forum (WEF), 2024). Income inequality, as measured by the Gini Index, stands at 0.408, with the share of income for the top 10% standing at 30.3% compared to 16% for the bottom 40% (Kenya National Bureau of Statistics, 2020). Inequalities in the distribution of growth and income remain key policy concerns in Kenya. In this section, we apply a human rights framework to budgets in Kenya at the local level in the context of the national process.

Human Rights Budgeting in Kenya

The Kenyan State has voluntarily taken on the duty to protect, promote, and respect human rights. This duty has been set out in the Constitution of Kenya under the Chapter on the Bill of Rights. Kenya established legislative and fiscal practices following its ratification of the International Covenant on Economic, Social and Cultural Rights, along with the adoption of Agenda 2030 on Sustainable Development. Kenya's public finance system was established under the 2010 Constitution and the Public Finance Management (PFM) Act of 2012. Both laws place a strong emphasis on fiscal transparency and participation in terms of the information and the timelines within which such information should be shared with the public. The criteria guaranteeing fiscal transparency require that fiscal information must be comprehensive, orderly, credible, timely, and of quality and integrity.

Transparency and Participation

Budget transparency is considered an integral part of the budget-making process in Kenya (Republic of Kenya, 2012). While the Kenyan Government may, for example, publish information on the fiscal balance and broad sector spending such as health and education, it fails to disaggregate the data at the sub-sector level, showing how much of the spending on health and education was also redistributed towards communities facing multiple and persistent forms of discrimination. Access to timely, comprehensive, and disaggregated budget information facilitates effective participatory processes, informing budget allocations and expenditures to meet the needs of communities.

Budget Allocations and Expenditures

The revenue generation cycle shows the different sources of revenue and forecasts made by the Government. The Constitution singles out Article 43 as the key provision setting out the State's economic and social rights obligations. The constitution protects against fiscal slippages that may corrode the equitable development and distribution of resources, especially for marginalized groups (Constitution of Kenya, 2010, art. 201(b)). For instance, Articles 10 (on sustainable development as part of the nation's governing policy) and 43 (on the right to health, housing, sanitation, food, water, social security, and education) of the Constitution are reflective of human rights obligations and should influence the State's sources of revenue and how they should be committed (art. 20(5), art. 21). The constitutional provisions under Chapter 12 on Public Finance explain the Government's obligation towards the progressive realization of its citizens' social and economic rights in the context of the state's fiscal capacity and powers.

Despite the legal framework providing the basis for allocating and spending resources in a way that advances the enjoyment of human rights, the country has underinvested in critical sectors linked to economic and social rights. According to OHCHR's budget analysis, the Kenyan Government has chronically underinvested in social sectors (Mulwa, 2022). In fiscal year 2022/23, the Government allocated 23.06% of its total budget to social sector investment (health, education, social protection, and water and sanitation), which represents 6.06% of GDP (UN Kenya, 2024). Social sector allocations as a share of the total budget have consistently decreased since 2019, from 26.49% to 23.06% in 2022, and as a share of GDP, decreased from 7.3% in 2019 to 6.06% in 2022 (UN Kenya, 2024). These allocations are inconsistent with the obligation to maximize available resources. In FY 2024/25, Kenya allocated an average of 27.5% of the total budget for the social sectors, a decrease from an average of 29.6% in FY 2023/24, and as a share of GDP, social sector investment decreased from a high of 7.4% in FY 2021/22 to 6.4% of GDP in FY 2024/25 (UN Kenya, 2024). This is despite the country experiencing real GDP growth of over 5% after the COVID-19 pandemic, which is inconsistent with Kenya's progressive realization obligation. This illustrates that the gains from growth are not adequately ploughed back into social spending. While there is no binding international benchmark for social spending, the current spending falls below the recommended international and regional minimum levels for social expenditure.[10] This low investment in the social sectors has implications for the realization and enjoyment of economic and social rights and attainment of the 2030 Agenda.

Outcomes and Feedback

Even though Kenya has a legal framework for human rights budgeting, the country faces challenges in producing budget outcomes that can facilitate the enjoyment of rights for all in a non-discriminatory manner. The right to health is a fundamental human right guaranteed in the Constitution of Kenya (2010) (art. 43 (1)(a)). Despite health being a human right, many Kenyans are unable to access quality healthcare due to financial constraints (KNBS, 2023). Only 26% of Kenyans had access to health insurance coverage (KNBS, 2023). Many Kenyans reported funding their health expenditures through out-of-pocket spending, which accounts for 27% of health expenditure and is twice the recommended WHO target of 12–15% (Ministry of Health, 2019). This demonstrates the need for effective human rights budgeting that relies on robust feedback mechanisms to assess the impacts of fiscal policies on human rights outcomes and informs future budget cycles in order to better serve the needs of all people and advance the enjoyment of rights for all.

Local-Level Human Rights Budgeting in Kenya

While national Governments participate in the UN human rights mechanisms directly, human rights law is binding on local Governments and provides beneficial policy guardrails. At the sub-national level, local Governments in Kenya operate with varying degrees of legal and political autonomy. The county Governments (i.e. sub-national level) have a major role to play in the governance and delivery of economic and social rights and achievement of SDGs as it relates to their budgets but remain dependent on the national Government for a significant portion of their budgets.

Transparency and Participation

County Governments are required by law to put in place regulatory frameworks, structures, and mechanisms and provide for appropriate spaces for all persons to participate in the budget process, i.e., women and men of all ages, those with disabilities, and those in difficult-to-reach areas. The PFM Act (2012) stipulates that county Governments should produce, publish, and publicize all key budget documents during the budget cycle. Comprehensive, adequate, accessible, reliable, timely, and user-friendly information is essential to facilitate meaningful and effective public participation in budget-making processes and enhance service delivery to beneficiaries. The constitution and the PFM Act mandate the county treasuries to prepare key budget documents within specified timelines for approval by the legislature.

Despite the existence of these structures and the processes laid out to facilitate increased participation, there are concerns about the time, method of communication, quality of the process, and engagement capacity of Kenyans. IBP's (2023) open survey results show that the average county budget transparency index in 2023 was 56 out of 100 points, compared to 41 out of 100 points in the previous year. This 15-point improvement was mainly driven by counties making more budget documents publicly available and providing more comprehensive information. However, this is short of a score of 61—the benchmark for indicating sufficient levels of budget information are publicly available and can support informed public debate on the budget (IBP, 2023). Some of the counties are falling behind. For instance, Trans Nzoia County did not publish 9 of the 11 budget documents that are required for effective and meaningful participation of citizens in the county (IBP, 2023). Garissa County, which has high levels of poverty,[11] also has low levels of fiscal transparency, as the county has never published its budget implementation report on its website (IBP, 2023).

The lack of comprehensive and adequate fiscal information limits public engagement in the budget-making process at all levels of governance, village, ward, sub-county, county, national levels. To address this deficiency, OHCHR Kenya has been working with local organizations to train and ensure rights holders are seen and heard within the county-level budget-making process. Training initiatives are conducted in collaboration with local organizations and county Government officials, by focusing on strengthening the three key aspects of human rights budgeting—participation and transparency in the process, alignment of budget allocations and expenditures with human rights obligations, and enhancing rights enjoyment through feedback mechanisms (OHCHR, 2023a). Community participation is fostered through meetings, outreach programmes, and radio talk shows, empowering human rights budget champions to advocate for greater transparency and inclusion (OHCHR, 2023b). This has led to stronger collaboration between county officials, CSOs, and marginalized groups, ensuring their voices and priorities are integrated into the budgeting process (OHCHR, 2023c). By prioritizing grassroots inputs, county-level budgeting can direct investments towards underserved areas (e.g., women and marginalized communities) and enhance the rights to water, sanitation, and healthcare. This localized focus can potentially improve the overall quality of life and well-being, fostering equity and reducing discrimination. This is meant to develop the capacity of CSOs in monitoring Government spending and assessing the alignment of budgetary decisions with human rights obligations, and to advocate for alternative policy choices for the enjoyment of human rights.

Budget Allocation and Expenditure

A context-specific, human rights-based analysis of the budget cycles at the sub-national level reveals the socio-economic and geographic widening gaps resulting from deficient funding across sectors implementing economic and social rights. For example, health is the most decentralized Government function in Kenya, with 99% of health facilities under county administration (IBP, 2023). More transparency and information are needed related to how county Governments allocate, manage, and account for resources for health priorities, as this impacts the ability of communities, civil society, and citizens to fully and effectively participate, monitor, and advocate for changes in decisions that impact them. Only six out of the 34 counties evaluated provided information on health personnel in their health budgets (KNBS, 2024).[12]

Outcome and Feedback

At the county level, feedback mechanisms embedded in participatory budgeting can create a more inclusive and rights-based approach to governance, ensuring that marginalized communities are active agents in shaping budget decisions. A human rights feedback loop using focus groups or crowdsourcing can provide useful information about the impacts of the spending. This approach not only enhances human rights by empowering marginalized communities to actively engage in decision-making but also provides critical feedback for refining future participatory processes and ensuring better alignment of budget allocations and expenditures with human rights standards. For instance, in Nakuru County—one of the counties OHCHR Kenya is supporting—the training of local organizations led to enhanced participation and transparency through community dialogues that also provide policymakers with direct feedback on the implementation of their policies. Increased public engagement, particularly among women and youth, influenced budget allocations, including funding for health, water, and social protection.[13] As a result, the women, youth, and socially disadvantaged groups who participated were able to gain influence over budget priorities, then monitor how the money was spent and indicate what went right and what went wrong. Their substantive engagement enabled systemic inequities in resource allocation to be addressed and resulted in the promotion of the rights to health, education, water and sanitation, and social protection.

Feedback mechanisms at the local level play a critical role in reducing discrimination and strengthening social and economic rights. By involving excluded groups, such as women and persons with disabilities, local Governments can address injustices and inequalities and enhance access to public services at the local level. They can also learn from these groups about the extent to which the changes in investments produced the desired change. These mechanisms not only amplify the voices of vulnerable groups but also foster accountability and trust between citizens and local Governments, ensuring that public spending aligns with human rights obligations. Ultimately, they bridge the gap between citizens and the local Governments, creating a more inclusive and equitable governance framework.

Based on the Kenya experience, more work is needed to develop a practical toolkit for Governments, particularly at the local level, for monitoring and creation of a feedback loop on the impact of budget allocations and expenditures. An even greater priority is clarifying the role of human rights in public budgeting and obtaining acceptance from local Government authorities of its importance and value added. Beyond being a legal obligation, human rights provide essential pathways to maximize benefits for individuals, communities, and the economy.

Conclusion

The human rights framework in local public budgets provides a pathway to ensure that macroeconomic policies serve the needs of people, particularly those in poverty, who often face multiple forms of discrimination. Through budgeting, the local Governments establish their priorities and commit to concrete actions, which may improve or limit the enjoyment of certain rights. A budget that is transparent and grounded in a State's human rights obligations, and implemented and monitored with multi-stakeholder participation, is essential for the realization of all human rights and the deepening of trust between the Government and its people. The content in the budget document reflects not only the Government's annual revenue and expenditures, but also its commitments to human rights, and steps to translate its development priorities and budgetary planning towards achieving the goals of the community and the nation. At the local level, Governments can play a central role in enhancing a human rights economy, as they can have stronger incentives to provide services consistent with local needs and preferences and their human rights obligations.

The case study shows that shifting from sectoral budget investments to human rights-centred methods requires an emphasis on fiscal transparency, citizen participation, and effective feedback mechanisms. While sectoral analysis provides a framework for resource appraisal, it frequently lacks the depth essential to achieve equitable results. Through the incorporation of participatory budgeting and effective feedback systems, local Governments can better align their budgetary policies with human rights obligations, ensuring that resource allocations reflect the needs of marginalized people. Therefore, the three aspects presented in this chapter, while independent, are deeply interconnected. As discussed, participatory processes inform budget content by highlighting unmet needs, particularly in vulnerable communities. Transparency ensures that allocated resources are effectively monitored, creating trust and enabling the measurement of outcomes. The monitoring of these outcomes from a human rights perspective, in turn, provides critical feedback for refining future participatory processes and ensuring better alignment of budget allocations and expenditures with human rights standards. This creates an iterative loop, where the principles, content, and outcomes continuously reinforce one another, fostering human rights enhancing budgets that evolve and adapt across budget cycles. Moreover, inclusive feedback mechanisms help Governments address systemic inequalities by involving communities in budget-making decisions.

The human rights framework presented in this chapter provides a plausible road ahead for countries looking to operationalize human rights economy and improve their level of respect for human rights and the multiple benefits this produces for societies and economies. More work is needed to further distil these experiences and others into a toolkit that can be easily applied by local as well as national Governments. Additional work is needed to create buy-in among local and national Government officials of the relevance of human rights to public budgets.

Notes

1 International Covenant on Economic, Social and Cultural Rights.
2 See CESCR General Comment No. 3: The Nature of States Parties' Obligations (Art. 2, Para. 1, of the Covenant), 1990. In addition, other UN human rights mechanisms, including the Committee on Economic, Social and Cultural rights (CESCR), the Committee on the Elimination of Discrimination against Women,

the Committee on the Elimination of Racial Discrimination, the Committee of the Rights of Persons with Disabilities, the Committee on the Rights of the Child, as well as the special procedures—provide country-specific observations and recommendations related to budgets.

3 For an assessment of the public availability and comprehensiveness of budget documents per country, see IBP *Open Budget Survey*.

4 CESCR, Concluding Observations: Namibia (23 March 2016) para 24; Republic of Macedonia (15 July 2016) 42.

5 For example, CESCR Concluding Observations: Ecuador (25 October 2019); South Africa (29 November 2018) paras 16–19.

6 CESCR, General Comment 3, para 10; OHCHR 'Report on austerity measures and economic and social rights'.

7 CESCR, General comment No. 19, para. 42.

8 The HDI is a summary measure for assessing achievement in three basic dimensions of human development: a long and healthy life, access to knowledge, and a decent standard of living.

9 This is an annual index that benchmarks the current state and evolution of gender parity across four key dimensions (economic participation and opportunity, educational attainment, health and survival, and political empowerment).

10 For the health sector, the Abuja Declaration and the World Health Organisation (WHO) recommend investments of 15% of the national budget and 5% of GDP, respectively. For education, the Incheon Declaration stipulates an investment of 20% of the total budget and/or an investment of 6% of GDP. For social protection, the International Labour Organisation (2024) estimates that low- and middle-income countries such as Kenya need to invest 3.3% of their GDP to provide a universal social protection package.

11 According to Kenya Poverty Report (2023), Garissa County is one of the counties with high levels of poverty and marginalization. The overall poverty level is 68.3%, child poverty is estimated at 69.5%, food poverty at 47.2%, and the Gini coefficient is 0.285.

12 The right of access to information is a central component of the right to freedom of expression. It is both the right of public access to information and the right of the media to access information (Universal Declaration of Human Rights (art. 19), ICCPR (art. 19.2), and regional human rights treaties).

13 The County Budget Transparency Survey 2023 showed improvement for Nakuru County from 51 to 62/100 points.

Bibliography

Brabham, D. C. 2015. *Crowdsourcing in the Public Sector*. Georgetown University Press.

Centre for Economic and Social Rights. 2020. *A Rights-Based Economy: Putting People and Planet First*.

Clark, B. Y., N. Zingale, J. Logan, and J. Brudney. 2016. "A Framework for Using Crowdsourcing in Government." *International Journal of Public Administration in the Digital Age* 3(4): 57–75.

Committee on Economic, Social and Cultural Rights (CESCR). 2016. *Concluding Observations on the Initial Report of Namibia: Committee on Economic, Social, and Cultural Rights*.

International Budget Partnership. 2024. *Open Budget Survey 2023; Global Report*. Washington, DC: International Budget Partnership.

International Budget Partnership. 2023. *Kenya's County Budget Transparency Survey 2023: Sustaining Progress in Sub-National Fiscal Openness*. Nairobi: IBP Kenya.

International Monetary Fund (IMF). 2019. *The Fiscal Transparency Code. Fiscal Transparency Principles*. Washington, DC: International Monetary Fund.
Kenya National Bureau of Statistics (KNBS). 2020. *Inequality Trends and Diagnostics in Kenya 2020: A Joint Report of the KNBS on Multidimensional Inequality*. Nairobi: Kenya National Bureau of Statistics.
Kenya National Bureau of Statistics. 2023. *Kenya Demographic Health Survey 2022*. Nairobi: Kenya National Bureau of Statistics.
Kenya National Bureau of Statistics. 2024. *Kenya Economic Survey 2024*. Nairobi: Kenya National Bureau of Statistics.
Ministry of Health. 2019. *Kenya National Health Accounts 2015/2016*. Nairobi: Kenya Ministry of Health.
Mulwa, M. 2022. *Human Rights Budget Analysis of Kenya's Budget 2022/23: What Do the Numbers Tell Us?* OHCHR Surge Initiative. Geneva: United Nations.
OHCHR. 1990. *CESCR General Comment No. 3: The Nature of States Parties' Obligations (Art. 2, Para. 1 of the Covenant)*. Adopted at the Fifth Session of the Committee on Economic, Social and Cultural Rights. Geneva: United Nations.
OHCHR. 2008 *CESCR. General Comment No. 19: The right to social security (Art. 9 of the Covenant), E/C.12/GC/19, 4 February 2008*. Geneva: United Nations.
OHCHR. 2012. *Human Rights Indicators: A Guide to Measurement and Implementation* (HR/PUB/12/5). Geneva: United Nations.
OHCHR. 2013. *Report on Austerity Measures and Economic and Social Rights*. General Assembly Resolution 48/141. Geneva: United Nations.
OHCHR. 2018. *Draft Guidelines for States on the Effective Implementation of the Right to Participate in Public Affairs*. Geneva: United Nations. https://docs.un.org/en/A/HRC/39/28
OHCHR. 2023a. *Fiscal Transparency, Participation and Accountability: Working Paper*. Geneva: United Nations.
OHCHR. 2023b. *Human Rights Economy Concept*. Geneva: United Nations.
OHCHR. 2023c. *Supporting a Human Rights Economy in Kenya*. Geneva: United Nations. https://www.ohchr.org/en/stories/2023/04/supporting-human-rights-economy-kenya
OHCHR and International Budget Partnership (IBP). 2017. *Realizing Human Rights Through Government Budgets*. New York / Geneva: OHCHR / International Budget Partnership.
Organization for Economic Cooperation and Development (OECD). 2017. *OECD Budget Transparency Toolkit: Practical Steps for Supporting Openness, Integrity and Accountability in Public Financial Management*. Paris: OECD Publishing.
Republic of Kenya. 2010. *The Constitution of Kenya: 2010*. Chief Registrar of the Judiciary. Government print.
Republic of Kenya. 2012. *County Government Act*. Government Print.
UN Kenya. 2024. *UN Joint Budget Analysis for Fiscal Year 2024/25*. Nairobi: United Nations.
United Nations. 1966. *International Covenant on Economic, Social and Cultural Rights*. General Assembly Resolution A, 2200. Geneva: United Nations.
United Nations Development Programme (UNDP). 2024. *Human Development Report 2023/2024: Reimagining cooperation in a polarized world*. New York: UNDP.
UNFPA. 2022. *Resource Planning and Budgeting*. New York: UNFPA. https://www.unfpa.org/admin-resource/resource-planning-and-budgeting
World Bank. 2003. *Case Study 2 - Porto Alegre, Brazil: Participatory Approaches in Budgeting and Public Expenditure Management*. Washington, DC: World Bank.

World Bank. 2008. *Success story in Kerala: Local governments and user groups plan and implement large water supply schemes*. Washington, DC: World Bank.
World Bank. 2024. *Macro Poverty Outlook: Country-by-Country Analysis and Projections for the Developing World*. Washington, DC: World Bank.
World Economic Forum. 2024. *The Global Gender Gap 2024: Insights Report*. Geneva: World Economic Forum.
World Health Organization. 2023. *Social Participation for Universal Health Coverage*. World Health Organization.

Part 2

Local–National–International Nexus

5 What Human Rights and the 5Rs Can Provide for the Reform of the Tax Architecture at the Global, National, and Local Levels

Maria Ron Balsera

Introduction

In an increasingly interconnected world, the design of tax systems remains a cornerstone of equitable and sustainable economic development and governance. A progressive, localized tax architecture, tailored to the needs of specific regions, can ensure fair revenue generation while addressing social inequalities and fostering sustainable development (United Nations, 1986). The question of tax reform, especially when framed in terms of progressivity, is a complex one. Progressive tax systems, where the wealthy are taxed at higher rates, are often hailed as a means to reduce income inequality by redistributing wealth. They can address the systemic challenges that affect marginalized communities, especially when progressive taxation is matched with progressive expenditure in gender responsive and inclusive public services. However, while many nations have made strides towards progressive taxation, global economic structures—shaped by institutions, policies, and international power dynamics—condition the capacity and will of local and national governments to implement these reforms effectively.

At both the local and national levels, tax policy is not created in a vacuum. It is influenced by external pressures from the global economy, the actions of multinational corporations, and international financial institutions such as the International Monetary Fund (IMF), the World Bank, the World Trade Organization, and the Organisation for Economic Co-operation and Development (OECD). This unequal global economic governance has created an environment where the sovereignty of states is increasingly compromised, limiting their ability to enact truly progressive tax policies.

The current international tax regime, primarily coordinated by the OECD, was established long before many colonies gained independence and inherently favours OECD member-states. As an institution mandated to represent and prioritize the interests of its 38 most industrialized members, the OECD's framework fails to address the needs and perspectives of the Global South adequately. The OECD's mandate does not include the promotion of human rights, and therefore, their policies and recommendations do not focus on raising revenue to resource rights, or even, in a right-aligned way.

DOI: 10.4324/9781003474845-8

The complexity of tax reform has increased in the era of digitalization, with challenges related to international taxation, particularly concerning multinational enterprises and illicit financial flows. On the one hand, multinational enterprises exploit tax loopholes through methods like shifting profits to lower tax nations to minimize tax liability, especially in digital corporations with no physical presence in many market jurisdictions. This creates a "race to the bottom" as countries lower corporate tax rates to attract foreign investment, resulting in revenue loss for low- and middle-income nations.

On the other hand, illicit financial flows result from tax evasion, involving the illegal movement of capital across borders. These flows are associated with various corrupt practices, including bribery and smuggling. They contribute significantly to the loss of tax revenue globally. The current non-inclusive and ineffective regime leaves the global tax system prone to abuse in the form of illicit financial flows and tax avoidance, disproportionately draining the coffers of low- and middle-income countries. Their hindered ability to mobilize domestic revenue through taxes results in the insufficient allocation of resources to fund public services, climate adaptation, and fulfil their human rights obligations. The urgency to stop the severe damage caused by burdensome debt and unfair tax practices has become even more critical amidst the poly crisis. Addressing these challenges requires a paradigm shift towards a fairer international tax regime, rooted in principles of fiscal justice. Such a regime not only holds the potential to mitigate inequality and curb tax abuse but also to enable greater domestic resource mobilization at the national and local levels that are essential for realizing human rights, climate action, and gender equality.

What a progressive, localized tax architecture looks like

In an era of increasing global inequality, climate change, and regional economic disparities, the need for a tax system that is both progressive and localized has never been more pressing. While national governments have long been the primary source of public revenue, there is a growing recognition of the need for tax systems that better reflect local realities and needs. A progressive, localized tax architecture—one that is tailored to local contexts but remains fair and equitable—can drive more effective governance, enhance social equity, and strengthen local economies (Kim and Dougherty 2018).

A localized, progressive tax system that ensures that individuals or entities with more economic resources contribute more as a proportion of their resources requires that tax policies and revenues are adjusted to reflect the unique needs, capacities, and challenges of specific regions, municipalities, or local governments. This could involve varying tax rates or types based on local factors such as income levels, cost of living, population density, or environmental concerns.

The core features of a localized, progressive tax architecture include: regional variability in tax rates, where local governments are empowered to set tax rates that respond to their particular circumstances. Wealth taxes, such as property or inheritance taxes, can be localized to capture disparities in local wealth to ensure that wealthier areas contribute a fair share to the community's development without exacerbating inequalities. Local governments can also impose taxes that reflect the environmental challenges or social needs of their areas. Similarly, taxes could fund social programmes that directly address local inequalities, such as education, healthcare, and other public services. In a progressive, localized tax system, regions and municipalities would have greater control over their fiscal policies, which would allow for more tailored solutions to local problems. Devolution of fiscal autonomy ensures that local governments can invest directly in the areas that need it most, whether through infrastructure development, social programmes, or public services (Kim and Dougherty 2018).

Progressive, localized tax architecture includes equity-driven revenue collection, ensuring that those with higher income or wealth contribute a larger proportion of their resources to public revenue. Localized tax systems can adapt this principle by implementing higher marginal tax rates on local high-income earners or wealthier businesses operating within the jurisdiction (IMF 2024); introducing property taxes based on market value, especially for luxury or speculative real estate (Transparency International 2020); enforcing tiered consumption taxes where essential goods are taxed at lower or zero rates, and luxury goods are taxed higher (World Bank 2022). A localized tax architecture should empower local governments to design and administer taxes that cater to regional priorities. This can include allowing municipalities to set tax rates on land, local businesses, or services to match their development needs (World Bank 2022); encouraging transparent and participatory budgeting where residents have a say in how tax revenues are allocated (Bogotá City Government 2019).

A progressive, localized tax architecture can help prioritize social investment by allocating revenue generated through these taxes on addressing inequality and improving public welfare, such as funding education, healthcare, and affordable housing programmes; investing in infrastructure projects that promote sustainable economic growth (IMF 2024); and/or offering targeted subsidies or tax credits to low-income households (OECD 2021).

Transparency is critical to ensure trust and compliance within localized tax systems. For that reason, governments should prioritize: Publishing detailed tax revenue and expenditure reports (Transparency International 2020) and setting up independent oversight bodies to audit tax collection and spending (World Bank 2022). Localized tax systems should strike a balance between incentivizing revenue generation and fostering local economic development by providing tax incentives for small and medium-sized enterprises (IMF 2019), while encouraging environmentally sustainable practices through green tax credits (United Nations Development Programme 2020).

Despite their advantages, localized tax systems face several challenges, including revenue disparities, capacity constraints, and tax evasion and avoidance, with the mobility of high-net-worth individuals and multinational corporations eroding the local tax base. The international community has a pivotal role in enabling and sustaining progressive, localized tax architectures. This includes: (1) Facilitating knowledge sharing and capacity building (OECD 2021). (2) Combatting tax evasion and avoidance, strengthening global cooperation on tax transparency by enforcing measures like the OECD's Common Reporting Standard and the Automatic Exchange of Information (OECD/G20 Inclusive Framework, 2021), and curbing profit shifting by multinational corporations through the implementation of global minimum tax rates (OECD 2021) and supporting the current UN Framework Convention on International Tax Cooperation (UNFCITC) process. (3) Financial support through grants or concessional loans to poorer regions to bridge revenue gaps and invest in tax collection infrastructure and build administrative capacity (IMF 2019; World Bank 2022). (4) Promoting regional coordination and harmonization agreements to prevent a "race to the bottom" in tax competition among neighbouring jurisdictions (OECD 2021) and facilitating cross-border collaboration on taxing multinational entities operating in multiple regions (OECD/G20 Inclusive Framework, 2021, UNFCITC Tax Convention process). (5) Strengthening legal and institutional frameworks, supporting the development of international tax dispute resolution mechanisms that assist local governments in handling disputes with multinational entities (OECD/G20 Inclusive Framework, 2021, Early Protocol of the UNFCITC Tax Convention process), and providing model tax legislation that can be adapted to local contexts, ensuring consistency with global standards while respecting local needs (IMF 2019).

For the international community to incentivize and support sustainable progressive tax systems at global, regional, national, and local levels, it must undergo a structural reform that aligns with human rights.

Why fiscal justice is key to resource human rights, climate justice, and gender equality

A just fiscal policy is essential for mobilizing the resources to guarantee human rights and tackle inequality. Tax and spending policies determine the contributions of different actors and benefits from efforts to realize rights and sustainable development. Therefore, fiscal justice, which is based on just, responsible, and progressive methods, is essential. Fiscal justice serves as the cornerstone for financing endeavours aimed at promoting human rights, climate justice, and gender equality, particularly when viewed through the prism of the 5Rs of taxation (Cobham 2005; Cobham 2015): revenue, redistribution, repricing, representation, and reparations.

Revenue

Fiscal justice guarantees that governments receive the funds required to support infrastructure and public services that are vital to the fulfilment of human rights. Sustaining human dignity and equality requires expenditures in social protection, healthcare, education, and environmental sustainability, all of which are made possible by adequate revenue. Human rights law is clear that countries have the obligation to use the maximum of their available resources to respect, protect, and fulfil economic and social rights (and all rights). For instance, the low levels of tax to GDP in sub-Saharan Africa countries such as Ghana, Kenya, and Uganda often result in underfunding of public services such as education. Even when these countries' policies stipulate that universal primary education is free and compulsory, schools request a myriad of fees to compensate for the systemic and historical underfunding, passed on from national to local education budgets, and children whose families cannot afford to pay those fees miss out on going to school (Ron Balsera 2018).

Redistribution

One of the main tenets of fiscal justice is progressive taxation, which makes redistribution easier by guaranteeing that those who can afford to contribute more do so proportionately. Fiscal policies can reduce economic gaps and promote social inclusion by redistributing resources from the affluent, those with higher wealth and income, to those with low or no income through higher taxes on wealth, property, inheritance, and corporate earnings. Wealth inequality is increasing at a higher rate than ever before. According to a recent report commissioned by the G20 Brazil presidency, a global minimum tax equal to 2% of the wealth of billionaires would raise $200–$250 billion per year globally from about 3,000 taxpayers; $100–$140 billion more could be mobilized if the tax was extended to those with more than $100 million. This amounts to about half of the money needed for developing countries to address climate challenges (Forgette 2024). Until countries can agree joint solutions to curtail the capital flight to tax havens and stop global tax abuse (ideally at the UN, although there were some advances at the G20 in Brazil), countries should consider adopting inheritance taxes, which are widely missing from lower-income countries.[1] It is estimated that Africans hold $500 billion in financial wealth offshore, the equivalent of 30% of all financial wealth held by Africans (Fjesldstad et al. 2017). Redistributive spending is just as important. Gender-responsive budgets emphasizing women's rights and interests are key to finance health, education, social services, and gender-based violence prevention. Women's rights and public services are directly undermined by tax loopholes and illicit financial flows (Hungwe and Ron Balsera 2025). Tax abuse results in the underfunding of public services, which in turn increases the care burden of women and girls, who involuntarily subsidize the economy through their unpaid care work of children, sick, and elderly due to the lack of access to schools, health facilities, care homes, etc. Redistribution could and should go beyond domestic boundaries.

Repricing

Repricing products and services to reflect their actual social and environmental costs can be accomplished through the use of taxes. Taxing environmentally damaging activities, such as pollution or carbon emissions, encourages sustainable behaviour and provides funding for adaptation and climate action programmes. Repricing through taxation can also help reduce gender gaps by providing financing for services and programmes that are sensitive to gender and support the rights and empowerment of women. The EU's carbon border adjustment mechanism (CBAM) is a tariff ostensibly designed to prevent carbon leakage.[2] A different example is the 2018 UK's sugar tax, which targeted drinks containing more than 8g of sugar per 100ml, being taxed 24p per litre, with the aim to reduce obesity, particularly childhood obesity (Thornton 2018). Much of the criticism around these taxes revolves on the unintended regressivity, where those with lower-income households pay disproportionately more than those in higher-income households, given that they tend to be sales taxes or passed on to consumers.

Representation

Transparent and accountable fiscal policies that take into account the interests and requirements of all societal groups, particularly the marginalized ones, are necessary for achieving fiscal justice. Governments can ensure that fiscal policies are sensitive to the different needs and ambitions of their communities and so advance social justice and democratic governance by incorporating citizens in the decision-making processes concerning taxes and public spending. Countries plighted by illicit financing flows and low tax-to-GDP ratios cannot properly discharge their human rights obligations (Ron Balsera, 2018); the lack of public services and adequate infrastructure contributes to the perception of government corruption. When citizens pay taxes but do not see public services and infrastructure in return, they feel disincentivized to do so. The drive for lower taxation, (particularly corporate income tax) and emphasis on privatization of public services such as health, water, or education, is resulting in the weakening of the social contract, questioning the role of the state (from provider to regulator or even market-creator) and leading to violations of human rights (Ron Balsera, 2011). Much can be done also at local level, from devolving certain powers of tax administration to raising awareness about how tax pays public services, like ActionAid has been doing for a decade. Ron Balsera (2020) shows how tax awareness can enable communities to mobilize and hold the state to account to provide free, quality education.

Reparations

Taxation can be used to redress current and historical legacies of colonialism and ecological damage, between and within countries (Mager and Chaparro 2023). Countries and groups who have least contributed to climate change are being most negatively impacted. Taxation can be used to reduce historic inequalities that stem from odious debt, corruption, colonial and neocolonial extractivism, or the gender and racially biased global fiscal governance.

The additional revenue could increase funds for climate finance to meet the Paris Agreement, including the Polluter Pays Principle. The Polluter Pays Principle declares that the entity responsible for pollution should bear the cost of mitigating that pollution, including redressing the damage caused by it; this should include historical polluters (CESR 2024b).[3] It would also enable the adequate financing of public services and human rights, increasing the maximum available resources. Taxation can also help with rebalancing, as it is a regulatory tool that directs economic activity in the direction of socially desirable goals. Governments can incentivize individuals and companies to invest in renewable energy, embrace sustainable practices, and advance gender equality in the workplace by imposing tax penalties and incentives. In addition to preventing detrimental behaviours like tax evasion and avoidance, re-regulation through taxes can guarantee that each player makes a fair contribution to the general welfare. The 'Cap and Share' method aims to tax fossil fuels at source, with the tax revenue going to an international fund which would then be allocated based on need and vulnerability to climate crises. Countries in the Global North, because of their disproportionate contribution to the climate crisis, have overriding responsibility to cease this conduct and to repair the losses and damages they have caused. After strong demands from climate justice movements, in 2022, the Loss and Damage Fund was established to assist vulnerable developing countries in responding to loss and damage. This fund can be seen as a small but important contribution to broader demands for reparations (CESR 2024a).

By using taxes as a tool to raise funds, redistribute income, change the cost of products and services, improve representation, and re-regulate economic behaviour, the state is able to address structural inequality and build a society that is more just, inclusive, and sustainable. However, the current global fiscal architecture favours wealthier countries, denying low- and middle-income countries the policy space and funding necessary to make investments in social security, environmental sustainability, and quality public services (Inter-American Commission on Human Rights 2017).

It is estimated that on a global scale abusive international tax practices lead to a loss of US$492 billion in tax revenue annually (Tax Justice Network 2024). Cross-border tax abuse by multinational companies contributes to lost revenue of US$347.6 billion, whereas the remaining US$144.8 billion is attributed to offshoring of wealth by high-net worth individuals. The research also reveals that the impacts are disproportionately felt by low- and middle-income countries, who lose out on significant portions of their total tax revenue while higher-income countries lose more revenue in absolute terms.

Additionally, studies indicate that most revenue losses from unfair international tax methods may be attributed to OECD nations. For example, 92% of the US$171 billion is borne by OECD nations and their dependencies. The global loss resulting from the offshoring of individual wealth is estimated to be US$158 billion annually. Approximately seven out of ten dollars that are lost are attributable to OECD member states and their dependencies. Furthermore, the majority of worldwide corporate tax evasion—69% in this instance, costing the global economy US$207 billion in missed corporation tax—occurs in OECD member nations and their dependent countries.

According to a recent study, the UK, along with its overseas territories and Crown Dependencies, is the single biggest enabler of global tax evasion, accounting for 24% of all corporate tax losses. Nearly half of the US$171 billion in taxes that the world loses to offshore wealth tax evasion each year, totalling nearly US$85 billion in lost revenue, is attributable to UK's Crown Dependencies and overseas territories. Multinational firms also shift US$262 billion in profits into the UK's Crown Dependencies and overseas territories annually, costing the global economy about US$72 billion in missed taxes due to corporate tax evasion. When accounting for tax losses resulting from private wealth offshoring, the overseas territories and Crown Dependencies of the UK are responsible for 33% of all tax losses suffered by countries around the world, costing countries over US$157 billion in lost revenue every year.

Lower-income nations, who rely substantially more on corporate taxes than higher-income nations, receive roughly 70% of their revenue from taxes. These nations can ill afford to lose the tax revenues to which they are rightfully due, and they confront significant obstacles in expanding their tax bases (Moore 2013). Investment tax incentives are one example. To encourage investment, most governments offer a wide range of tax breaks. These include tax expenditures made to draw in foreign direct investment, such as tax vacations, patent boxes, and special fiscal regimes provided in special economic zones. But the public's scrutiny of these incentives has increased recently due to worries about lost tax income and the financial stability of local governments (De Gruyter 2019). However, they do function as tools of tax competition that weaken the tax bases of other economies.

Domestically, if progressive tax policy is structured so that the wealthiest taxpayers contribute proportionately more, it has the potential to significantly increase revenue in an equitable manner and reduce inequality. Although wealth, property, inheritance, capital gains, and corporate taxes are crucial progressive tools, they are underutilized in developing nations. On the other hand, regressive overreliance on consumption taxes unjustly encumbers the low-income households, having disproportionate impact on girls and women and other disadvantaged groups (Inter-American Commission on Human Rights 2017).

The idea that wealthier people ought to pay more to support public goods and services has gained traction in the wake of the COVID-19 outbreak. Here, it is pertinent to note that income and wealth are not the same thing. Income is the flow of revenues during a certain time period, whereas wealth is the net worth of an individual or corporation (i.e., the excess stock of assets over the accompanying obligations at a specific point in time). This discrepancy becomes crucial, for instance, when certain people earn a lot of money but do not necessarily possess equivalent wealth, or the other way around. A tax jurisdiction's ability to tax wealth contributes to the reduction of wealth concentration at the top of the wealth pyramid. Wealth-based progressive taxes guarantee that people pay taxes that correspond with their wealth, thus taxpayers with higher net worths pay higher marginal tax rates. Wealthier people gain more from a nation's institutions, resources, and opportunities; as a result, they should pay a proportionate share of the government's costs for public goods and services (UN Committee of Experts on International Cooperation in Tax Matters' Subcommittee on Wealth and Solidarity Taxes 2023).

Along the same lines, another useful tool to generate revenue and redistribute is windfall taxes. A windfall tax is a levy imposed on unforeseen gains or profits that come to people or businesses as a result of outside circumstances like advantageous market conditions or acts by the government. This tax is meant to make sure that the advantages of these unanticipated riches are distributed throughout society as a whole, instead of being restricted to a small group of people (Tax Justice Network 2022). Windfall taxation also aids in rebalancing economic behaviour. For instance, a company might be more inclined to take risks in the future if it gains a windfall from an abrupt increase in the value of its stock. Levying windfall taxes can discourage such behaviour and promote entities to act responsibly.

Unfortunately, recent taxing measures have been less focused on targeting the wealthy. One example of this is the EU's recently instituted CBAM (European Commission 2023). The CBAM is a tariff ostensibly designed to prevent carbon leakage, the rise in carbon emissions resulting from corporations moving their operations to regions with less stringent regulations. Unfortunately, the tariff was passed without any protections or exceptions for low-income countries and could lead to African countries losing billions as a result (African Climate Foundation 2023). Furthermore, the measure was passed without any input from the ten countries on which it will have the greatest impact, completely abandoning notions of inclusivity and representation within the process (Trachtman and Yves Remy 2023).

In the state of poly crisis that the world is facing, fiscal policy is severely constrained by unsustainable debt burdens that divert resources to lenders, often under neocolonial arrangements (EURODAD 2020). Restructuring and debt relief are crucial, and they must be based on lender and borrower accountability. After resources are freed up, they can be used for sustainable development and rights.

Fiscal justice is also a prerequisite for climate justice. Resources are needed for vulnerable nations that are most adversely affected by climate change to adapt and increase resilience. To deliver climate money, calls for global collaboration and strong leadership from wealthy polluting countries are necessary. Fiscal flexibility is crucial since funding climate action also requires mobilizing domestic revenue (Initiative for Human Rights Principles in Fiscal Policy 2021). CESR's work in this area has focused on communities impacted by the climate crisis to attain a stronger role in fiscal decision-making processes (CESR 2017).

Fiscal policy should be guided by human rights concepts such as accountability, transparency, equality, and participation (Inter-American Commission on Human Rights & REDESCA 2019). Governments have an obligation to use "maximum available resources" to advance the realization of economic and social rights, which means they must raise and allocate funds in a way that minimizes inequality and gives priority to underprivileged populations (UN CESR 1990). States need to create more equitable global fiscal governance and restructure domestic policies when resources are limited by international debt and tax regulations (Initiative for Human Rights Principles in Fiscal Policy 2021).

These principles, according to regional human rights bodies, dictate budgetary policy as a whole. However, the current approach frequently ignores rights and promotes austerity, in response to pressure from international organizations, linked to budgetary constraints due to insufficient revenue mobilization through taxes and the pursue of the so-called 'fiscal consolidation', which exacerbates inequality (Independent Expert on foreign debt and human rights 2018). As a result, public confidence in the government declines, decreasing representation and, eventually, leading to the delegitimization and dismantling of the state (Inter-American Commission on Human Rights & REDESCA 2019). In order to rebuild public confidence and facilitate inclusive budgetary agreements among states, individuals, and corporations, greater openness, involvement, and accountability are essential. Human rights should serve as a yardstick for assessing various policy options, and fiscal policy should aim to ensure both equity and rights. Fiscal policy grounded in the concepts of climate justice and human rights may turn around economies and fund sustainable development that puts people first. It is key to shift fiscal policy from the human rights agenda's periphery to its centre.

Wealthy individuals and multinational enterprises evade taxes at astronomical rates

The gross impact of global tax avoidance is staggering. The TJN's State of Tax Justice 2023 found that countries are losing $480 billion a year due to tax abuse. The brunt of that harm is falling on lower-income countries, whose tax losses equate to roughly 49% of their public health budgets. In comparison, higher-income countries suffered tax losses of just 9% of their public health budgets. In Africa, corporate tax accounts for nearly twice the amount as in OECD countries, more than any other region in the world. Another report by the EU Tax Observatory found that, despite recent "ambitious policy initiatives … a persistently large amount of profits is shifted to tax havens: $1 trillion in 2022".

Multinational enterprises have long engaged in abusive tax practices because existing international tax law requires companies to have a "physical presence" in a country to be classified as having permanent establishment and thus having its profits taxed in that jurisdiction (Ovonji-Odida et al. 2020). Highly digitalized businesses, such as Uber, Facebook, and Amazon, have continued to lobby international economic governance spaces, arguing that their online services in developing countries do not meet the criteria under the physical presence test (despite being used by many residents in those countries and creating economic value). Companies have historically been able to dodge tax obligations by shifting their international headquarters to jurisdictions like Ireland or the Cayman Islands, where corporate tax rates ranged from low to non-existent.

These flaws in the international tax regime and the damage stemming from their exploitation have long been recognized and understood. Indeed, they were precisely what the OECD set out to fix when it began to develop the Inclusive Framework in 2016. The analysis below delves into the Inclusive Framework, highlighting its shortcomings while ultimately advocating for a new, more inclusive approach that builds upon its strengths.

For over a decade, the OECD has invested huge resources into fighting the Base Erosion and Profit Shifting to stop tax evasion and avoidance that lead to the undermining of countries' abilities to grow. The promising Inclusive Framework "to level the playing field" (which started in 2016), with its two pillars, has been a historic missed opportunity. The minimum corporation tax was reduced last minute from 25% to an insufficient 15%, leading a new race to the bottom to attract foreign investment. It also added the option of carve-outs for further tax exemptions.

The urgent need to tax the digital economy, to ensure that companies such as Uber, Microsoft, and Google pay taxes where the activities are carried out and profits are made, has not been much more fruitful. The current agreement largely favours high-income countries, such as the United States, where most of these corporations are headquartered. It establishes an arbitrary threshold of $750 million in profits (which with the current schemes it'd mean that Amazon would be exempt) (CICTAR 2022). Yet, despite supporting the measures and encouraging every country to sign the agreement, the United States was tempted to sign. Countries, especially low- and middle-income countries, should think twice before ratifying this Inclusive Framework agreement that could lead to giving up their taxing rights to collect revenue from these corporations. The EU Tax Observatory estimates that the potential revenue gains (from implementing Pillar 1 Amount A) would be just "0.17% of current tax revenues for developing countries and 0.15% for developing and least developed countries" (Barake and Le Pouhaër 2023). That is why countries should consider alternatives, such as digital services taxes or withholding taxes that are estimated to generate similar or more revenues.

How the OECD Inclusive Framework has fallen short of realizing human rights obligations

The Inclusive Framework instituted a "two-pillar" approach to the issues of profit-sharing and tax havens outlined above. The first pillar has sought to alter the "physical presence" requirement by awarding some taxing rights to destination countries (where companies sell goods and services and employ workers) rather than solely to residence countries (where companies are headquartered). The new taxing rights ostensibly allow for multinational enterprises to be taxed according to their participation in local economies. In practice, however, the current number of thresholds that a company must overcome to qualify to be taxed for their economic presence in a region is much too high. A recent estimate from Oxfam found that these new tax rights were generating revenues equivalent to just 0.026% of GDP in developing countries (Oxfam 2022). This approach directly contradicts state obligations under Article 3 of the 1986 UN Declaration on the Right to Development, which compels all states to ensure "developing countries have the appropriate means and facilities to foster their comprehensive development", and Article 4, requiring that states "fulfil their duties in such a manner as to promote a new international economic order based on sovereign equality … and cooperation" (United Nations 1986).

Another defect in the Inclusive Framework's first pillar is its infringement on developing countries' sovereign right under international law to undertake national measures to tax. As noted above, an increasing number of highly digitalized businesses take advantage of operating in low-income countries without exposing themselves to tax liability. Some states have sought to remedy this by imposing digital service taxes, such as India's 2016 levy of 6% on digital advertising services. The first pillar of the Inclusive Framework attempts to prohibit these taxes, and the United States has imposed trade sanctions on countries who implement them (Office of the US Trade Representative 2025). Ironically, the Oxfam report estimated that digital services levies of 3% would engender revenues roughly equivalent to those produced by the new taxing rights, rendering developing states' participation in the first pillar essentially a wash.

The second pillar of the Inclusive Framework is unfortunately also plagued with problems that disproportionately harm developing countries. The second pillar creates a global corporate minimum tax to which all 140 member jurisdictions of the Inclusive Framework must adhere. The concept behind the institution of such a tax is sound. Establishing a floor rate for global taxation should in theory temper the global "race to the bottom" by governments eager to attract foreign investment by offering rock-bottom corporate taxes. Unfortunately, the 15% minimum tax rate established by the second pillar is well *below* that of most nations, meaning that the "minimum" rule, as currently proposed, incentivizes countries to treat the 15% number as a ceiling rather than a floor.

Additionally, substantial carve-outs embedded within the second pillar permit multinational enterprises to reduce their profits subject to the minimum corporate tax if they locate employees and assets in different jurisdictions. This lowers the effective tax rate below the already-too-low 15%, substantially negating its efficacy (Barake et al. 2021). Even worse, the second pillar's global minimum corporate tax is collected where multinational corporations are headquartered, predominantly high-income countries. Developing countries are worst affected by tax avoidance and illicit financial flows and thus should receive the first claim on taxable revenues.

Many of the human rights issues in the Inclusive Framework stem from a lack of transparency and inclusivity in decision-making. The Maastricht

Principles on the Extraterritorial Obligations of States in the Area of Economic, Social, and Cultural Rights (a distillation of states' extraterritorial obligations in the fiscal arena) clarify that "(states) must observe international rights standards, including the right to ... participate in decision-making ... transparency, and accountability" (CIEL 2015). The IF violates these principles by exhibiting a total lack of formal rules regarding decision-making and procedure. OECD documents vaguely describe a decision-making process with a "two-layer structure". The first layer includes working groups of member jurisdictions (which have limited developing country participation) and a second layer, the Committee on Fiscal Affairs, which makes decisions on an unclear basis of "consensus". This lack of transparency inhibits criticism and input from less influential and less represented developing countries.

Nevertheless, despite its deficiencies, the fundamental principles underpinning the Inclusive Framework remain important. It correctly diagnoses profit-sharing, tax havens, and other forms of tax abuse as significant problems. Furthermore, the framework's shifting of taxing rights and creation of minimum corporate taxes hold the potential to ameliorate these problems, but only if these actions are implemented in a more progressive way that prioritizes the developing countries that suffer the most from tax abuse. The UNFCITC represents a new opportunity to offer a truly participatory and much-needed international tax reform.

Why should the UNFCITC incorporate human rights?

Bringing norm and standard-setting on international tax concerns under the UN's purview, where all states have an equal "seat at the table", would be greatly aided by the UN Framework Convention on International Tax Cooperation (UNFCITC). The UN Convention's promise to "level the playing field" in concerns of international taxation is one of the main advantages for nations in the Global South. A UN Convention would also need to acknowledge international human rights legislation as a fundamental basis, since global economic governance institutions frequently do not, given the importance of human rights to the UN Charter. It would make it possible to harmonize public or private legal norms with the normative framework of international human rights law in areas such as finance, accounting, tax, and fiscal problems (Center for Economic and Social Rights et al. 2022).

The continuous fight for more fair and just international debt and tax arrangements has a lot to do with human rights. Human rights will support the progressive reform measures' legitimacy from a moral, political, and legal standpoint. They provide poorer nations with a strong legal basis to demand that wealthier states and international organizations respect, preserve, and assist in securing their fiscal space (Saiz 2021). The future is bleak for lower-income nations as long as the wealthier states are not held properly responsible for their human rights commitments. Together with the previously discussed principles of maximum available resources, non-retrogression, extraterritorial obligations, and participation, the UNFCITC must also include the following international human rights principles:

Right to self-determination

The International Covenant on Civil and Political Rights, the Universal Declaration of Human Rights, and the ICESCR all recognize the right to self-determination. This means that any global tax reforms must take into account power imbalances between states in the Global North and South and establish fiscal policies through inclusive, democratic processes. The unquestionable racial component of the right to self-determination for both indigenous people and historically colonized states necessitates the decolonization of the global economic system and the admission that the Global South is a net creditor.

Non-discrimination and substantive equality

Explicitly gender-responsive fiscal policies are necessary for substantive gender equality. These policies must also recognize that women and girls are disproportionately affected by IFFs, tax havens, and austerity measures because of their increasing reliance on public services.

When combined with gender equality, substantive racial and gender equality strengthens the need for tax spillover assessments for tax policies that have disproportionate effects on women, girls, and other vulnerable groups outside of a state's borders. Realizing that one way to make up for historical racial subordination is through the creation of a just and equitable international order. Intersecting discrimination and disadvantage on a variety of grounds, including race, caste, gender, sexual orientation, gender identity, migrant status, disability, and social origin, must also be addressed by equality. To uphold substantive equality, the Convention must also address the unfair and discriminatory effects of regressive taxes as well as the states' excessive dependence on them.

Right to development

States should realize their rights and carry out their obligations in a way that promotes a new international economic order based on sovereign equality, interdependence, mutual interest, and cooperation among all states, as well as to encourage the observance and realization of human rights. States bear the primary responsibility for creating national and international conditions favourable to the realization of the right to development. States also have a duty to cooperate with one another in ensuring development and eliminating obstacles to development. The equitable allocation of taxing rights is mandated by the right to development.

Conclusion

Taxation is fundamentally intertwined with the protection and promotion of human rights, ranging from gender and racial equality to climate justice and economic and social rights. The current global tax landscape is fraught with loopholes and inconsistencies, allowing multinational corporations and wealthy individuals to exploit tax havens and avoid paying their fair share of contributions which are essential for budgeting for human rights. National tax sovereignty is constrained by the international financial architecture, which favour multinational corporations and high-net worth individuals, at the expense of domestic resource mobilization. Although promising, the OECD effort to address the problems and rewrite the international tax rules appears to have fallen short of its obligations under human rights law. It lacks universality and inclusivity in agenda setting and decision-making mechanisms and has been disproportionately detrimental to low- and middle-income nations.

The United Nations possesses the unique ability to bridge this gap by creating a truly participatory and transparent global forum that promotes fairness, state accountability, and the role of human rights and development in global tax debates. A UN Tax Convention can and must work together with the OECD. A substantive UNFCITC on International Tax Cooperation and its protocols would offer human rights guarantees necessary for human rights economies at the national and local levels.

Notes

1 According to the IMF (2024), wealth taxes can be found in Colombia, Liechtenstein, The Netherlands, Norway, Spain, Switzerland (all OECD countries) and the following non-OECD countries: Algeria, Argentina, Bolivia, Suriname, Uruguay, Venezuela. Countries cited in this paper as having an inheritance plus gifts tax are: Algeria, Angola, Belgium, Bolivia, Brazil, Burkina Faso, Chile, Democratic Republic of the Congo, Croatia, Denmark, Ecuador, Equatorial Guinea, Finland, France, French Guiana, Germany, Greece, Guinea, Ireland, Italy, Japan, Korea, Lebanon, Luxemburg, Mali, Montenegro, The Netherlands, Poland, São Tomé and Príncipe, Senegal, Spain, Tunisia, Türkiye, Venezuela, Vietnam. https://www.elibrary.imf.org/view/journals/061/2024/001/article-A001-en.xml.

2 The CBAM is a tariff ostensibly designed to prevent carbon leakage, the rise in carbon emissions resulting from corporations moving their operations to regions with less stringent regulations. Unfortunately, the tariff was passed without any protections or exceptions for low-income countries and could lead to African countries losing billions as a result. Furthermore, the measure was passed without any input from the ten countries on which it will have the greatest impact, completely abandoning notions of inclusivity and representation within the process.

3 Full and effective reparation includes restitution, compensation, rehabilitation, satisfaction, and guarantees of non-repetition. For more information, see CESR 2024b. Climate Finance, Reparations and Human Rights. Key concepts. https://www.cesr.org/key-concepts-climate-finance-reparations-and-human-rights/.

Bibliography

African Climate Foundation. 2023. "EU's CBAM: Africa Could Lose up to $25b per Annum as a Direct Result - the African Climate Foundation." *The African Climate Foundation - Pushing the Frontier of Climate, Development and Economic Transformation in Africa*, May 9, 2023. https://africanclimatefoundation.org/blog/eus-cbam-africa-could-lose-up-to-25b-per-annum-as-a-direct-result/

Barake, M., P. E. Chouc, T. Neef, and G. Zucman. 2021. "Minimizing the Minimum Tax? The Critical Effect of Substance Carve-Outs." *EU Tax Observatory*. https://www.taxobservatory.eu/publication/minimizing-the-minimum-tax-the-critical-effect-of-substance-carve-outs/

Barake, M., and E. Le Pouhaër. 2023. Tax Revenue from Pillar One Amount A: Country-by-Country Estimates. *halshs-04039288*. https://www.taxobservatory.eu/www-site/uploads/2023/03/wp_202312_.pdf

Center for Economic and Social Rights (CESR). 2017. "Fighting Fiscal Injustice and Human Rights Risks across the Andean Region." *Center for Economic and Social Rights*, September 27, 2017. https://www.cesr.org/fighting-fiscal-injustice-and-human-rights-risks-across-andean-region/

Center for Economic and Social Rights (CESR), et al. 2022. "Submission to the Independent Expert on Foreign Debt, Other Related International Financial Obligations and Human Rights Ahead of the 77th Session of the General Assembly." https://www.cesr.org/cesr-and-partners-call-for-human-rights-aligned-global-tax-reforms/

Center for Economic and Social Rights (CESR). 2024a. "CESR Submission for the Second Session of the UN Framework Convention on International Tax Cooperation (UNTC)." https://cesr.org/strengthening-the-human-rights-dimension-of-the-untc-cesr-and-allies-weigh-in-on-terms-of-reference-zero-draft/

Center for Economic and Social Rights (CESR). 2024b. "Key Concepts: Climate Finance, Reparations, and Human Rights." https://www.cesr.org/key-concepts-climate-finance-reparations-and-human-rights/

CICTAR. 2022. "Amazon: The World's Largest Company Is Subsidised by You." https://cictar.org/all-research/amazon

CIEL. 2015. "Maastricht Principles on Extraterritorial Obligations of States in the Area of Economic, Social and Cultural Rights." https://www.ciel.org/wp-content/uploads/2015/05/Maastricht_ETO_Principles_21Oct11.pdf

Cobham, A. 2005. "Taxation Policy and Development." *The Oxford Council on Good Governance*. https://www.taxjustice.net/cms/upload/pdf/OCGG_-_Alex_Cobham_-_Taxation_Policy_and_Development.pdf

Cobham, A. 2015. "Taxing Multinationals: A Research Agenda for #FFD3." *The Uncounted*. https://uncounted.org/tag/5rs-of-tax/

De Gruyter. 2019. "Tax Expenditure and the Treatment of Tax Incentives for Investment." *Economics: The Open-Access, Open-Assessment E-Journal*. https://doi.org/10.5018/economics-ejournal.ja.2019-12

EURODAD. 2020. "Global Week of Action for Debt Cancellation." *Open Letter to All Governments, International Institutions and Lenders*. https://d3n8a8pro7vhmx.cloudfront.net/eurodad/pages/768/attachments/original/1610355046/DSSI-briefing-final.pdf?1610355046

European Commission. 2023. "Carbon Border Adjustment Mechanism (CBAM) Starts to Apply in Its Transitional Phase." *European Commission*, September 23, 2023. https://ec.europa.eu/commission/presscorner/detail/en/ip_23_4685

Fjeldstad, O. H., S. K. Jacobsen, P. Ringstad, and H. P. Ngowi. 2017. *Lifting the Veil of Secrecy: Perspectives on International Taxation and Capital Flight from Africa*. Bergen: Chr. Michelsen Institute. https://www.cmi.no/publications/6382-lifting-the-veil-of-secrecy

Forgette, M. 2024. "Financing a Green Future: Tax Strategies to Bridge the Climate Funding Gap." *CESR Blog*. https://www.cesr.org/financing-a-green-future-tax-strategies-to-bridge-the-climate-funding-gap/

Hungwe, M., and M. Ron Balsera. 2025. "Progressive Taxation for a Gender-Transformative Social Organisation of Care." *Global Tax Justice Blog*. https://globaltaxjustice.org/news/gdoa-2025-demand-1/

IMF. 2019. Tax Expenditure reporting and its Use in Fiscal Management: A Guide for Developing Economies. 2019 (002). https://doi.org/10.5089/9781498303217.061

IMF. 2024. *How to Tax Wealth*. By Shafik Hebous, Alexander D. Klemm, Geerten Michielse, and Carolina Osorio Buitron (eds.). International Monetary Fund. https://doi.org/10.5089/9798400266881.061. https://www.elibrary.imf.org/view/journals/061/2024/001/article-A001-en.xml

Independent Expert on Foreign Debt and Human Rights. 2018. "Report of the Special Rapporteur on Extreme Poverty and Human Rights (A/73/396)." https://undocs.org/A/73/396

Initiative for Human Rights Principles in Fiscal Policy. 2021. "Principles and Guidelines on Human Rights in Fiscal Policy." https://derechosypoliticafiscal.org/en/

Inter-American Commission on Human Rights. 2017. "Report on Poverty and Human Rights in the Americas (OEA/Ser.L/V/II.164 Doc.147)." https://www.oas.org/en/iachr/reports/pdfs/Poverty-HumanRights2017.pdf

Inter-American Commission on Human Rights, and REDESCA. 2019. "Business and Human Rights: Inter-American Standards." http://oas.org/en/iachr/reports/pdfs/BusinessHumanRights.pdf

Kim, J., and S. Dougherty, eds. 2018. *Fiscal Decentralisation and Inclusive Growth. OECD Fiscal Federalism Studies*. Paris: OECD Publishing; Seoul: KIPF. https://doi.org/10.1787/9789264302488-en

Mager, F., and S. Chaparro. 2023. "Delivering Climate Justice Using the Principles of Tax Justice: A Guide for Climate Justice Advocates." *Position Paper*. https://taxjustice.net/wp-content/uploads/2023/06/Delivering-climate-justice-using-the-principles-of-tax-justice-Tax-Justice-Network-June-2023.pdf

Moore, M. 2013. "Obstacles to Increasing Tax Revenues in Low Income Countries." *International Centre for Tax and Development Working Paper* 15. https://ssrn.com/abstract=2436437

OECD. 2021. Tax Policy Reforms 2021. Special Edition on Tax Policy During The COVID-19 Pandemic. https://www.oecd.org/content/dam/oecd/en/publications/reports/2021/04/tax-policy-reforms-2021_35c401b1/427d2616-en.pdf?utm_source=chatgpt.com

Office of the US Trade Representative. 2025. "Section 301 – Digital Service Taxes." https://ustr.gov/issue-areas/enforcement/section-301-investigations/section-301-digital-services-taxes

Ovonji-Odida, I., V. Grondona, and S. V. Makwe. 2020. "Assessment of the Two-Pillar Approach to Address the Tax Challenges Arising from the Digitalization of the Economy: An Outline of Positions Favourable to Developing Countries." *South Center Tax Initiative Report*. https://www.southcentre.int/wp-content/uploads/2020/12/Assessment-of-the-Two-Pillar-Approach-to-Address-the-Tax-Challenges-Arising-from-the-Digitalization-of-the-Economy-reduced.pdf

OXFAM. 2022. "The Effect of the OECD's Pillar 1 Proposal on Developing Countries." https://www.oxfamamerica.org/explore/research-publications/the-effect-of-the-oecds-pillar-1-proposal-on-developing-countries/

Ron Balsera, M. 2011. "Does the Human Capital Discourse Promote or Hinder the Right to Education? The Case of Girls, Orphans and Vulnerable Children in Rwanda." *Journal of International Development* 23 (2): 274–287. https://doi.org/10.1002/jid.1769

Ron Balsera, M. 2018. "Why Should Tax Justice Be Part of the Solution to Finance Free Good Quality Education? A Multi-country Study: Pakistan, Ghana, Kenya and Uganda." *Education Finance, Equality, and Equity*, 39–49. https://doi.org/10.1007/978-3-319-90388-0_3

Ron Balsera, M. 2020. "Why Progressive Tax Reform Is Essential to Reach SDG4 in Pakistan?" In David Archer (ed.), *Domestic Financing, Tax, and Education*. Norrag Special Issue 05. https://www.norrag.org/nsi-05-domestic-financing-tax-and-education/

Saiz, I. 2021. *Freeing Fiscal Space: A Human Rights Imperative in Response to COVID-19*. Development and Peace Foundation (SEF). https://www.cesr.org/freeing-fiscal-space-a-human-rights-imperative-in-response-to-covid-19/

Tax Justice Network. 2022. "Taxing Unearned Profits." https://taxjustice.net/2022/11/03/taxing-unearned-profits/

Tax Justice Network. 2024. "The State of Tax Justice 2024." https://taxjustice.net/wp-content/uploads/2024/11/State-of-Tax-Justice-2024-English-Tax-Justice-Network.pdf

Thornton, J. 2018. "The UK Has Introduced a Sugar Tax, but Will It Work?" *London School of Hygiene and Tropical Medicine*, June 2018. https://www.lshtm.ac.uk/research/research-action/features/uk-sugar-tax-will-it-work

Trachtman, J., and J. Y. Remy. 2023. "Comment: The EU's Carbon Border Tax Is a Blow to Climate Justice. Here's How to Fix It." *Reuters*, November 15, 2023. https://www.reuters.com/sustainability/boards-policy-regulation/comment-eus-carbon-border-tax-is-blow-climate-justice-heres-how-fix-it-2023-11-15/

Transparency International. 2020. Real estate data: Shining a light on the corrupt. *Transparency International*. https://www.transparency.org/en/publications/real-estate-data-shining-a-light-on-the-corrupt

UN Committee on Economic, Social and Cultural Rights (CESCR). 1990. "CESCR General Comment No. 3: The Nature of States Parties' Obligations (Art. 2, Para. 1, of the Covenant) (E/1991/23)". https://tbinternet.ohchr.org/_layouts/15/treatybodyexternal/Download.aspx?symbolno=INT%2fCESCR%2fGEC%2f4758&Lang=en

UN Committee of Experts on International Cooperation in Tax Matters' Subcommittee on Wealth and Solidarity Taxes. 2023. "Draft Guidance Document, as of 27 September 2023." https://financing.desa.un.org/sites/default/files/2023-10/CPR.27%20Annex%20Wealth%20Tax%20Subcommittee%20Paper.pdf

United Nations. 1986. "Declaration on the Right to Development. Adopted December 4, 1986, by the General Assembly Resolution 41/128." https://www.ohchr.org/en/instruments-mechanisms/instruments/declaration-right-development

World Bank. 2022. Decentralization, multilevel governance, and intergovernmental relations: A primer. *World Bank*. https://documents1.worldbank.org/curated/en/099225502022314300/pdf/P1754490a5d87e07d0915e0e165e739dbf5.pdf

6 Biosphere Defenders Operationalising the Prevention Principle in Climate Adaptation through Territorial Planning

Indraraj Gunasekara and Claudia Ituarte-Lima

Introduction

Traditional economic models, particularly of the neoclassical vein, tend to take a predominantly anthropocentric character, prioritising economic growth, property rights, and resource exploitation, and treating land and water as commodities (Lumby 2007; Prudham 2015). However, this perspective can be problematic as it reflects a prioritisation of economic efficiency and resource commodification to drive growth over broader social considerations, such as with water governance policies (Roberts 2008). Moreover, such models often involve monetary valuation of the environment and frame well-being through a continual increase in the consumption of goods and services instead of reaching a point of satiation where needs are adequately met. This can lead to the removal of decision-making power from certain communities at subnational levels and cause degradation of the environment, overuse of natural resources, and increased pollution (Beder 2000; Brand-Correa et al. 2022). The academic literature has addressed the importance of incorporating human rights in climate change policies at the national level, such as in national determined contributions (Glemarec 2019; Toussaint and Martínez Blanco 2019; Bach 2016). However, the role of various subnational-level actors in advancing the integration of human rights in climate adaptation, particularly through supporting biosphere defenders as agents of change, is not well understood. Shifting focus to subnational-level efforts is crucial for transitioning from global economic models based on the exploitation and degradation of ecosystems to those of regenerative economics (Turner and Wills 2022).

This chapter discusses how biosphere defenders challenge these traditional assumptions, proposes an alternative epistemology that recognises humans as part of the biosphere rather than its owners, and advocates for territorial planning that respects ecological limits and fosters sustainable economic practices. In this connection, the conceptualisation of a human rights economy as described by the Office of the Human Rights Commissioner of the United Nations provides principles for aligning economic practices with human rights, including reconciling economic growth with climate and environmental action (OHCHR 2023). However, this framework, while important, may be limited in

DOI: 10.4324/9781003474845-9

its reliance on economic growth as a means to achieve sustainability as there is a growing body of literature suggesting that economic growth is irreconcilable with the required climate and environmental action (Tscherrig and João Parreira 2024; Hickel 2019). Instead, we suggest a paradigm shift that prioritises moving beyond economic growth and highlights the importance of adopting principles that reflect regenerative economic practices and ecological health. The aforementioned human rights economy framework highlights critical principles and emphasises state- and business-driven initiatives, as they are often the primary duty-bearers. However, this approach may overlook the contributions of subnational actors and right-holders such as biosphere defenders who provide localised, participatory solutions that complement this framework. Accordingly, this chapter holds that to fully realise the potential of a human rights economy, recognition must be given to biosphere defenders as agents of change and their initiatives, which offer transformative pathways that prioritise equity, participation, ecological health, and regenerative economic practices while recognising the State as primary duty-bearer.

Environmental human rights defenders (EHRDs) often face human rights violations such as loss of life and the risk thereof, threats, lack of access to information, and forms of judicial harassment (Human Rights Watch 2023a, 2023b; Business & Human Rights Resource Center 2023; Yusuf 2023). Inadequate or ineffective legal systems, alongside toxic narratives such as being framed as "anti-development", discredit their efforts and amplify the risks they face (Global Witness 2019). This may reinforce deep-seated social, political, or economic inequalities and sustain disparities in resources, living standards, and power, which are exacerbated by limited intergenerational social mobility (ECLAC 2018). Despite this, EHRDs are not merely victims in need of protection, but agents of change (Ituarte-Lima, Nardi, and Varumo 2024a). As this chapter discusses, the realisation of their rights is key to operationalise the Prevention Principle in climate adaptation, which simultaneously addresses systemic inequities that perpetuate social and economic poverty (Hamilton and Bisnath 2024). As such, there is growing consensus in international and regional fora of the need to increase action to respect, protect, and fulfil the rights of EHRDs. For example, the UN General Secretary, António Guterres, in the Global Call for Action on Human Rights (2020) has called for protecting the rights and supporting the work of EHRDs (United Nations Secretary-General 2020). Similarly, the UN Human Rights Council (2023) (A/HRC/RES/52/23) highlighted the need to promote a safe, enabling environment for individuals, civil society organisations, and EHRDs to work without threats or insecurity. Moreover, the Regional Agreement on Access to Information, Public Participation and Justice in Environmental Matters in Latin America and the Caribbean (Escazú Agreement) became the first treaty to specify the rights of EHRDs (Article 9) (UN and ECLAC 2022). Organisations supporting the work of defenders often connect defenders with land. For example, Global Witness (n.d.) calls them "land and environmental defenders", and International Work Group for Indigenous Affairs (n.d.) calls them "land defenders". Yet, how to create an enabling environment for defenders engaged in climate-sensitive land use planning and the role of various actors at interacting scales (subnational, national, transnational) in the process of preventing the negative impacts of climate change is not well understood.

The "prevention principle" in human rights law involves reducing various types of harms, including human rights abuses, conflicts, and crises, through the anticipation of risks and advanced preparation to mitigate them (de Greiff 2024).[1] Therefore, human rights are central to this principle, as recognised by the Secretary-General to the UN Security Council, who stated, "There is no better guarantee of prevention than for Member States to meet their human rights responsibilities" (United Nations Secretary-General 2020). Despite this, the term "prevention" has remained ambiguous, having differing roles depending on the context, whether conflict prevention, public health, or climate change adaptation, due to a siloed approach focusing on crisis prevention instead of long-term systemic prevention efforts which address the root causes of crises (Center for International Cooperation 2023). In this chapter, we are interested in human rights law not only as a mechanism for redress towards violations of rights of biosphere defenders but as a means of prevention with a focus on climate risk-sensitive land and water use planning, particularly at the local level. This chapter addresses the question: how can the realisation of biosphere defenders' rights in the context of climate adaptation help operationalise the prevention principle?

To do this, this chapter utilises the Defend-Biosphere Framework, which goes beyond the traditional silos of biodiversity, climate, and ocean defenders, to undertake a comprehensive approach to environmental law and governance, including the right to a clean, healthy, and sustainable environment (right to a healthy environment (RTHE)), recognised by the UN General Assembly (2022) to advance pathways to sustainability (Ituarte-Lima 2023; Ituarte-Lima, Nardi, and Varumo 2024a). Previous research conducted by Ituarte-Lima on projects on defenders and prevention has contributed to inform this chapter. While access to information and public participation are among the procedural elements of the RTHE, a safe climate, clean air and water, and healthy biodiversity and ecosystems are some of the substantive elements (United Nations Environment Programme et al. 2022). As such, this framework promotes collaboration across actors and thematic areas, nurturing an enabling environment for defenders to exercise their civil and political rights while rethinking and addressing multi-dimensional economic, social, and cultural challenges simultaneously. Accordingly, this framework highlights the importance of addressing structural challenges faced by defenders and ecosystems, particularly those rooted in the organisation of social and economic hierarchies, instead of merely reacting to crises.

This chapter defines biosphere defenders as "individuals, groups and organisations who play a role in advancing pathways for just sustainability including by using the law to enact positive change for people and nature".[2] Biosphere defenders address climate adaptation by recognising the interconnected nature of biodiversity, ecosystems, and climate change, using a composite of strategies, including the law, to trigger social change in a manner that contributes towards intergenerational protection of the RTHE. To make prevention a reality for all, the Defend-Biosphere Framework recognises the intersecting identities, capabilities, and vulnerabilities of biosphere defenders, including social, political, and economic obstacles they overcome, as they participate from various groups of society.

In a subnational context, this chapter utilises examples of women and girls, such as those from the Bochahi Village in Nepal, and from Botswana's Bobirwa (sub-district), Chobe (district), and Mahalapye (town); members of rural communities and/or indigenous peoples, such as the Garo Tribe in the Northeast Indian state of Meghalaya; and youth biosphere defenders, such as those from the city of Kampot, Cambodia, to address the aforementioned question. The identities of these biosphere defenders do not fall into distinct categories but exist within a spectrum of socio-legal categorisation. For example, female biosphere defenders may also be youth, while indigenous defenders may live in a diverse range of ecosystems, from forests to deserts and urban areas.

To challenge the ontological fragmentation between people and nature, we use both the term "biosphere" and "territory" (Ituarte-Lima et al. 2024b). While the "biosphere" – the sum of all ecosystems or thin layer of Earth where life flourishes – helps us place the discussion in the context of Earth System's science and the interconnected global and local dynamics, the notion of "territory" contributes to ground the discussion on a relational understanding of land, not only in terms of the land titles provided by a particular State, but the relationship between specific human societies and the place they inhabit, the land, water, and ecosystems and the biocultural values placed therein (Chaparro 2021; Escobar 2008; López Sandoval et al. 2017; Lyons 2022; Ojeda 2022). These concepts allow us to gain a more accurate understanding of both the climate-adaptive contributions and the specific vulnerabilities of biosphere defenders. We focus on unpacking five levers used in the Defend-Biosphere Framework: (a) incentives and mobilisation of capacities, (b) cross-sectoral coordination, (c) adaptive decision-making, (d) pre-emptive action, and (e) laws for achieving the RTHE's substantive outcomes.

Biosphere Defenders as Catalysts for Local Climate Resilience

Participation as a Lever for Catalysing an Enabling Environment

Inclusive public participation creates an enabling environment for biosphere defenders to challenge inequities, contribute to adaptive decision-making, and advocate for solutions that balance ecological sustainability with community economic needs. Accordingly, public participation is to be seen as a dynamic process with clear objectives and with the systematic representation of relevant right-holders and duty-bearers and where trust and mutual learning are actively cultivated.[3] Furthermore, historical entrenched inequalities need to be tackled, as inter-group inequalities often arise from dominant groups' strategic efforts to preserve their social hierarchy (Darity, Hamilton, and Stewart 2015). For example, Participatory 3-Dimensional Mapping (P3DM) was used in Bochahi Village in Nepal, where the RTHE has been recognised, but vulnerability is deeply tied to caste-based power structures (Gaillard et al. 2013). P3DM facilitated an enabling environment for the critical knowledge of so-called lower castes, women, and children to influence climate adaptation decision-making, leveraging the capabilities and reducing the vulnerabilities of the whole village. Although not initially invited, women detailed essential understandings of household risks and vulnerabilities, including houses with elderly members, children, and pregnant women, shaping the community's comprehensive flood vulnerability assessment. Moreover, children contributed through their unique spatial insights by mapping playgrounds and other areas with which adults were less familiar, and for which safe spaces were not previously considered by adults, highlighting the importance of intergenerational knowledge sharing.

The P3DM process promoted cross-sectoral coordination between Western and Nepalese geographers and local NGO staff; identified social divisions and knowledge gaps; improved collaboration and trust; and facilitated relatively more equal participation across different castes, genders, and ages, allowing them to tangibly contribute their respective knowledge for adaptive decision-making. Over 18 months, this built a shared incentive among distinct castes to construct a bio-engineered dike for flood protection in the village, a significant step to pre-empt climate-related challenges. The P3DM project also had transnational dimensions as it was facilitated by the French National Research Agency. This example highlights the increasing need to recognise the intersectional dimensions of biosphere defenders' rights, as emphasised by the heightened obligations placed on subnational-level governmental institutions to ensure an enabling environment for their meaningful participation and well-being in climate adaptation.

Gendered and Generational Dimensions of Climate Adaptation

Empowering women and children biosphere defenders can help to address the disproportionate social and economic impacts of climate change they face (Stoet and Geary 2019), while leveraging their unique contributions to community resilience and sustainable development. Accordingly, the Convention on the Elimination of All Forms of Discrimination against Women (CEDAW) contributes to specify State's obligations, requiring them to account for rural women's unique challenges and significant economic contributions, including unpaid work, and ensuring the Convention's provisions apply to them (Article 14) (United Nations General Assembly 1979). While clarifying these obligations is important, there is significant work needed to ground them at subnational and local level to prevent disproportionate harm towards certain groups in practice. During the 2004 tsunami, four times as many women than men were killed in Indonesia, Sri Lanka, and India because men were taught how to swim and climb trees at young ages, while women were not (MacDonald 2005). Therefore, deliberate empowerment of women and girls to act as biosphere defenders in climate adaptation is essential as it better positions them to define their own priorities, challenges, and opportunities, and actively inform climate-sensitive territorial planning. Research highlights women's agency in enhancing household and community resilience despite being disproportionately affected by climate change when compared to men (UNDP 2019; Ituarte-Lima et al. 2020), as seen in Nepal, where during extreme events and with high rates of male outmigration, many women take on extra caregiving responsibilities (Ministry of Population and Environment 2017). Even under these circumstances, women in Nepal contribute 60.5% of the agricultural economy, which is vital to food security (Gurung and Bisht 2014).

Thus, not only recognising rights but also actively catalysing an enabling environment at the local level for adult and children biosphere defenders to exercise their rights is necessary. The Convention on the Rights of the Child (United Nations 1989) explicitly links children's rights to environmental protection through Article 24, which requires States to combat disease and malnutrition while considering environmental pollution, and Article 29, which entails the education of the child to be directed towards respect for the natural environment, recognising that a healthy environment is crucial to a child's well-being and development. Accordingly, there are other initiatives, such as in the city of Kampot, Cambodia, in which community members, including children and youth, together with other groups are restoring mangroves to help prevent climate change-related hazards by reducing the impacts of storm waves and flooding while also providing shelter to various types of fish, which is essential for the community's economic sustainability as 3,500 families in Kampot rely on fishing for their livelihood (United Nations Development Programme 2019). When such local knowledge is integrated through climate-sensitive territorial planning, the agency of vulnerable groups is strengthened by identifying their capabilities, which helps to prevent future hazards by promoting resilient land and water use strategies.

In Zambia, Malawi, Zimbabwe, Lesotho, and South Africa, girl biosphere defenders have contributed to climate adaptation, supported by GIRRL (Girls In Risk Reduction Leadership) Program, designed in 2007 through the African Centre for Disaster Studies at North-West University, South Africa (Forbes-Genade and Van Niekerk 2017). As inequality and human rights violations were root causes of girls' vulnerability to climate change, GIRRL encouraged social structural changes through inclusivity and participation, increasing community resilience, while highlighting the agency of adolescent girls in the five countries. This Program utilised a Participatory Action Research methodology, emphasising planning, action, reflection, and evaluation, which enabled girls to participate in informed decision-making for resilience building and risk reduction. Key activities included relationship building, role and responsibility identification, collaborative decision-making, data collection, and action planning. GIRRL utilised a human rights-based approach focused on accountability, information, non-discrimination, and participation.

Girls in Zambia contributed towards public health by conducting water quality testing and communicating results to their families and schools, and by advocating for better menstrual hygiene conditions in schools. The latter led to institutional commitments to improve sanitary conditions and addressed existing absenteeism and dropout rates linked to inadequate menstrual care, allowing more girls to participate in school and engage in biosphere defence leadership activities. In Malawi, girls addressed food scarcity by securing community lands from local elders to actively participate in small plot farming, and tackled the effects of droughts by participating in irrigation projects. Their contribution was particularly powerful, as they were often disproportionately affected during food scarcity due to gendered feeding practices. In South Africa, where disaster management efforts traditionally excluded youth, and girls in particular, participants from the towns of Ikageng and Tshwelelang collaborated with the local government (Fire Department and Public Safety/Disaster Management) on fire safety and disaster prevention campaigns. The girls from Ikageng also volunteered with a local youth organisation to host sessions on sexual health, team-building, coping strategies, and community awareness.

In Lesotho, girls planted trees, directly impacting local construction needs and providing firewood. They also participated in a conservation agriculture project in their school and helped to disseminate the technology to their community. These activities led to public visibility of their technical skills in an environment where girls had little say in ecosystems management. In Zimbabwe, groups gained financial literacy through training in the Village Savings and Loan Scheme, offering a potential pathway out of poverty in a context where girls often faced economic exclusion. This provided greater economic resilience in an environment where economic stability was directly affected by climate-related challenges. Relatedly, Zimbabwe's CARE Leader reported that girls were developing their leadership and information access and sharing skills concerning climate-related disaster risk prevention.

Traditional and Intersectional Approaches to Climate Adaptation

Traditional ecological knowledge (TEK) is grounded in local place-based conservation and use of the territory. Integrating TEK with scientific approaches can strengthen climate resilience and foster economic strategies that are both sustainable and culturally aligned with local communities. In terms of peasants biosphere defenders, the UN Declaration on the Rights of Peasants and Other People Working in Rural Areas (UN Human Rights Council 2018) requires States to protect their RTHE and ensure they can participate in shaping and implementing climate policies, incorporating traditional knowledge and practices (United Nations Human Rights Council 2023). A valuable example of collaborative, climate-sensitive land-use planning is the "Adaptation at Scale in Semi-Arid Regions" project, part of which involved Oxfam Great

Britain training researchers at the University of Botswana on conducting Vulnerability and Risk Assessments (VRA; Morchain et al. 2019). In the sub-district of Bobirwa, Botswana, rural farmers adopted climate-adaptive practices utilising traditional knowledge, such as using indigenous crops and seasonal farming, while mopane caterpillar harvesters (mostly women and youth) provided an additional income to meet basic needs and buffer against climate-related challenges like droughts (Masundire et al. 2016). Yet, the VRA process, supported by local officials such as district economic planners from Bobirwa, identified that drought-related water shortages, worsened by climate change, resulted in reduced mopane caterpillars and crop yields, further limiting income generation due to inadequate alternatives to agriculture-based livelihoods. The VRA facilitated the recognition of otherwise underrepresented groups like the caterpillar harvesters and integrated their traditional knowledge into decision-making structures. It also proposed climate-adaptation responses such as exploring the use of groundwater for crop irrigation and human consumption and communicating drought management strategies (Morchain et al. 2019, 28, 30).

Following this VRA workshop, cross-sectoral and cross-jurisdictional follow-up processes strengthened the capacities of subnational government officials to conduct participatory processes. For instance, a VRA training for District Officers nationwide was held in the town of Mahalapye in August 2018, proposed by national-level government officials working alongside the University of Botswana. Building on Bobirwa's successful VRA workshop and the VRA training in Mahalapye, the trained officials conducted another VRA workshop in Chobe District in January 2019, displaying adaptive decision-making capacity (Ibid., 33). Participatory assessments which nurture collaboration between peasants, biosphere defenders, and subnational and national governments can help examine climate change-associated vulnerabilities and governance challenges, and identify ways for multiscale governments to support defender's place-based ecological knowledge and capabilities. Indigenous biosphere defenders contribute significantly to climate change adaptation and biodiversity conservation due to their distinct relationships with nature and TEK. Recognising this, international frameworks have provided heightened human rights obligations for States towards indigenous peoples. For example, Article 29 of the UN Declaration on the Rights of Indigenous Peoples (UNDRIP) (United Nations General Assembly 2007) affirms the right of indigenous peoples to protect and sustainably manage the productive capacities and resources of the environment on their territories, thus reinforcing their role as biosphere defenders. Moreover, UNDRIP enshrines their rights to participate in decision-making processes which would affect their rights, requiring their free, prior, and informed consent (Articles 18 and 10). Similarly, the Convention on Biological Diversity (2011) requires party States to respect indigenous rights over lands, territories, resources, and TEK, warranting their participation in decision-making, while Operational Target 22 in the Kunming-Montreal Global Biodiversity Framework (Conference of the Parties to the

Convention on Biological Diversity 2022) necessitates inclusive, equitable, and gender-responsive indigenous participation in biodiversity decisions alongside access to justice and information.

The Garo Tribe of the Northeast Indian state of Meghalaya illustrates unique traditional ecological practices deeply intertwined with its hilly landscape, contributing towards biosphere protection (Sarma and Yadav 2013). For instance, the Garo people's primary occupation is jhum cultivation, a form of slash-and-burn agriculture involving clearing forest patches, cultivation, and extended fallow periods for regeneration. The community also protects "sacred groves", which act as biodiversity hotspots, remaining untouched by human activities, and engages in multispecies cropping systems relying on permaculture principles, growing crops such as potato, ginger, and turmeric, and fruits such as orange, pineapple, and lemon, demonstrating a degree of economic resilience and biodiversity conservation within agroecological systems. The tribe further displays their TEK through bamboo drip irrigation to navigate the hilly terrain while conserving water and reducing soil erosion.

Women play a crucial role in sustainably using, maintaining, and enhancing biodiversity, spending most of their productive lives in land-based production processes. They contribute towards food security and disaster prevention by managing wood, water, and fodder on a daily basis in addition to looking after their children, and act as important risk communicators through various communal networks. Despite this, cyclones and droughts resulting from environmental stress and climate impact have damaged the area, and a shift to economically valuable cash crops such as pineapple and areca nut, which increased income in some areas, degraded traditional crop diversity crucial for climate variability resilience. Moreover, reduced jhum cycles resulted in shorter fallow periods which caused sheet erosion exacerbated by heavy rainfall, all of which contributed towards economic vulnerability due to their reliance on agriculture and forest products. When coupled with a lack of basic infrastructure such as health and education facilities, this left them particularly affected by climate change and perpetuated intergenerational poverty.

To address these challenges, a Community-Based Vulnerability and Capacity Assessment utilising purposive sampling was co-led by the Garo Hills District Council in collaboration with the Meghalaya Forest Department, local NGOs such as the Wildlife Trust of India (WTI) and the Samrakshan Trust, village elders, community leaders/Nokmas (who are women), farmers, hunters, and other stakeholders. We see the mobilisation of capacities, for example, at the village level, where the Nokmas undertook leadership roles in coordinating forest management projects, cooperating with government agencies to integrate traditional governance structures into modern conservation efforts. Further, farmers applied bamboo matting across flood-prone channels to trap silt and prevent soil erosion during heavy rains and expanded the bamboo irrigation system to improve water efficiency in agriculture, particularly during droughts. Moreover, the Samrakshan Trust trained village members in eco-tourism management, diversifying income sources, and WTI worked with the community to restore degraded lands and create Village Reserve Forests, which provided ecological benefits and employment for over 100 days annually to village residents, incentivising climate-sensitive employment and regenerative economic activities.

Discussion

Systemic change requires contextualising and challenging systemic social, political, cultural, and economic inequalities that perpetuate historical and institutionalised systems of oppression. The Defend-Biosphere Framework, uniting human rights law with science and policy, contributes to visibilise the vital role of local actors directly depending from nature as agents of change in an interconnected world. Beyond unpacking human rights violations, this framework has contributed to envisioning pathways for the realisation of human rights and sustainability by deepening our understanding of levers for sustainability pathways in the context of climate-sensitive territorial planning. The framework bridges traditional and practical place-based knowledge on land and water governance with global understandings of social-ecological processes and power dynamics.

Below we zoom-in to discuss insights of three levers: incentives and mobilisation of capacities, coordination across sectors and jurisdictions, and laws for achieving the RTHE's substantive outcomes. We find that the levers of adaptive decision-making and pre-emptive action are cross-cutting to these three levers.

Incentives and Mobilisation of Capacities

By recognising *all* contributions towards climate resilience, Defend-Biosphere Framework reveals a broad range of contributors' agencies and empowers them by valuing both their actions and capacities. *Incentives play a fundamental role in mobilising the capacities of such agents*, not only through direct economic benefits but also by recognising the social value of biosphere defenders' participation in climate adaptation initiatives. Similarly, the *pre-emptive action* lever complements mobilisation when specific structural issues are targeted via government strategies. For instance, the P3DM process in Bochahi Village facilitated the participation of marginalised groups traditionally excluded in climate-related decision-making, simultaneously enhancing community resilience and women's leadership. The recognition and mobilisation of these groups incentivised *adaptive decision-making*, specifically a shift from exclusive decision-making by elites to more inclusive participation, highlighting the power of collective action.

This shift was not merely altruistic, but incentivised through the potential of obtaining tangible benefits, both material (flood protection) and social (unleashing community solidarity), exemplified by the creation of a bio-engineered dike which benefitted the whole community. Moreover, incorporating such marginalised knowledge into climate adaptation strategies acted as a pre-emptive lever towards dismantling caste-based exclusion by demonstrating its practical value. Similarly, the GIRRL Program tackled climate change vulnerabilities by utilising the collective capacities of girls by engaging them in water purification projects, public health advocacy, and food security initiatives, which enhanced the community's climate resilience while concurrently strengthening girls' leadership roles.

This programme reveals layered incentives for girls. On the one hand, they benefit from material improvements in community resilience like better access to clean water and increased food security. On the other hand, their actions in leadership roles resulted in the social recognition of their capabilities, challenging gendered hierarchies. *Economic independence* through financial literacy also provided girls with tools for continued involvement in climate resilience strategies. Youth skill development, particularly marginalised youth, acts as a preventative step against future climate risks and existing structural challenges. In both examples, mobilised capacities and incentives worked hand-in-hand with pre-emptive action to safeguard biosphere defenders' rights, activating their latent capacities to effectively address local climate risks.

Coordination across Sectors and Jurisdictions

The Defend-Biosphere Framework also highlights existing tensions between TEK and Western scientific and/or technocratic knowledge systems, where TEK is often devalued, causing epistemic injustice, commonly rooted in the power dynamics inherent in knowledge production, operating at an intersection of education, colonial legacies, and governance structures. The lever of *cross-sectoral and cross-jurisdictional coordination* addresses this by integrating both knowledge systems in climate adaptation strategies by broadening the scope of participation as a means of *pre-emptive action*. For example, horizontal coordination in Botswana mobilised farmers, harvesters, district economic planners, and local NGOs to tackle the overlapping challenges of economic vulnerability and environmental degradation. Vertical coordination through the extension of the VRA process beyond local level to involve subnational and national government bodies, such as conducting a VRA workshop in the Chobe District, demonstrates how *adaptive decision-making* can be institutionalised across jurisdictions, enabling different locations to adopt similar resilience strategies while tailoring them to their unique circumstances. Likewise, the GIRRL Program in Southern Africa targeted climate vulnerabilities by including the participation of girls across the region, facilitating coordination between schools, local communities, and government agencies, which was crucial to its success.

Unpacking the role of biosphere defenders in climate adaptation therefore sheds light on adaptive decision-making and how a diverse range of allies of defenders can support evidence-based planning and decision-making in the context of climate-sensitive land and water governance. This conceptualisation of biosphere defenders opens opportunities to unleash values of responsibility and solidarity with a broad and diverse skill base, not limited to allies in the human rights community, such as collaboration to prevent flooding between local NGOs, local and Western geographers via the P3DM in Nepal.

Like the P3DM, the participatory VRA in Southern Africa (Morchain et al. 2019) shows the tool's effectiveness in highlighting the contributions and capacities of otherwise marginalised communities to local stakeholders, and larger subnational, national, and international bodies. The VRA catalysed locals to further engage in biosphere defence, amplifying the influence of those involved in sustainable farming and caterpillar harvesting in regional climate-sensitive land and water use planning and decision-making, while also promoting alliances between various groups to address the root causes of vulnerabilities to climate change. In each instance, the utility of tools like the P3DM and VRAs and the resulting integration of TEK into the fabric of broader governance frameworks unleashed the capabilities of relevant individuals and groups and facilitated a multi-layered response to climate change.

Laws for Achieving the RTHE's Substantive Outcomes

While international legal frameworks like CEDAW and UNDRIP aim to disrupt the perpetuation of repressive social dynamics by institutionalising empowerment, it is important to recognise the existence of resistance to change within legal and governance systems as a key barrier to effective climate adaptation. In turn, this highlights the importance of the lever of *creating, reforming, and/or implementing laws towards realising the RTHE.* Although the GIRRL Program and the VRA process in Botswana show the effectiveness of legal frameworks when aligned with local needs and capacities, the Garo Tribe's shift towards cash crops due to economic hardship emphasises the need of *pre-emptive action* through creating effective mechanisms and allocating sufficient resources that ensure the enforcement of laws and their implementation at the local level.

We find that international legal frameworks must be supported by robust implementation mechanisms in local and subnational processes through the use of interdisciplinary tools such as VRAs and VCAs in the context of climate-sensitive water and land use planning to operationalise the prevention principle. The empowerment gained by these tools contributes to an enabling environment for communities to advocate for institutional and legal reforms to protect their rights, as illustrated by the commitments undertaken to improve menstrual hygiene as a result of advocacy by girls facilitated through the GIRRL Program. Without empowered communities with influence in *adaptive decision-making*, legal frameworks remain abstract commitments lacking meaningful ground-level translation. As such, we find that is important to recognise biosphere defenders not only as individuals that resist exploitation, but also as a diversity of individuals and collectives who are change-makers, generating proactive strategies to advance climate resilience and sustainability, for example, through initiatives that integrate TEK and scientific knowledge to respond to contemporary social-ecological challenges. In this connection, biosphere defenders bridge the domains of biodiversity conservation and climate adaptation, having a vital role in preventing large-scale human rights violations connected to the climate crises and ecosystems degradation.

Conclusion

In sum, this chapter has shown that biosphere defenders' participation in territorial planning at different subnational levels is critical in addressing interconnected climate, biodiversity, ecosystem, social, and economic challenges in a preventive way. Furthermore, examining their agency and associated obstacles in the context of climate-sensitive land and water use planning serves to unpack levers to operationalise the prevention principle. To overcome structural inequalities, coordination across sectors and jurisdictions is needed. This coordination can also contribute towards the recognition of diverse knowledge systems and epistemic justice, strengthening the decision-making process by unleashing values of responsibility and solidarity by various groups and triggering collective action and adaptive decision-making. Whether engaging in ecotourism, integrating TEK into adaptive strategies, or fostering inclusion and cross-sectoral collaboration, legal and governance reforms, when combined with administrative tools like VRAs, the P3DM, and GIRRL Program, have catalysed actions that safeguard against ecosystem, social, and economic shocks. This works by empowering diverse actors, strengthening and diversifying sustainable income sources, and increasing financial literacy and social mobility to create an enabling environment for biosphere defenders to act as agents of change. An enabling environment for biosphere defenders in climate-sensitive territorial planning helps operationalise the prevention principle by pre-emptively addressing climate risks in a participatory manner. Therefore, we hold that reforming legal and governance frameworks to support this enabling environment is vital for advancing a local regenerative economy aligned with Earth's life support systems.

Notes

1 See more on the role of prevention at "A Framework Approach to Making Prevention a Reality | Powered by Box." March 2024. https://app.box.com/s/9p9oildfxgk3fsd3gxsbfzoo16zq466q.

2 Coined by the co-author of this chapter in Ituarte-Lima, "Biosphere Defenders Leveraging the Human Right to Healthy Environment for Transformative Change", and further developed in Ituarte-Lima, Nardi, and Varumo, "Just Pathways to Sustainability", 352.

3 For more on public participation as a dynamic process, see Reed, Mark S. 2008. "Stakeholder Participation for Environmental Management: A Literature Review". *Biological Conservation* 141(10): 2417–31.

Bibliography

Bach, Tracy. 2016. "Human Rights in a Climate Changed World: The Impact of COP21, Nationally Determined Contributions, and National Courts." *Vermont Law Review* 40 (forthcoming). Vermont Law School Research Paper No. 1–16. Available at SSRN: https://ssrn.com/abstract=2734992 or http://dx.doi.org/10.2139/ssrn.2734992

Beder, Sharon. 2000. "Costing the Earth: Equity, Sustainable Development and Environmental Economics." *New Zealand Journal of Environmental Law* 4 (January): 227. https://ro.uow.edu.au/artspapers/30/

Brand-Correa, Lina, A. Brook, M. Büchs, P. Meier, Y. Naik, and D. W. O'Neill. 2022. "Economics for People and Planet—Moving Beyond the Neoclassical Paradigm." *The Lancet Planetary Health* 6 (4): e371–79. https://doi.org/10.1016/s2542-5196(22)00063-8

Business & Human Rights Resource Centre. 2023. "Uganda: Environmental Defenders Raising Concerns about the East Africa Crude Oil Pipeline Project Continue to Experience Attacks." December 20, 2023. https://www.business-humanrights.org/en/latest-news/uganda-continued-attacks-against-environmental-defenders-protesting-against-totalenergies-oil-pipeline-project-incl-company-response/

Centre for International Cooperation. 2023. "An Integrated Approach to Prevention." March 2, 2023. https://cic.nyu.edu/resources/an-integrated-approach-to-prevention-the-links-between-prevention-the-2030-agenda-and-sustaining-peace/

Chaparro, A. 2021. "Territorio habitado y territorio como derecho: reflexiones desde el caminar Kichwa Lamista." *Revista de Antropologia y Sociología: Virajes* 23 (1): 118–147. https://doi.org/10.17151/rasv.2021.23.1.6

Convention on Biological Diversity. 2011. *Convention on Biological Diversity*. Secretariat for the Convention on Biological Diversity. https://www.cbd.int/doc/legal/cbd-en.pdf

Darity, William A., D. Hamilton, and J. B. Stewart. 2015. "A Tour de Force in Understanding Intergroup Inequality: An Introduction to Stratification Economics." *The Review of Black Political Economy* 42 (1–2): 16.

de Greiff, Pablo. 2024. *A Framework Approach to Making Prevention a Reality*. Prevention Project, March 2024.

Economic Commission for Latin America and the Caribbean. 2018. *The Inefficiency of Inequality*.

Escobar, A. 2008. *Territories of Difference: Place, Movements, Life, Redes*. Durham and London: Duke University Press.

Forbes-Genade, Kylah, and D. Van Niekerk. 2017. "The GIRRL Program: A Human Rights Based Approach to Disaster Risk Reduction Intervention in Southern Africa." *International Journal of Disaster Risk Reduction* 24 (April): 507–514.

Gaillard, Jean Christophe, C. Monteil, A. Perrillat-Collomb, S. Chaudhary, M. Chaudhary, O. Chaudhary, F. Giazzi, and J. R. D. Cadag. 2013. "Participatory 3-Dimensional Mapping: A Tool for Encouraging Multi-Caste Collaboration to Climate Change Adaptation and Disaster Risk Reduction." *Applied Geography* 45 (October): 158–166.

Glemarec, Yannick. 2019. "Aligning National Interests and Global Climate Justice: The Role of Human Rights in Enhancing the Ambition of Nationally Determined Contributions to Combat Climate Change." *Fudan Journal of the Humanities and Social Sciences* 12(3): 309–327. https://doi.org/10.1007/s40647-018-0249-4

Global Witness. 2019. *Enemies of the State*? London, UK: Global Witness. https://www.globalwitness.org/en/campaigns/environmental-activists/enemies-state/

Global Witness. n.d. "Environmental Activists: Land and Environmental Defenders." https://www.globalwitness.org/en/campaigns/environmental-activists/.

Gurung, D. D., and S. Bisht. 2014. "Women's Empowerment at the Frontline of Adaptation: Emerging Issues, Adaptive Practices, and Priorities in Nepal." *ICIMOD Working Paper 2014/3*.

Hamilton, Darrick, and Savitri Bisnath. 2024. *Racial and Gender Inclusion through Economic Policies Informed by Economic and Social Rights*. Institute on Race, Power & Political Economy, The New School.

Hickel, Jason. 2019. "The Contradiction of the Sustainable Development Goals: Growth Versus Ecology on a Finite Planet." *Sustainable Development* 27 (5): 873–884. https://doi.org/10.1002/sd.1947

Human Rights Watch. 2023a. "Uganda: Oil Pipeline Protests Stifled." November 2, 2023. https://www.hrw.org/news/2023/11/02/uganda-oil-pipeline-protests-stifled

Human Rights Watch. 2023b. "Working On Oil is Forbidden." November 2, 2023. https://www.hrw.org/report/2023/11/02/working-oil-forbidden/crackdown-against-environmental-defenders-uganda

International Work Group for Indigenous Affairs. n.d. "Land Defence and Defenders." https://iwgia.org/en/land-defence-defenders.html

Ituarte-Lima, Claudia. 2023. "Biosphere Defenders Leveraging the Human Right to Healthy Environment for Transformative Change." *Environmental Policy and Law* 53: 1–13.

Ituarte-Lima, Claudia, V. Bernard, D. Paul, S. San, M. M. Aung, C. Dany, T. Chavisschindha, D. Paramita, T. M. Aung, and N. Saenphit. 2020. *Prosperous and Green in the Anthropocene: The Human Right to a Healthy Environment in Southeast Asia*. Raoul Wallenberg Institute of Human Rights and Humanitarian Law.

Ituarte-Lima, Claudia, M. A. Nardi, and L. Varumo. 2024a. *Just Pathways to Sustainability*. Raoul Wallenberg Institute of Human Rights and Humanitarian Law.

Ituarte-Lima, Claudia, Natalia Urzola, Valentina Lomanto, Neshan Gunasekera, Maria Andrea Nardi, and Juan Antonio Samper. 2024b. *Discussion Paper on Biosphere Defenders in Latin America and the Caribbean & Written Comments to the Escazú Agreement's Draft Regional Action Plan on Human Rights Defenders in Environmental Matters*. Submitted to the Economic Commission for Latin America and the Caribbean (ECLAC) in January 2024. Glawcal Lab at the Raoul Wallenberg Institute and the Global Network for Human Rights and the Environment.

Kunming-Montreal Global Biodiversity Framework. 2022. *Conference of the Parties to the Convention on Biological Diversity*. https://www.cbd.int/doc/decisions/cop-15/cop-15-dec-04-en.pdf

López Sandoval, M.F., et al. 2017. "Space, Power, and Locality: The Contemporary Use of Territorio in Latin American Geography." *Journal of Latin American Geography* 16 (1). https://doi.org/10.1353/lag.2017.0009.

Lumby, Ab. 2007. "The Current Orthodoxy in Environmental Economics: A Review and a Challenge." *South African Journal of Economic and Management Sciences*. https://sajems.org/index.php/sajems/article/view/1056/353

Lyons, K. 2022. "Nature and Territories as Victims: Decolonizing Colombia's Transitional Justice Process." *American Anthropology*, 1–14. https://doi.org/10.1111/aman.13798.

MacDonald, Rachel. 2005. "How Women Were Affected by the Tsunami: A Perspective from Oxfam." *PLoS Med* 2(6): e178. https://doi.org/10.1371/journal.pmed.0020178

Masundire, H., D. Morchain, N. Raditloaneng, S. Hegga, G. Ziervogel, C. Molefe, and K. Omari. 2016. *Vulnerability and Risk Assessment in Botswana's Bobirwa Subdistrict: Fostering People-Centred Adaptation to Climate Change*. Cape Town: University of Cape Town.

Ministry of Population and Environment (MoPE). 2017. *Vulnerability and Risk Assessment Framework and Indicators for National Adaptation Plan (NAP) Formulation Process in Nepal*. Kathmandu.

Morchain, Daniel, D. Spear, G. Ziervogel, H. Masundire, M. N. Angula, J. Davies, C. Molefe, and S. Hegga. 2019. "Building Transformative Capacity in Southern Africa: Surfacing Knowledge and Challenging Structures through Participatory Vulnerability and Risk Assessments." *Action Research* 17 (1): 19–41. https://doi.org/10.1177/1476750319829205

Office of the United Nations High Commissioner for Human Rights. 2023. "Building Economies That Place People's Human Rights at the Center." April 6, 2023. https://www.ohchr.org/en/stories/2023/04/building-economies-place-peoples-human-rights-center

Ojeda, D. 2022. "Beyond Land as Property: A Feminist Perspective." In *The Oxford Handbook of Land Politics*, edited by Saturnino M. Borras Jr. and Jennifer C. Franco. Oxford: Oxford University Press. https://doi.org/10.1093/oxfordhb/9780197618646.013.17

Prudham, Scott. 2015. "Property and Commodification." In *The Routledge Handbook of Political Ecology*. https://scottprudham.org/wp-content/uploads/2017/01/Prudham_Handbook-of-PE-2015-proof.pdf

Reed, Mark S. 2008. "Stakeholder Participation for Environmental Management: A Literature Review." *Biological Conservation* 141(10): 2417–2431.

Roberts, Adrienne. 2008. "Privatizing Social Reproduction: The Primitive Accumulation of Water in an Era of Neoliberalism." *Antipode* 40 (4): 535–560. https://doi.org/10.1111/j.1467-8330.2008.00623.x

Sarma, P. Y. K. 2013. "A Framework for Indigenous Community-Based Climate Vulnerability and Capacity Assessment in the Garo Hills, North-East India." *Journal of Biodiversity Management & Forestry*, January.

Stoet, Gijsbert, and D. C. Geary. 2019. "A Simplified Approach to Measuring National Gender Inequality." *PLoS One* 14 (1).

Toussaint, Patrick, and A. Martínez Blanco. 2019. "A Human Rights-Based Approach to Loss and Damage under the Climate Change Regime." *Climate Policy* 20 (6): 743–757. doi:10.1080/14693062.2019.1630354

Tscherrig, and J. Parreira. 2024. "Embracing a Beyond Growth Approach for Sustainable Futures." *SDG Knowledge Hub*. July 13, 2024. https://sdg.iisd.org/commentary/guest-articles/embracing-a-beyond-growth-approach-for-sustainable-futures/

Turner, Rebecca A., and J. Wills. 2022. "Downscaling Doughnut Economics for Sustainability Governance." *Current Opinion in Environmental Sustainability* 56: 1–10.

UN. Human Rights Council (39th Sess.: 2018: Geneva). 2018. "United Nations Declaration on the Rights of Peasants and Other People Working in Rural Areas: Resolution /: Adopted by the Human Rights Council on 28 September 2018." *United Nations Digital Library System*, October 8, 2018. https://digitallibrary.un.org/record/1650694?ln=en&v=pdf

United Nations. 1989. . "Convention on the Rights of the Child." Treaty Series 1577 (November): 3.

United Nations Development Programme. 2019. *Gender, Climate and Disaster Resilience*.

United Nations Environment Programme (UNEP), United Nations Development Programme (UNDP), A. Steiner, V. Türk, and I. Andersen. 2022. "What Is the Right to a Healthy Environment?" *Information Note*. https://www.undp.org/sites/g/files/zskgke326/files/2023-01/UNDP-UNEP-UNHCHR-What-is-the-Right-to-a-Healthy-Environment.pdf

United Nations General Assembly. 1979. "Convention on the Elimination of All Forms of Discrimination Against Women." December 18, 1979. https://www.ohchr.org/sites/default/files/Documents/ProfessionalInterest/cedaw.pdf

7 Water Governance and Human Rights Economies

LaDawn Haglund

Introduction

Water is foundational to both human rights and planetary health. The human right to water, traditionally understood, comprises access, affordability, reliability, and quality of supply. However, water-related human rights transcend potable water to include the right to sanitation (toilets, sewage treatment, and waste disposal), health and hygiene, agriculture and livelihoods, and healthy ecosystems. Water is also central to traditional cultural, spiritual, and economic practices and, by extension, the rights of Indigenous peoples. From pipes to water bottles to conduits to drainage basins, water is irrevocably linked to local economies, local and national budgets, multilevel governance choices, and human rights.

Despite water's crucial importance, two billion people lack safe drinking water and four billion lack sanitation, a 100% increase since 2002 (compared to a 29% population increase) (Arrojo-Agudo 2023). Simultaneously, environmental disasters with water at their core – floods, droughts, fires, hurricanes, and climate change – are intensifying. The challenges of governing this precious substance in ways that protect human rights and the planet are steep. The place-based reality of hydrological systems means that subnational and local governments are central players in satisfying this responsibility. Given the substantial capacity needed for water governance, policymakers are tempted to pursue public-private partnerships, offering incentives to companies for private investment, often with few strings attached. The tension between public duties and private investment is well documented in the water sector (Bakker 2013). "Human rights economies" (HREs) are relevant in this context, as they seek to ensure that economic policies, processes, and mechanisms at subnational levels are "put in service to promote, fulfill, and respect human rights for all, including a clean, healthy, and sustainable environment" (Bisnath, this volume).

Three key dimensions of water governance shape the capacity of HREs to achieve water-related human rights: the social, ecological, and economic *principles* that vie for primacy; the ebb and flow among state, community, and private *institutions*; and *who decides* which objectives are most important and how to achieve them. In this chapter, I compare the principles and practices reflected

DOI: 10.4324/9781003474845-10

United Nations General Assembly. 2007. "United Nations Declaration on the Right of Indigenous Peoples." *UNGA Res 61/295*. September 13, 2007. https://www.un.org development/desa/indigenouspeoples/wp-content/uploads/sites/19/2018/11 UNDRIP-E-web.pdf

United Nations General Assembly. 2022. "The Human Right to a Clean, Healthy, an Sustainable Environment." *A/RES/76/300*, July 28, 2022. https://digitallibrary.u org/record/3983329?ln=en

United Nations Human Rights Council. 2023. "The Human Right to a Clean, Healt and Sustainable Environment." *A/HRC/52/L.7*, March 23, 2023. https://undocs.o Home/Mobile?FinalSymbol=A%2FHRC%2F52%2FL.7&Language=E DeviceType=Desktop&LangRequested=False

United Nations Secretary-General. 2020. *The Highest Aspiration: A Call to Action Human Rights*. https://www.un.org.peacebuilding/sites/www.un.org.peacebuildi files/documents/2020_sg_call_to_action_for_hr_the_highest_aspiration.pdf

Yusuf, Mohammed. 2023. "Rights Group Claims Company Intimidates Communi Along Tanzania-Uganda Oil Pipeline." *VOA News*, December 8, 2023. https://w voanews.com/a/rights-group-claims-company-intimidates-communities-alc tanzania-uganda-oil-pipeline/7389853.html in the "transformative commitments" of human rights-based water governance (UN News 2023) with empirical evidence from interviews and sociolegal analyses from the Global North and South[1] and secondary sources. I evaluate transformative potential using a framework for social transformation that analyzes rights realization across three iterative "moments" of change (Haglund and Stryker 2015). Moments #1 and #2 attend, respectively, to how *beliefs and perceptions* about a particular norm evolve, and to mechanisms that spur *action* on these norms. Moment #3, the focus of this chapter, analyzes how actions cumulate to *meaningful social change* – in our case, a society that largely respects, protects, and fulfills water-related human rights.

Three interconnected drivers shape broader social transformations at Moment #3: (1) cultural assumptions and narratives, (2) structural conditions, and (3) power dynamics (Stryker and Haglund 2015). Ostensibly, HREs would shift all three to produce rights-responsive water governance:

1. Adoption of human rights principles should change *the way we talk* about water and *the assumptions we make* about appropriate priorities and processes;
2. Policies, processes, and mechanisms of HREs should challenge *structural* barriers to providing potable water, sanitation, and healthy hydrological systems;
3. Water would be distributed first and foremost to life-threatening exclusions based on collective wisdom discerned through participatory, *power-sharing* processes.

In short, HREs would challenge beliefs and perceptions that contradict human rights principles, structural conditions that reproduce existing inequities, and power dynamics that impede life-affirming water governance. The focus on subnational governance includes a recognition that these conditions and dynamics operate within and across multiple institutions and levels of governance.

The "three pillars" in HREs

Human rights entail a distinctive set of principles, structures, and power dynamics that imbue the social, environmental, and economic "pillars" of sustainability with meaningful content (Murphy 2012). In terms of *principles*, the social pillar for HR2WS is framed as access to affordable, potable water for households and basic sanitation; the inseparability of different human rights (water, health, housing, food, and livelihoods; Van Koppen et al. 2017; Satterthwaite 2021); and participatory governance (Schiel, Langford, and Wilson 2020). The environmental pillar in HREs foregrounds protection of water ecosystems as essential to all life and incorporates polluter pays and precautionary principles. A key *economic* framing for water in HREs is as a *public good*, which prioritizes the promotion of human rights over other economic interests when they come into conflict and employs indicators beyond GDP to measure progress (UNGA 2024).

Table 7.1 Dimensions of a "human rights economy" for sustainable water governance

Pillar	*Principles/framings*	*Structures*	*Power*
Social	Equitable access; indivisibility of water and right to health, housing, food, and livelihoods; stakeholder inclusion	Establish basic minimums, HR2WS protected by courts, policies to prevent and mitigate health emergencies, adequate housing policies, participatory mechanisms	Democratized decision-making; participation support for marginalized groups
Ecological	Water is essential to all life, polluter pays, precautionary principle	Environmental regulation/fines, licensing/permitting review, policies to reduce consumption, promote sustainable farming, and prevent and mitigate ecological emergencies	Nature as rights-holder
Economic	Water as a public good; rights take precedence over other economic uses; human rights indicators complement GDP	State investment and progressive realization using "all available resources"; transparency; new indicators for monitoring, accountability	Human rights prioritized over economic interests; participatory budgeting

Institutionalized human rights principles underpin *structural* change (Table 7.1, Column 3) by holding governments accountable to their obligations through monitoring and assessment (Yamin 2005). "Progressive realization" of the HR2WS requires national and subnational governments to marshal "all available resources" – laws, budgets, policies, programs, and investments – to prioritize HR2WS and create conditions for interrelated health, housing, and participatory rights. In water governance, this might mean reassessing regulations, licenses, permits, and penalties to align with the ideals above, as well as creating new policies to reduce consumption and limit agricultural and industrial pollution (Arrojo-Agudo 2023).

HREs challenge standard economic priorities of market efficiency, growth, and stability with fiscal, trade, and sectoral approaches that "redress barriers to equality, justice and sustainability" (Türk 2023). Fiscal policy would entail transparent, inclusive budgeting rather than insider processes that create "elaborate loopholes to free the wealthy from fair taxation" (Türk 2023). IFI and development interventions would ensure "that governments are not forced to undercut investments in rights to repay their foreign debt" or comply with austerity policies (Türk 2023). Trade agreements would incorporate worker and environmental rights and promote circular economies (UNGA 2024). Sectoral policies would prioritize "small-scale water users while targeting and enforcing regulatory licenses to the few high-impact users" (Van Koppen et al. 2017, p. 130).

HREs can also challenge *power relations* (Table 7.1, Column 4). Power analysis (Gaventa 2005) highlights how HREs address *spaces, levels, and forms* of power that undermine rights-based water governance. *Closed spaces* (where elites make decisions behind closed doors) limit empowerment, while *invited spaces* (where stakeholders engage in predefined conversations) and *claimed spaces* (where marginalized groups articulate their own priorities) tend to equalize power. Decentralization can bring power to the *local level* but requires resources and coordination *across* the hydrological system. Finally, *visible* power (laws and policymaking) is only one *form*; *hidden* power (agenda-setting) and *invisible* power (embodied in cultural narratives) also perpetuate inequities. Attending to these dynamics fosters inclusivity, accountability, and prioritization of human rights and ecological wellbeing.

HREs democratize *spaces* of power by giving marginalized groups (and even nature itself) a voice in decision-making. Rights-holders and advocates gain power through meaningful opening of closed spaces, for example by *inviting* civil society actors into dialogue and implementation architecture through ongoing partnerships (Arrojo-Agudo 2023), offering a sense of efficacy for rights-holders and legitimacy for rights claims (Kozikis and Winkler 2020, p. 474). The independently articulated priorities of marginalized groups in *claimed* spaces go further to facilitate self-generated dialogue and priorities that HREs can incorporate into consequential decisions. Structural reforms strengthen these spaces through capacity building for local stakeholders and protecting water defenders' civil and political rights.

State power predominates in the water sector, unless the government intentionally gives its power away through, for example, privatization or trade agreements. HREs democratize decision-making by *decentralizing* governance as much as possible to the local level. They also shift state duties from meeting general human "needs" to creating accountability for identifiable "rights" (Young 2019).

The *visible power* of laws and policies can reprioritize HRE goals. HRE reforms counter *hidden forms* of agenda-setting by powerful groups through, for example, human rights due diligence that "ensures business operations do no harm" and sectoral investments, cross-subsidies, and tax incentives that prioritize human rights "instead of favouring the private interests of monied lobbies" (Türk 2023). HREs can counter the *invisible power* of hegemonic economic narratives by emphasizing that "human rights are obligations, not aspirations" (Türk 2024). In short, HREs are about bringing transparency and "rebuilding new kinds of relationships between social actors, based on greater equality and trust" (Türk 2023).

The following sections explore signs of progress and remaining challenges to adopting rights-responsive principles, altering structural conditions, and empowering historically marginalized actors through local HREs. While there is reason for optimism regarding the transformative potential of HREs, countervailing tendencies continue to create barriers to HRE goals in the water sector. The chapter concludes with a comment on what might need to change to overcome these barriers.

Adoption of Human Rights Principles

Signs of Progress

By 2021, 91% of national constitutions explicitly or implicitly recognized the HR2WS (Satterthwaite 2021) and a majority recognized a right to a healthy environment (Knox 2020). IFIs have also increasingly adopted human rights language (Ochoa 2003), and the UN Guiding Principles on Business and Human Rights have encouraged incorporating human rights into corporate social responsibility and national and local action plans (UNHCR 2024). In the U.S., the Biden administration's Justice40 initiative sought to "concurrently elevate equity, climate action, and economic health" – the three pillars – "as core principles guiding the federal government's work" (Fu and Shipp 2022). This trickled down to local water governance practices through, for example, new EPA mandates for removing lead water pipes and reversing legacy contamination in marginalized communities (David and Hughes 2024). Regional and local policies and programs like the "Right to the City", "SDG Cities", and SURGe initiatives have also embraced human rights principles, with implications for water governance, urban planning, and policy (Right2City, 2024; SDG Cities, 2024; UN Habitat 2024). At the subnational level, many cities have submitted Voluntary Local Reviews that include assessments of SDG 6 (UN DESA n.d.).

Business as Usual

Although human rights as a discursive phenomenon have proliferated, water governance strategies still reflect principles that conflict with the HR2WS and healthy ecologies: economic orthodoxies that downplay public contributions and frame water as a productive input or property in the service of growth and investor returns; technocratic overconfidence that reimagines ecologies without regard to Indigenous warnings to respect natural logics; and neo-colonial approaches that seek "development" at all costs, seeing water as a resource for state- and territory-building projects without due regard to extractive, polluting, and discriminatory outcomes (Boelens et al. 2016). Antipathy toward public governance and investment is clear in the language of IFIs, despite greater attention to human rights. IFI documents continue to extoll the virtue of private sector water governance (Voegele, Gouled, and Tafara 2024) and emphasize growth, capital markets, "bankable" projects, "conducive business environments", and risk mitigation for investors (Global Partnership 2019). This language is a far cry from grassroots and Indigenous declarations on water's sanctity for all life (Hellum and Kameri-Mbote 2015; The People's Water Forum 2023).

Even for UN representatives, the language of growth and the epistemology of GDP sit uncomfortably alongside calls for more human rights-responsive measures. The UN Special Rapporteur on the human rights to safe drinking water and sanitation expressed disappointment in the 2023 Water Conference's economic framings that crowded out water as a public good, as well as its recommended forms of stakeholder engagement that sidelined the knowledge of traditional communities and other "water defenders" (Arrojo-Agudo 2023). Overconsumption is also marginally discussed, perhaps due to a perceived tension between preserving water resources and ensuring the HR2WS. This conflict arises primarily when water use is framed in terms of reducing household demand rather than the far more wasteful uses in agriculture and industry (Bond 2011). Protecting hydrological systems thus requires language that explicitly acknowledges the outsized role of production as a source of environmental harm and inequitable resource allocation.

Structural Shifts in HREs

Signs of Progress

Economic thinking informed by human rights principles should improve structural supports for rights-based water governance (Brunner et al. 2015). Constitutionalization correlates with "enforceable law provisions" (Kaletski et al. 2016, p. 433) and better water sector outcomes when accompanied by "democratic governance" (Schiel, Langford, and Wilson 2020). HR2WS indicators (Meier et al. 2014) and human rights impact assessments (OHCHR 2018) have advanced and as indicators have improved, so has "economic access" to sanitation (Giné-Garriga et al. 2017). These initiatives underscore the impact of going beyond GDP to monitor and hold states accountable to "progressive realization" using "all available resources". In 2021, California became the first US state to measure progressive realization with an interactive web tool (CalHRTW 1.0) and report, Achieving the Human Right to Water in California: An Assessment of the State's Community Water Systems (OEHHA 2021).

The World Bank (WB), International Monetary Fund (IMF), and other IFI policies impact the "policy space" available to governments for local water governance (Muller and Bellmann 2016). IFI policies have evolved to better reflect human rights principles, though often to place conditions on governments rather than themselves. The WB Environmental and Social Framework (2018) requires borrowing countries to follow labor, community health and safety, and engagement standards before receiving assistance. The WB acknowledges Indigenous peoples' rights to free, prior, and informed consent (FPIC) for projects impacting their land/resources and of communities adversely affected by WB-funded projects to file complaints (World Bank Inspection Panel 2025). The International Finance Corporation and regional development banks have similar mechanisms (CAO n.d.; ADB 2024; AfDB n.d.), although the IMF has yet to establish redress mechanisms for its own policies (Caliari 2024).

Governments have also proactively enacted legislation incorporating the polluter pays principle,[2] sought clarifications before the Inter-American court on their climate change obligations (Gamboa 2024), and requested exemptions for water services under the World Trade Organization's General Agreement on Trade in Services (GATS). The fact that *zero* countries have opted to include their water sectors in GATS (World Bank n.d.) shows the importance of retaining control over this essential public good and preserving regulatory autonomy. Policies supporting the HR2WS have also gained traction in the U.S., with California leading the way in 2012 by declaring that "every person in the state has a right to clean, safe, and affordable drinking water" and providing funding to secure this right in 2019 (OEHHA 2021). Even in the notorious Flint and Detroit, Michigan cases, a visit and statement by the UN Special Rapporteur on the Right to Water empowered advocates and legislators to secure state (General Fund) and federal (COVID, BID/IILA) funding to protect human and environmental rights (Senate Democratic Caucus n.d.)

Legal innovations to promote human rights at national and local levels have also grown, with courts in Latin America, Eastern Europe, South Asia, and South Africa "reviewing legislation and policy for economic and social rights infringements, and ordering remedies upon findings of their breach" (Young 2019, p. 16). Human rights principles have been adjudicated to prevent local water suppliers from cutting off essential services due to inability to pay (Côrtes and Côrtes 2021), limit austerity policies interfering with government investments (Scheppele 2003), and reaffirm corporate responsibility for mining pollution (*Harmony Gold* 2013).

These legislative, regulatory, and legal changes shift the structural conditions for local-level water governance, enabling alternatives to business as usual. Progress in fiscal policy is also evident. Participatory budgeting processes have allowed citizens to demand the prioritization of basic water and sanitation, as well as influence project selection, design, and implementation (Calisto Friant 2019). While few studies indicate whether embracing HREs has led to more progressive taxation, rights-adjacent principles have historically led to better public goods outcomes (Stiglitz 2012). Rights-responsive investments in basic services, watershed management, and climate action have positively impacted human rights (Haglund 2014; Felice and Fuguitt 2020).

Federal investment resurged in the U.S. under the Biden administration's Justice40 initiative, the Inflation Reduction Act, and the Bipartisan Infrastructure Bill. These committed billions to support climate-resilient water and sanitation infrastructure, with Justice40 directing 40% of federal expenditures to disadvantaged communities. These investments sought to reverse environmental injustices by supporting local governments in replacing lead pipes, building safer water infrastructure, and cleaning up contamination. In addition, new blended (public-private) capital sources have emerged for climate resilience, adaptation, and mitigation, such as localized green banks (U.S. EPA 2023), while the global "loss and damage fund" designed to help poor countries withstand the impacts climate change (including in water sectors) is seeing its first deposits trickling in as of COP 29 in 2024.

Corporate monitoring and accountability have evolved more slowly, with some states creating national action plans and businesses adopting voluntary monitoring, assessment, and mitigation practices in response to the UN Guiding Principles on Business and Human Rights (George 2021). Efforts to reduce consumption often come down to cost-based mechanisms. The human rights approach promotes cross-subsidies, block tariffs, and free basic water for households. Educational efforts to reduce household consumption exist, though reducing consumption for paying customers also means reducing income for providers. Cost recovery and reduced consumption can be achieved with steeper tariffs for heavy users, as demonstrated in Cape Town after the 2011–18 drought, resulting in a shift away from luxury uses (lawns and swimming pools) toward reduction and reuse (Alexander 2019).

Business as Usual

The domination of market discourses continues to legitimize capitalist property relations, resource control, and decision-making. This impacts structural transformation across all three pillars of sustainability (Table 7.1, Column 3). Under the social pillar, states' ability to ensure basic services depends greatly on revenue. Full cost recovery cannot cover water infrastructure costs, especially in poor areas (Brunner et al. 2015), and states must raise revenue to invest. However, as state activity is "rolled back", its role in service provision is hobbled (Peck and Tickell 2002). Simultaneously, as market-friendly mechanisms are "rolled out" (ibid), HRE goals such as polluter pays and precautionary principles become difficult to regulate. Emblematic of recent rollbacks was the decision by the Supreme Court of the United States to overturn longstanding doctrine of judicial deference to agency decision-making, thereby limiting the authority of regulatory agencies (Howe 2024).

Courts in other jurisdictions have attempted to support the social pillar in water governance, but rulings do not necessarily build state capacity. Efforts to hold polluters accountable can be derailed if funds are not set aside for remediation, as in the *Harmony Gold* case in South Africa, where lack of funds for acid mine drainage clean-up and limited accountability of corporate actors with powerful attorneys made "paying a fine much cheaper [for big companies] than disposing of chemical waste in an appropriate manner."[3] Limited state capacity can also mean an inability to restrict heavy users, who operate "without any state regulation of their water use and waste discharge" (Van Koppen et al. 2017, p. 140).

Fiscal constraints and private markets undermine not only the social but also the environmental pillar of water sustainability. As services are commodified, heavy users with money consume without constraint while poor households struggle to meet basic needs (Bond and Dugard 2008) The 2023 Water Conference failed to address industrial and agricultural consumption, despite their outsized role in freshwater extraction (OECD 2017), greenhouse gas emissions (Fanzo & Downs 2021), and deforestation (FAO 2017). States like California have created policies to limit extraction (California DWR n.d.), incentivize sustainable practices (CDFA n.d.), and promote alternatives (Nitta 2024), but business interests seeking to maintain the status quo retain the upper hand against such efforts (Mirumachi et al. 2021).

Structural changes to the economic pillar have been the most intransigent. Water privatization continues despite its terrible track record, with multinationals "promot[ing] their role in the sector, particularly in middle-income countries", and "local private companies [emerging] as the new face of privatisation" in developing countries (Langford 2017, p. 464). Despite hundreds of reversals of privatization between 2000 and 2019, one of the most respected public water companies in Latin America – the São Paulo state water company, SABESP – was privatized in 2024 (Heller 2024).

Additionally, "new private actors, such as equity and pension funds, targeting water infrastructure ownership for financial super-profits" have become ubiquitous (Loftus 2019, p. 4), extracting value from the sector while neglecting human needs. Infrastructure investment is being led by asset firms like Australian financial services group Macquarie, with devastating outcomes for public goods sectors:

> Asset managers focus on optimizing returns on the assets they control by maximizing the income they generate, while minimizing operating and capital costs. Many users of infrastructure that has come under asset manager ownership have suffered, as service rates have risen quickly and service quality has deteriorated.
>
> (Christophers 2023)

Private sector duties in the water sector are often voluntary (Figueroa, Lee, and Jepson 2022) while "accountability" is framed mainly as state rather than market "failure" (Karunananthan 2019). Corporate disclosure of water quality and access data has been largely inadequate (Hazelton 2013).

Attempts to direct global resources toward water and climate resilience have met similar constraints. The "loss and damage fund" is, at the time of this writing, less than 0.5% of what has been pledged (and even less that what is needed). The "misalignment between national budgets and capital markets" was also the refrain at 2024 Financing for Development Dialogues (UN 2025). While rights claims "may have helped individuals and communities to articulate rights as against the (territorial) state", they are less effective against the incursions of private capital (Satterthewaite 2021, pp. 374–5).

Empowerment in HREs

As with discursive and structural shifts, power relations in water sectors governed by human rights principles have seen both signs of progress and barriers to change, depending on the nature of engagement in spaces (closed, invited, claimed), across governance levels (local to global), and in different forms (visible, hidden, invisible) (Institute of Development Studies. n.d.).

Signs of Progress

Mechanisms like participatory budgeting and watershed committees represent invited spaces that strengthen local community engagement. Evidence strongly supports the power of participation in promoting better outcomes: consumer satisfaction, tariff payments, equal access, time savings, and belief in the system (Prokopy 2005). Experiments in participatory budgeting originating in Porto Alegre, Brazil, have spread to 1,700 municipalities in 40+ countries, contributing "significantly to innovating and improving basic service delivery in cities, with a higher awareness of spatial and social justice, the democratization of governance, and the modernization of local governments" (Cabannes 2015, p. 280). Although the amounts to be distributed can be small, the impact of investments in water and sanitation infrastructure, bottle-refilling stations, fountains, environmental awareness, climate adaptation, and a raft of other initiatives globally represents a substantive change from earlier forms of governance.

Indigenous and land-based communities are *claiming* new spaces that challenge historical power dynamics and affirming their sovereignty through the principle of FPIC, embodied in the United Nations Declaration on the Rights of Indigenous Peoples (UNDRIP). Throughout the history of colonization, both states and industry extracted and disfigured the lands and environments of these communities at will. However, with FPIC, "Indigenous groups now *expect* consultation as part of customary law" (Leo quoted in Haglund, 2019, p. 12). While FPIC has not shifted power everywhere, it has allowed communities to repoliticize water governance and challenge "the legitimacy of state natural resources decision-making" (Curran 2019, p. 7).

As HREs open spaces, governments at all levels are more hesitant to employ market mechanisms with negative track records (Hall et al. 2005). Instruments like UNDRIP at the *global level* provide resources for demanding inclusion at lower levels of governance, while participatory budgeting links *local* concerns to broader governmental resource allocation. Decentralization has gained prominence as another strategy for improving policy formulation, implementation, and public service delivery through municipal control and incorporation of local businesses and communities in decision-making (Agrawal and Ribot 1999). However, state *capacity* is often more determinative of local empowerment than decentralization *per se* (decentralization.net).

The policies and mechanisms of HREs discussed above challenge not only *visible power* through formal inclusion, but also *hidden power* by contesting the formulation of budget priorities and policy agendas by elites (Curran 2019). The *invisible power* of hegemonic anthropocentric thinking is also shifting. Even before Stone (1972) posed the provocative question "Should Trees Have

Standing?" environmentalists and Indigenous peoples sought to advocate for the natural world. This has manifested in the (still anthropocentric) notion of the rights of future generations (WCED 1987), "Earth Jurisprudence" (Burdon 2014), rights of nature (UN n.d.), and "ecocide" at the international level (Stop Ecocide International n.d.). These epistemic shifts have led to an explosion of local-level actions defending rivers, glaciers, streams, and watersheds (GARN n.d.), forcing governments and corporations to consider ecosystems in ways that were inconceivable only a decade ago.

Business as Usual

While invited water governance spaces can broaden participation, they may reproduce existing power dynamics if not accompanied by mobilization or support for less powerful stakeholders (Abers and Keck 2006). Empowerment and inclusivity in decision-making also depend on the design of participatory mechanisms and who they engage (Montambeault and Papillon 2023). Participatory budgeting, for example, may have little substantive impact if budgets are small, and regardless, remains rare. More common are closed spaces, where water governance decisions are made without community input. While the claimed spaces discussed above hold promise, they rarely culminate in enforceable rights; in the case of FPIC, this leaves Indigenous communities without veto power over critical decisions (Martinez-Cruz et al. 2024, p. 11).

The contribution of decentralization to local empowerment is complicated. While local control is desirable, the complexity of water governance often requires strong institutions and better coordination between governance levels (Eakin and Lemos, 2006). When responsibilities are decentralized but not financial and institutional capacity, expectations of higher-level administrators and actual service requirements misalign. Some municipalities, usually smaller ones with fewer revenue streams, have turned to full-cost recovery and even privatization. Without careful design, such interventions can exacerbate HR2WS violations (Empinotti, Gontijo, and de Oliveira 2018). Lack of coordination between international frameworks and local implementation also creates barriers to addressing systemic inequities and pollution.

Elite power remains visible in the water sector, where mechanisms like FPIC are far from respected. Indigenous Peoples' "lands and waters are constantly being grabbed and polluted by extractive industries (including industrial agriculture) and other projects that violate their right to self-determination, their rights to self-development, and FPIC" (Martinez-Cruz et al. 2024, p. 11). Hidden elite agenda-setting is evident in the sidelining of marginalized groups from meaningful participation in forums like the 2023 Water Conference (Arrojo-Agudo 2023). Even when human rights are a stated policy priority, the abstraction of "The Economy" is used to prioritize investor and private sector interests. The invisible power of hegemonic ideas entrenches profit-driven and anthropocentric narratives that prioritize economic growth over environmental protection and human rights. By comparison, "rights of nature" lack a broadly accepted cost-benefit framework for adjudicating among policy options in complex hydrological systems (Guim and Livermore 2021). Legal system intricacies further complicate justiciability and can lead to overturned cases (Kahui, Armstrong, and Aanesen 2024). Finally, when human and non-human priorities conflict, human systems tend to favor anthropomorphic concerns.

Conclusion and Discussion: Three Transformations in HREs for Water Governance

This chapter proposed a framework for analyzing the transformative potential of HREs in water governance, focused on three elements:

1. The impact of adopting human rights principles on *the way we talk* about water and *the assumptions we make* about appropriate priorities and action
2. The capacity of policies, processes, and mechanisms of HREs to challenge *structural* barriers to HR2WS and protection of hydrological systems
3. Redistribution of power and decision-making that would allow priorities to shift away from business as usual to fully embrace human rights and rights-adjacent principles.

As the evidence indicates, economic frameworks do not generally concern themselves with the protection and fulfillment of the right to water. Rather, water governance bends and molds itself to the prevailing political economy – the demands, priorities, capacities, and financial resources of powerful actors. For HREs to manifest in broad social transformations (Moment #3 from the introduction), actors and agencies must believe in and be willing and able to implement policy interventions that take human rights seriously and state duties as inviolable. Although some localities have implemented rights-based and/or participatory elements of HRE interventions, they are rare. Achieving HREs that live up to the promise of promoting equitable and sustainable water governance would require cultural, structural, and power-based shifts. The following recommendations emerge from this analysis.

Recommendations for Cultural Transformation

Conventional water governance approaches, even in HREs, often draw on economic principles of efficiency, developmentalism, and technical fixes. The analysis above suggests a *narrative shift* to reframe water not merely as a developmental input but as a common good. Market-friendly valorization of "bankable" projects (World Bank 2019) and "cost recovery" would be replaced with a recognition of the value of public investment, civil service, ecological reciprocity, and collective responsibility. This shift requires a more honest look at the impacts of consumptive, extractive culture on people and the planet. Although polluter pays and precautionary principles are not new, GDP and traditional economic indicators must be coupled with metrics measuring the full social and environmental impact of current practices. Less "efficient" or profitable governance strategies are needed to limit consumption and curb harmful marketing practices.

Various strategies to support such a cultural shift are already practiced in a "pluriverse" of contexts (Kothari et al. 2019). Public education and engagement can help by emphasizing human-nature interdependence, challenging technocratic quick-fixes, and elevating Indigenous perspectives that view water as life and nature as a relative. Humanist approaches could use art and storytelling to reveal the non-monetary and spiritual importance of water. These strategies represent a change from treating communities as passive consumers to living, breathing beings with a stake in equity, sustainability, and the collective good.

Recommendations for Structural Transformation

Institutionalizing alternative framings and stakeholder rights, including those of Indigenous groups, is crucial for transformative water governance. Innovative HRE policies and governance frameworks exist but additional interventions are needed to ensure equitable access for underserved and marginalized communities. Public investments in infrastructure and green economies, robust regulatory agencies, and fiscal and technical support for subnational governments would reduce market dependence, strengthen polluter pays and precautionary principles, and promote less damaging production practices. Supporting cooperative, community-led, and traditional stewardship models would challenge technocratic dominance, democratize decision-making, and advance rights-based water management. Participatory budgeting could ensure local priorities guide financial allocations to support community-based and sustainable projects.

Reimagining economic metrics and fiscal policy provides additional pathways to rights-responsive governance. Indicators like Human Rights Impact Assessments and CalHRTW could complement GDP, with success measured by how well the economy "delivers on people's rights … disaggregated to make sure that discrimination, and other forms of structural inequality, are clearly visible and can be addressed" (Türk 2023). Fiscal and monetary policies, employing tools like green bonds, progressive taxation, cross-subsidies for poor households, and ecological restoration funds would make right-responsive goals economically feasible. Reinforcing public ownership, eschewing financialization, advocating for trade policies that exempt water from commodification, and preventing IFIs from prioritizing debt and austerity over public investment are other keys to aligning multilevel governance with human rights.

Given the reality of corporate power, HREs would need to implement more robust mechanisms for monitoring human rights impacts and corporate accountability. Laws and regulations enhancing corporate responsibility in the water sector would need meaningful enforcement mechanisms, binding commitments, and channels for local redress, which unfortunately has a negative track record in many places (Türke 2018).

Recommendations for Redistributing Power

Expanding the reach of HREs requires addressing the spaces, levels, and forms of power discussed above. Invited spaces like participatory budgeting and governance processes are crucial to ensure decision-making is not closed to marginalized groups. Financial and technical support to build capacity can improve the quality of engagement in disadvantaged communities. Participatory budgeting of a greater percentage of public funds can increase commitment and build trust in government. Claimed spaces should be recognized as legitimate platforms for ongoing dialogue for Indigenous groups, water defenders, women, youth, and civil society actors. These align with the UN Special Rapporteur on the Right to Water's recommendation to integrate civil society actors fully into governance frameworks (Arrojo-Agudo 2023).

Reforms must strengthen local decision-making while addressing systemic inequalities at national and global levels. Legal recognition and enforcement of FPIC must offer Indigenous groups veto power over projects affecting their lands and water. Global mechanisms are needed to protect communities from extractive incursions and provide recourse for past harms. Corporations should be held to global standards for human rights and environmental due diligence, with binding regulations and penalties for violations, preventing "regulatory arbitrage" to find "pollution havens" (Berry, Kaul, and Lee 2021). Mandatory transparency in corporate water use, quality data, and impacts on rights and ecosystems is essential for accountability to local communities and natural systems.

Visible power dynamics perpetuating inequities are addressed by state policies that prioritize rights-based governance over profit-driven interests. The hidden power of agenda-setting can be countered through structural reforms such as human rights impact assessments, tax incentives for rights-responsive policy, and sectoral investments prioritizing community needs over corporate profits (Türk 2023). Invisible power can be challenged by replacing anthropocentric ideologies with narratives of ecological reciprocity and sustainability. Establishing legal guardianship for nature, as proposed by Kahui, Armstrong, and Aanesen (2024), would allow ecosystems to hold enforceable rights, ensuring their protection through liabilities.

In sum, while HRE principles provide inspiration for more just and sustainable approaches to water governance, their public, democratic, participatory, and ecocentric vision will require more work to achieve.

Notes

1 This material is based on work supported by the National Science Foundation under Grant Numbers 1324248 and 2417874. Any opinions, findings, conclusions, or recommendations expressed in this material are those of the author and do not necessarily reflect the views of the National Science Foundation.

2 Examples include the European Union's Environmental Liability Directive (ELD) (2004/35/EC); the US Comprehensive Environmental Response, Compensation, and Liability Act (CERCLA or Superfund) (1980) and Oil Pollution Act (OPA)

(1990); and similar legislation in Canada, Australia, New Zealand, Switzerland, Japan, South Korea, France, Brazil, India, China, South Africa, Nigeria, Kenya, Indonesia.

3 Quote from SA10, Senior Manager, City of Johannesburg, Department of Infrastructure and Services, interview with the author, 11 Mar 2014; SA01, Senior Researcher, Wits University, interview with the author, 18 Feb 2014.

Bibliography

Abers, Rebecca, and M. E. Keck. 2006. "Muddy Waters: The Political Construction of Deliberative River Basin Governance in Brazil." *International Journal of Urban and Regional Research* 30 (3): 601–22.

Agrawal, Arun, and J. Ribot. 1999. "Accountability in Decentralization: A Framework with South Asian and West African Cases." *The Journal of Developing Areas* 33 (4): 473–502.

Alexander, Christian. 2019. "Cape Town's 'Day Zero' Water Crisis, One Year Later." *CityLab* April 12 2019. https://www.citylab.com/environment/2019/04/cape-towns-day-zero-water-crisis-one-year-later/585899/.

Arrojo-Agudo, Pedro. 2023. "What's Next: The Legacy of the UN Water Conference." *UN Special Rapporteur on the Human Rights to Safe Drinking Water and Sanitation. Statement following the 2023 UN Water Conference.* Accessed August 3, 2024. https://www.ohchr.org/sites/default/files/documents/issues/water/statements/SR-water-sanitation_Assessment_UN_Water_Conference_20240404.pdf

Bakker, Karen. 2013. *Privatizing Water: Governance Failure and the World's Urban Water Crisis.* Cornell University Press.

Berry, Heather, A. Kaul, and N. Lee. 2021. "Follow the Smoke: The Pollution Haven Effect on Global Sourcing." *Strategic Management Journal* 42 (13): 2420–50.

Boelens, Rutgerd, J. Hoogesteger, E. Swyngedouw, J. Vos, and P. Wester. 2016. "Hydrosocial Territories: A Political Ecology Perspective." *Water International* 41 (1): 1–14.

Bond, Patrick. 2011. "South Africa's 'Rights Culture' of Water Consumption." In *Water, Cultural Diversity & Global Environmental Change: Emerging Trends, Sustainable Futures.*

Bond, Patrick, and J. Dugard. 2008. "The Case of Johannesburg Water: What Really Happened at the Pre-Paid Parish Pump." *Law, Democracy & Development* 12: 1, 2, 8.

Brunner, Norbert, V. Mishra, P. Sakthivel, M. Starkl, and C. Tschohl. 2015. "The Human Right to Water in Law and Implementation." *Laws* 4: 413.

Burdon, Peter D. 2014. *Earth Jurisprudence: Private Property and the Environment.* Routledge.

Cabannes, Yves. 2015. "The Impact of Participatory Budgeting on Basic Services: Municipal Practices and Evidence from the Field." *Environment and Urbanization* 27 (1): 257–84.

Caliari, Aldo. 2024. "IMF Human Rights Accountability: A Pragmatic Way to Break the Deadlock." *Perspectives.*

Calisto Friant, Martin. 2019. "Deliberating for Sustainability: Lessons from the Porto Alegre Experiment with Participatory Budgeting." *International Journal of Urban Sustainable Development* 11 (1): 81–99.

Christophers, Brett. 2023. "Why Are We Allowing the Private Sector to Take Over Our Public Works?" *New York Times*, May 8 2023. https://www.nytimes.com/2023/05/08/opinion/inflation-reduction-act-global-asset-managers.html

Côrtes, Lara, and A. Côrtes. 2021. "Right to Water and Courts in Brazil: How Do Brazilian Courts Rule When They Frame Water as a Right?" *Water* 13 (23): 3362.

Curran, Deborah. 2019. "Indigenous Processes of Consent: Repoliticizing Water Governance through Legal Pluralism." *Water* 11 (3): 571.

David, Olivia, and S. Hughes. 2024. "Ten Years Later: How Water Crises in Flint and Detroit Transformed the Politics of US Water Policy." *The Forum* 22 (1): 161–75. De Gruyter.

Eakin, Hallie, and M. C. Lemos. 2006. "Adaptation and the State: Latin America and the Challenge of Capacity-Building under Globalization." *Global Environmental Change* 16: 7–18.

Empinotti, Vanessa Lucena, W. C. Gontijo, and V. E. de Oliveira. 2018. "Federalism, Water, and (De)centralization in Brazil: The Case of the São Francisco River Water Diversion." *Regional Environmental Change* 18: 1655–66.

Fanzo, Jessica C., and S. M. Downs. 2021. "Climate Change and Nutrition-Associated Diseases." *Nature Reviews. Disease Primers* 7 (1).

FAO (Food and Agriculture Organization). 2017. *The Future of Food and Agriculture – Trends and Challenges*. Rome.

Felice, William F., and D. Fuguitt. 2020. *Human Rights and Public Goods: The Global New Deal*. Rowman & Littlefield.

Figueroa, Cindy, K. Lee, and W. Jepson. 2022. "Corporate Social Responsibility in the Water Industry: A Critical Review." *Wiley Interdisciplinary Reviews: Water* 9 (6): e1607.

Fu, Samantha, and A. Shipp. 2022. *Positioning Justice40 for Success: A Policy and Practice Playbook*. Washington, D.C.: Urban Institute, November 15 2022. https://www.urban.org/apps/positioning-justice40-success

Gamboa, Liliana. 2024. "A Seminal Case for Climate Litigation: Climate Change Presents States with New Obligations. Chile and Colombia Are Asking What Those Are." *Carnegie Endowment for International Peace*, June 26 2024. https://carnegieendowment.org/research/2024/06/a-seminal-case-for-climate-litigation?lang=en&center=europe.

Gaventa, John. 2005. "Reflections on the Uses of the 'Power Cube' Approach for Analyzing the Spaces, Places and Dynamics of Civil Society Participation and Engagement." Prepared for Dutch CFA Evaluation, Assessing Civil Society Participation as Supported In-Country by Cordaid, Hivos, Novib and Plan Netherlands.

George, Erika. 2021. *Incorporating Rights: Strategies to Advance Corporate Accountability*. Oxford University Press.

Giné-Garriga, Ricard, Ó. Flores-Baquero, A. Jiménez-Fdez de Palencia, and A. Pérez-Foguet. 2017. "Monitoring Sanitation and Hygiene in the 2030 Agenda for Sustainable Development: A Review through the Lens of Human Rights." *Science of the Total Environment* 580: 1108–19.

Global Partnership for Effective Development Cooperation MDB Working Group. 2019. "Multilateral Development Banks and Private Sector Engagement for Sustainable Development." Accessed September 9, 2024. https://ppp.worldbank.org/public-private-partnership/sites/ppp.worldbank.org/files/2022-03/mdbs-private-sector-sustainable-development.pdf

Guim, Mauricio, and M. A. Livermore. 2021. "Where Nature's Rights Go Wrong." *Virginia Law Review* 107 (7): 1347–1419.

Haglund, LaDawn. 2014. "Water Governance and Social Justice in São Paulo, Brazil." *Water Policy* 16 (S2): 78–96.

Haglund, LaDawn. 2019. "Human Rights Pathways to Just Sustainabilities." *Sustainability* 11 (12): 3255.

Haglund, LaDawn, and R. Stryker, eds. 2015. *Closing the Rights Gap: From Human Rights to Social Transformation*, 1sted. University of California Press.

Harmony Gold Mining Company Ltd v. Regional Director: Free State Department of Water Affairs and Others. 2013. (971/12) [2013] ZASCA 206; [2014] 1 All SA 553 (SCA); 2014 (3) SA 149 (SCA) (December 4 2013).

Hazelton, James. 2013. "Accounting as a Human Right: The Case of Water Information." *Accounting, Auditing & Accountability Journal* 26 (2): 267–311.
Hall, David, E. Lobina, and R. de la Motte. 2005. "Public Resistance to Privatisation in Water and Energy." *Development in Practice* 15 (3–4): 286–301.
Hellum, Anne, and P. Kameri-Mbote, eds. 2015. *Water Is Life: Women's Human Rights in National and Local Water Governance in Southern and Eastern Africa*. African Books Collective.
Howe, Amy. 2024. "Supreme Court Strikes Down Chevron, Curtailing Power of Federal Agencies." *SCOTUSblog*, June 28 2024. https://www.scotusblog.com/2024/06/supreme-court-strikes-down-chevron-curtailing-power-of-federal-agencies/
Institute of Development Studies. n.d. *Power Cube: Understanding Power for Social Change*. Accessed January 16, 2025. https://www.powercube.net
Kahui, Viktoria, C. W. Armstrong, and M. Aanesen. 2024. "Comparative Analysis of Rights of Nature (RoN) Case Studies Worldwide: Features of Emergence and Design." *Ecological Economics* 221: 108193.
Kaletski, Elizabeth, L. Minkler, N. Prakash, and S. Randolph. 2016. "Does Constitutionalizing Economic and Social Rights Promote Their Fulfillment?" *Journal of Human Rights* 15 (4): 433–53.
Karunananthan, Meera. 2019. "Can the Human Right to Water Disrupt Neoliberal Water Policies in the Era of Corporate Policy-Making?" *Geoforum* 98: 244–53.
Knox, John H. 2020. "Constructing the Human Right to a Healthy Environment." *Annual Review of Law and Social Science* 16 (1): 79–95.
Kothari, Ashish, A. Salleg, A. Escobar, F. Demaria, and A. Acosta, eds. 2019. *Pluriverse: A Post-Development Dictionary*. New Delhi: Tulika Books.
Kozikis, Sabrina, and I. T. Winkler. 2020. "The Paradox of Framing Water as a Human Right in the United States: An Analysis of Power and Resistance." *Journal of Human Rights* 19 (4): 464–83.
Langford, Malcolm. 2017. "Privatisation and the Right to Water." In M. Langford and A. F. S. Russell (eds.), *The Human Right to Water: Theory, Practice and Prospects*. Cambridge University Press.
Martinez-Cruz, Tania Eulalia, L. Adelman, L. Castañeda-Quintana, and D. Mejía-Montalvo. 2024. "Water Is More than a Resource: Indigenous Peoples and the Right to Water." *Social Sciences & Humanities Open* 10: 100978.
Meier, Benjamin Mason, J. G. Kestenbaum, G. L. Kayser, U. Q. Amjad, and J. Bartram. 2014. "Examining the Practice of Developing Human Rights Indicators to Facilitate Accountability for the Human Right to Water and Sanitation." *Journal of Human Rights Practice* 6: 159–81.
Mirumachi, Naho, A. Duda, J. Gregulska, and J. Smetek. 2021. *The Human Right to Drinking Water: Impact of Large-Scale Agriculture and Industry*. Policy Department for External Relations, Directorate General for External Policies of the Union, European Parliament.
Montambeault, Françoise, and M. Papillon. 2023. "Repoliticising Indigenous Participation: FPIC Protocols in Canada and Brazil." *The International Journal of Human Rights* 27 (2): 335–58.
Muller, Mike, and C. Bellmann. 2016. *Trade and Water: How Might Trade Policy Contribute to Sustainable Water Management?* Geneva: International Centre for Trade and Sustainable Development (ICTSD).
Murphy, Kevin. 2012. "The Social Pillar of Sustainable Development: A Literature Review and Framework for Policy Analysis." *Sustainability: Science, Practice and Policy* 8 (1): 15–29.
Ochoa, Christiana. 2003. "Advancing the Language of Human Rights in a Global Economic Order: An Analysis of a Discourse." *Boston College Third World Law Journal* 23: 57.

OECD. 2017. "Water Risk Hotspots for Agriculture." In *OECD Studies on Water*. Paris: OECD Publishing.

OEHHA (Office of Environmental Health Hazard Assessment). 2021. *Achieving Health Risk Targets for Water and Health in California: A Report to the California State Water Resources Control Board*. Sacramento: California Environmental Protection Agency. https://oehha.ca.gov/media/downloads/water/report/hrtwachievinghrtw2021f.pdf

OHCHR. 2018. *Human Rights Impact Assessments for Economic Reform Policies*. A/HRC/40/57. Geneva: United Nations, December 19 2018. *Presented to the 40th Session of the Human Rights Council*, 2019.

Peck, Jamie, and A. Tickell. 2002. "Neoliberalizing Space." *Antipode: A Radical Journal of Geography* 34: 380–404.

Prokopy, Linda Stalker. 2005. "The Relationship Between Participation and Project Outcomes: Evidence from Rural Water Supply Projects in India." *World Development* 33 (11): 1801–19.

Right2City. 2024. "Right to the City." Accessed May 6, 2024. https://www.right2city.org/

Satterthwaite, Margaret L. 2021. "Assessing the Rights to Water and Sanitation: Between Institutionalization and Radicalization." *Georgetown Journal of International Law* 52: 315–79.

Schiel, Rebecca, M. Langford, and B. M. Wilson. 2020. "Does It Matter: Constitutionalisation, Democratic Governance, and the Human Right to Water." *Water* 12 (2): 350.

SDG Cities. 2024. Accessed May 6, 2024. https://www.sdg-cities.org/

Stiglitz, Joseph E. 2012. *The Price of Inequality: How Today's Divided Society Endangers Our Future*. New York: W. W. Norton & Company.

Stone, Christopher D. 1972. "Should Trees Have Standing? Towards Legal Rights for Natural Objects." *Southern California Law Review* 45: 450–501.

Stop Ecocide International. n.d. "Developing Ecocide Law." Accessed January 16, 2025. https://www.stopecocide.earth/

Stryker, Robin, and L. Haglund. 2015. "Conclusion: Emerging Possibilities for Social Transformation." In L. Haglund and R. Stryker (eds.), *Closing the Rights Gap: From Human Rights to Social Transformation*. University of California Press.

The People's Water Forum. 2023. "The Water Justice Manifesto." *The People's Water Forum*, February 28, 2023. Accessed September 18, 2025. https://thepeopleswaterforum.org/2023/02/28/water-justice-manifesto/.

Türk, Volker. 2023. "Statement by UN High Commissioner for Human Rights on Human Rights and the Economy." *United Nations Office of the High Commissioner for Human Rights* April 20 2023. Accessed August 3, 2024. https://www.ohchr.org/en/statements-and-speeches/2023/04/statement-un-human-rights-chief-human-rights-economy

Türk, Volker. 2024. "High Commissioner Address at UNCTAD60 Global Leaders Forum." *United Nations Office of the High Commissioner for Human Rights*, June 13 2024. https://www.ohchr.org/en/statements-and-speeches/2024/06/high-commissioner-address-unctad60-global-leaders-forum

Türke, Mariana Aparecida Vilmondes. 2018. "Business and Human Rights in Brazil: Exploring Human Rights Due Diligence and Operational-Level Grievance Mechanisms in the Case of Kinross Paracatu Gold Mine." *Revista de Direito Internacional* 15 (2): 221–41.

UN. 2025. "Harmony with Nature: Rights of Nature." Accessed January 16, 2025. http://harmonywithnatureun.org/rightsOfNature/

UN DESA. n.d. "SDG Localization and the Voluntary Local Reviews." Accessed January 11, 2025. https://sdgs.un.org/topics/voluntary-local-reviews

UNGA. 2024. "Pact for the Future, Global Digital Compact, and Declaration on Future Generations." General Assembly Resolution A/RES/79/1, September 2024.
UN Habitat. 2024. "Overview of the Options for the Operationalization of the Sustainable Urban Resilience for the Next Generation (SURGe) Initiative." HSP/EB.2024/INF/5. Executive Board of the United Nations Human Settlements Programme, April 2024.
UNHCR. 2024. "National Action Plans on Business and Human Rights." Accessed December 2, 2024. https://www.ohchr.org/en/special-procedures/wg-business/national-action-plans-business-and-human-rights
UN News. 2023. "Turn the Tide on Water Crisis with Game-Changing Commitments, Urge Co-Hosts of UN Conference." Quote by Yoka Brandt (ed.), *Permanent Representative of the Kingdom of the Netherlands*. Accessed April 16, 2025. https://www.un.org/sustainabledevelopment/blog/2023/03/interview-turn-the-tide-on-water-crisis-with-game-changing-commitments-urge-co-hosts-of-un-conference-2/
U.S. Environmental Protection Agency. 2023. "Green Banks." Accessed June 4, 2023. https://www.epa.gov/statelocalenergy/green-banks
Van Koppen, Barbara, A. Hellum, L. Mehta, B. Derman, and B. Schreiner. 2017. "Rights-Based Freshwater Governance for the Twenty-First Century: Beyond an Exclusionary Focus on Domestic Water Uses." In *Freshwater Governance for the 21st Century*, 129–43.
Voegele, Juergen, M. Gouled, and E. Tafara. 2024. "Scaling Up Finance to Ensure a Water-Secure Future for All." *World Bank Blogs*, March 19, 2024. https://blogs.worldbank.org/en/voices/scaling-up-finance-to-ensure-a-water-secure-future-for-all
World Bank Inspection Panel. 2025. Accessed January 16, 2025. https://www.inspectionpanel.org/
World Bank. 2019. *Financing Climate Change Adaptation in Transboundary Basins: Preparing Bankable Projects*. World Bank. Accessed January 16, 2025. https://openknowledge.worldbank.org/server/api/core/bitstreams/a2557d64-4c25-5087-8455-4d7ea5e11447/content
World Bank. n.d. "GATS – Fact and Fiction." Accessed January 17, 2025. https://www.wto.org/english/tratop_e/serv_e/gatsfacts1004_e.pdf
WCED (World Commission on Environment and Development). 1987. *Our Common Future (The Brundtland Report)*. Oxford: Oxford University Press.
Yamin, Alicia Ely. 2005. "The Right to Health Under International Law and Its Relevance to the United States." *American Journal of Public Health* 95 (7): 1156–61.
Young, Katharine G. 2019. "Rights and Queues: On Distributive Contests in the Modern State." *Columbia Journal of Transnational Law* 57: 1–64.

8 Human Rights as a Key to Unlock a Just Transition for the Built Environment

John Morrison and Giulio Ferrini

Introduction

Accounting for almost two-thirds of global emissions, the built environment sector will have to rapidly transform over the coming decades. Cities, responsible for most of these emissions, are not only at the forefront of this challenge but also where climate action most clearly intersects with social equity.

This chapter argues that human rights can provide a key framework to ensure that the transformative changes required for net zero do not negatively impact marginalised communities, that they create equal access to opportunities and benefits, that potentially affected groups have agency to hold decision-makers accountable, and that change is leveraged to transform systems.

With these key elements in place and by implementing the overarching principles of accountability, participation, non-discrimination, and transparency, cities can lead the way in demonstrating how the climate transition can help create a more equitable and resilient future for all.

Just Transition

The built environment—buildings, roads, and other public infrastructure—accounts for approximately 37% of global energy-related greenhouse gas emissions through its construction and operations (UNEP 2023). When combined with emissions from the transport sector, this figure rises to almost two-thirds of global emissions (UN 2021).

Most of these emissions are generated in urban centres, making cities a focal point of both the climate challenge and its potential solutions. Urban areas are particularly vulnerable to climate change impacts: by 2050, rising sea levels are projected to directly affect at least 800 million people living in 570 cities (C40 Cities 2018), and the heat island effect makes heat stress particularly severe. Most of the world's population lives in cities, and, despite these risks, people continue to migrate to urban areas, adding pressure to limited resources, increasing commute times, and driving demand for further construction.

DOI: 10.4324/9781003474845-11

This context underscores the urgency of radically transforming how we design, build, and manage the built environment to achieve net zero carbon emissions by 2050.

The sweeping transformation required to mitigate and adapt to climate change will radically transform jobs, lifestyles, and economic systems across the globe. As with every change, some impacts will be positive, in the form of improved wages or reduced costs, while others will be negative, in the form of job losses, increased competition for resources, and higher costs. The concept of a just transition addresses how these opportunities and risks are distributed, with a particular focus on ensuring that efforts to combat climate change do not exacerbate existing inequalities.

A transition that does not carefully identify and address the negative impacts on certain workers, residents, and communities will lead to their resistance, which may ultimately jeopardise the transition itself. Moreover, it risks perpetuating extractive dynamics such as resource exploitation, unequal trade, and labour abuses that undermine global peace and prosperity.

However, achieving a just transition is complex. For instance, newly created jobs in green industries, such as energy efficiency bio-based material production, may emerge far from where fossil-fuel-reliant jobs are lost, require different skills, offer lower wages or poorer working conditions. Further complications arise from competing demands for critical resources like copper, lithium, and rare earth metals, which are essential for renewable technologies. At the same time, global financial systems remain ill-prepared to mobilise the necessary trillions of dollars required for equitable transitions, particularly in low-income countries.

The just transition paradigm is embedded in the 2015 Paris Climate Agreement and UNFCCC work processes (UNFCCC 2015). Yet, it lacks a single definition, and the concept continues to evolve. COP27, the UN's 2023 Climate Conference, expanded the term's understanding from its original focus on workers in fossil fuel industries and towards broader socio-economic factors, emphasising inclusive, participatory approaches that ensure no one is left behind (UNFCCC 2022). As the term gains prominence, there is a risk of dilution into a vague concept devoid of substantive meaning. This risk is particularly relevant because its true meaning is subjective at its core: a transition must only be considered "just" when those affected—workers, communities, and indigenous peoples—feel it to be so (Morrison 2024).

While this framing is crucial for implementation and accountability, the global nature of the challenge requires aligned frameworks, approaches, and guardrails. Internationally recognised human rights, also cited in the preamble to the 2015 Paris Agreement, offer the appropriate lens through which the rights of all those affected can be understood, as well as the duties of governments and the responsibilities of non-state actors such as business.

In 2022, the Institute for Human Rights and Business (IHRB) convened an international meeting of 55 experts at Wilton Park to identify the cornerstones of what is, and what is not, a just transition approach (IHRB 2022a). Four key elements were identified, the absence of any one indicating the transition process might not align with international understandings of what might legitimately be called a just transition process (Wilton Park 2022). These are:

Element 1: Risks and Impacts

Many of the negative social impacts of the green transition are predictable and avoidable if governments and businesses plan proactively to protect affected communities. The United Nations Guiding Principles on Business and Human Rights (UNGPs), endorsed by the UN Human Rights Council in 2011, offer a clear framework for this (UNOHCHR 2011):

- Governments must protect individuals against human rights violations, including those involving private businesses.
- Businesses must respect human rights by avoiding harm.
- All economic actors, whether private or public, must provide remedy for any adverse impacts they cause or are linked to.

While the UNGPs are widely endorsed, they are not yet fully integrated into climate action frameworks. Embedding these principles would help mitigate risks during the shift to a green economy, such as displacement from urban renewal projects or the exploitation of communities affected by the extraction of new construction materials.

Element 2: Opportunities and Benefits

A foundational tenet of the just transition is ensuring that the positive benefits of decarbonisation are fairly distributed among affected workers, communities, indigenous peoples, and consumers. Beyond that, however, the transition offers an opportunity for broader socio-economic reform and the reduction of pre-existing inequalities. For instance, land use decisions should integrate indigenous stewardship and collective ownership models, which often align with long-term sustainability goals.

To achieve these outcomes, climate transitions require careful planning and deliberate action. Crucially, these efforts must be driven by those most affected by the transition, considering their perspectives on equity and justice alongside cultural, spiritual, and economic values. The human rights framework is a critical tool in this process, guiding policymakers in managing risks, opportunities, and trade-offs in a principled and accountable way. Human rights are not merely "benefits" but essential conditions for equitable transition planning. Governments and businesses should integrate human rights fulfilment into their transition models, breaking down silos across departments to achieve socially responsible and equitable outcomes. Despite the current immaturity of public and private climate policies, socio-economic planning rooted in human rights must become a key strategy for climate action.

Element 3: Agency and Accountability

A just transition requires an inclusive planning and implementation process that recognises workers, communities, indigenous peoples, consumers, and other affected groups as agents of change rather than passive observers. When these groups have access to information and can engage in decision-making, for example regarding a neighbourhood retrofit project, climate actions are more likely to simultaneously address other social issues, minimise harm, and ultimately gain widespread support.

Transparency from governments and businesses is therefore critical for accountability, enabling stakeholders to understand the balance and distribution of risks and benefits. Additionally, capacity-building initiatives are essential, as many impacted groups may lack the sector-specific knowledge to meaningfully contribute and shape outcomes. Governments and businesses must provide the knowledge and resources to empower effective participation in transition planning, particularly in areas marked by conflict, racism, discrimination, or inequality.

Accountability extends beyond providing remedies for harm; it addresses the power dynamic between decision-makers and those impacted by their actions. Although empowering affected groups is crucial, some authority must still rest with those in power to ensure swift climate action. Thus, future efforts should focus on ensuring that those with power serve and protect the interests of impacted communities.

Element 4: Transformational Systems Change

Ultimately, a successful just transition should fundamentally reshape the systems responsible for both inequality and the climate crisis: unsustainable extraction, production, and consumption patterns; fossil fuel dependency; inequitable trade relationships; inadequate jobs; unequal land distribution; and the failure to create shared prosperity.

For workers, communities, indigenous peoples, and consumers to be in better positions post-transition, decarbonisation must include diversification away from mono-industries, repurposing infrastructure, resource-efficiency innovations, stronger social protection systems, and reforms to the international debt and financial systems. Initiatives such as the Bridgetown Agenda, the UN's Loss and Damage fund (UNFCCC 2023), and the recently proposed global billionaire tax (Zucman 2024) do so while prioritising the needs of low-income countries, which often bear the brunt of climate impacts while lacking the resources for effective adaptation.

By grounding these initiatives in rights-respecting practices, the transition will be just, not only addressing climate goals but also advancing broader socio-economic justice. IHRB is currently collecting examples of how these four elements can be combined in local transition processes as part of the *Just Stories* programme (IHRB 2024h). There is much to be learned (both in terms of positive and negative lessons) from the transition out of coal in countries such as Germany, Spain, and the UK, as well as contemporary energy transitions in South Africa, Indonesia, and Colombia (Morrison 2024). Learning about transitions within the built environment is more nascent and at present is more at the level of statements of intent (such as the Just Transition Charters for cities such as London and Bristol).

Managing Climate Transitions

A global framework is crucial for collective action, but climate transitions are inherently local and context specific. Over the next 25 years, thousands of local transitions will unfold simultaneously—each interconnected with each other and within global supply chains. Communities affected by these transitions are well-networked and expect fairness; if they perceive significant disadvantages for themselves or future generations, resistance will likely arise. Misinformation can exacerbate fears, leading some to argue against ambitious Net Zero targets or dismiss climate change as exaggerated.

Each transition must be grounded in local realities, a principle central to IHRB's two-year research project on a just transition in the built environment. With protests against fuel tax increases in France (BBC News 2018), heat pumps in Germany (DW News 2023), and gas stoves in the USA (Milman 2023) highlighting how easily transitions can falter, IHRB organised visioning workshops in eight cities around the world (IHRB 2024a). These brought together representatives of civil society organisations, unions, businesses, and government to craft local visions for a just transition in their city, with clear actions for all stakeholders.

Efforts to transition inherently involve risks, as evidenced by 30 years of climate discourse. Today's challenge centres not on the "why" but the "how" and "when" of transitions. To illustrate how local authorities and communities can ensure a just transition, we will in the following consider human rights in the built environment, including mobility.

Cities are uniquely positioned to design and implement place-based climate solutions. Not only do they generate 70% of global emissions (Lugman et al. 2023), but they are also where inequality is often most visible, with significant levels of poverty and marginalisation. Across the EU, cities and regions are responsible for implementing 70% of climate mitigation measures and 90% of adaptation policies (ECR 2024).

At the city level, the envisioned transitioned state involves a dynamic urban landscape operating within planetary boundaries. This includes accessible green spaces, efficient public transport, flood-resistant infrastructure, sustainable affordable homes, and a robust economy that generates sustainable jobs. While it's easy to unite around this vision, the challenge lies in the journey, ensuring that the benefits of these changes are equitably distributed and that vulnerable populations are not left behind. To achieve this, an internationally agreed-upon framework, such as human rights, becomes essential for guiding analysis, diagnosis, and action.

The Right to Housing and Addressing Inequality

At the heart of built environment transition challenges lies the right to adequate housing: the right to live in a home in peace, security, and dignity, which includes security of tenure, availability of services, affordability, habitability, accessibility, appropriate location, and cultural adequacy (UNOHCHR 2025).

The 2022 report from the UN Intergovernmental Panel on Climate Change (IPCC) emphasises the urgent need for healthy, affordable, and sustainable housing as foundational in addressing climate change, as well as promoting well-being, employment, and health (IPCC 2022). Yet, 1.8 billion people globally either lack homes or live in grossly inadequate housing (UNOHCNR 2025)—a crisis also visible in high-income regions, with 895,000 unhoused people in Europe alone (FEANTSA 2023).

This housing deficit coexists with unsustainable emissions from the building sector. Total emissions, encompassing both embodied carbon (emissions from materials and construction) and operational carbon (emissions from the building's use), continue to rise rather than reduce (UNEP 2023).

As referenced in the Global Alliance for Building and Construction's recent report on Sufficiency in the Built Environment, radically different approaches are needed depending on the economic context (GlobalABC 2024). In Europe, for instance, where there are 38 million empty homes (Eurostat 2011) and up to 72 million people facing energy poverty (Maier & Dreoni 2024), the focus must be on retrofitting. In lower-income countries, however, where there are insufficient homes, new construction will be required, and efforts must concentrate on minimising associated whole-life carbon emissions. The financial resources exist to drive this change, with real estate accounting for two-thirds of global real assets, or net worth (Woetzel et al. 2021). The right to housing provides a key framework to guide capital towards making housing affordable and sustainable rather than an investment asset.

The IPCC report underscores the need to move from incremental approaches to transformative strategies. For example, the "housing first" approach, originating in New York in the 1990s but most successfully adopted in Finland, has been promoted by multiple UN Special Rapporteurs on the Right to Adequate Housing as a way to prioritise the right to adequate housing in all policy and practice areas (UNOHCHR 2021).

A housing-first approach entails safeguards against evictions, transparency in land and building ownership, strong tenant protections, a healthy social housing stock, and active tenant and owner associations. IHRB's research shows that in cities where these are in place, the social costs and benefits of decarbonisation initiatives are distributed more equitably, protecting residents living pay cheque-to-pay cheque, particularly those from historically marginalised backgrounds (IHRB 2024b).

This systemic approach is crucial because, without it, the benefits and costs from the burgeoning green economy will fall along existing power lines: primarily benefiting more privileged populations—historically the highest emitters—while marginalised communities—who are already most vulnerable to climate change—bear the brunt of costs.

The future of our cities depends on recognising and addressing the intersection of housing and climate vulnerability. By prioritising adequate housing for all, cities can build stronger, more resilient communities capable of adapting to the ever-evolving challenges posed by climate change. A housing-first approach, therefore, is not merely a housing policy; it is a comprehensive strategy that intertwines social equity and environmental sustainability, creating more equitable, sustainable cities where no one is left behind.

IHRB's recent publication, *Advancing Just Transitions in the Built Environment*, analyses a range of city-level decarbonisation initiatives to determine whether they exacerbate or address social issues (IHRB 2024b). These include retrofitting existing buildings, developing energy-efficient new ones, implementing circular economy practices, and increasing green spaces.

Retrofitting buildings presents unique social challenges. The European Union has invested heavily in this area, but, as housing remains a member state competence, disparate local frameworks have determined how the costs and benefits have been distributed. In Lisbon and Athens, for instance, short rental contracts and easy termination clauses allow landlords to claim subsidies, complete renovations, and increase rents, often displacing tenants (IHRB 2024b)—a phenomenon known as "renovictions". In contrast, Brussels' policy framework prevents this by capping rental increases to inflation. To incentivise retrofits, rents are frozen for the least energy-efficient properties, while for average-performing ones, rents can be increased by half the rate of inflation. Only for the most energy-efficient buildings can annual rental increases match inflation (IHRB 2023a). This example shows clearly how the underlying social foundation shapes the outcomes of decarbonisation initiatives.

The circular economy offers opportunities to align environmental and social outcomes. For example, reusing existing spaces and materials reduces carbon emissions while creating new homes and jobs. Cities like Brussels and Milan have mapped vacant buildings (IHRB 2023a) and are reclaiming them for public purposes (Carolan 2024). These initiatives can foster the emergence of businesses like Inclusio which, by focusing on empty buildings and reusing materials, is able to rent homes at 70–75% of the market rate, often to previously unhoused people and migrants (IHRB 2024c). Vancouver, Canada, has introduced a 2% annual tax on empty homes to encourage their return to the market (IHRB 2023a).

With sufficiency taking priority across Europe, the construction sector is adjusting to move away from large new builds to a focus on retrofit. While this could benefit workers—retrofit jobs tend to be more labour intensive and increase demand—evidence from Copenhagen highlights greater risk of human rights violations in smaller jobs, which often have more complex supply chains and less transparency (IHRB 2024b). Oslo has tackled this issue through its "Oslo Model" which limits public procurement to one step (Lindahl 2018), although its long-term impact on supply chain competition is yet to be seen.

Re-skilling has understandably been the focus of just transition discussion, with cities in Bulgaria, Ireland, France, and Spain including mandatory training clauses in public procurement contracts (IHRB 2023a). However, working conditions are equally important, with mixed evidence on whether green jobs have better pay and security than the "brown" ones they replace (IHRB 2024d). Given the sector's widespread labour shortages, attracting a workforce that can deliver the transition will require collective action to ensure historical issues of safety, precarity, and poor working conditions are addressed.

Adaptation to climate impacts poses additional challenges, with many coastal cities having to respond to rising sea levels. Copenhagen's coastal protections will include a controversial new island, which will house 35,000 residents, while Indonesia is relocating its capital to an entirely new city, with the future of the sinking Jakarta unclear (IHRB 2024e). In Lagos, Nigeria, the new Eko Atlantic City promises to be a new low-carbon development that provides coastal protection for the often-flooded city. However, prices in the development are unaffordable to practically all Nigerians, and the project has forcibly displaced 80,000 traders, cleaners, waiters, and clerks who lived informally on the previously public land (IHRB 2024b).

Equitably tackling existing inequalities is a big challenge for cities. For example, wealthier neighbourhoods often have greater access to green space. In Athens, this uneven distribution means that the most extreme temperatures are recorded in the most deprived parts of the city (IHRB 2024f). An equitable approach may seek to rebalance this by building new green spaces in historically disadvantaged areas, but this may come at the expense of additional housing and may ultimately end up increasing prices through green gentrification, a widespread phenomenon in Copenhagen (IHRB 2023b).

This example demonstrates the need for a clear, strategic-level approach. For instance, the "Just Transition Declaration for Bristol" centres on community expertise and prioritises accessible communication, as well as defining principles to ensure that the transition process actively involves and empowers marginalised populations (Bristol 2023). Similarly, Oakland, California's Equity Indicators take an equity-led approach to decision-making that seeks to reduce disparities experienced by different marginalised groups (Oakland 2018), and the region of Catalunya has developed a strong regional strategy (Catalonia 2022) to guide its just transition that is now being applied across policy areas.

A clear golden thread emerging from IHRB's research is that the decarbonisation initiatives that achieve just transition objectives are those that are grounded in human rights and follow the four elements identified at Wilton Park:

- Risk and adverse impact prevention;
- Equal access to opportunities and benefits;
- Accountability to, and agency of, potentially affected groups; and
- Transformational systems change.

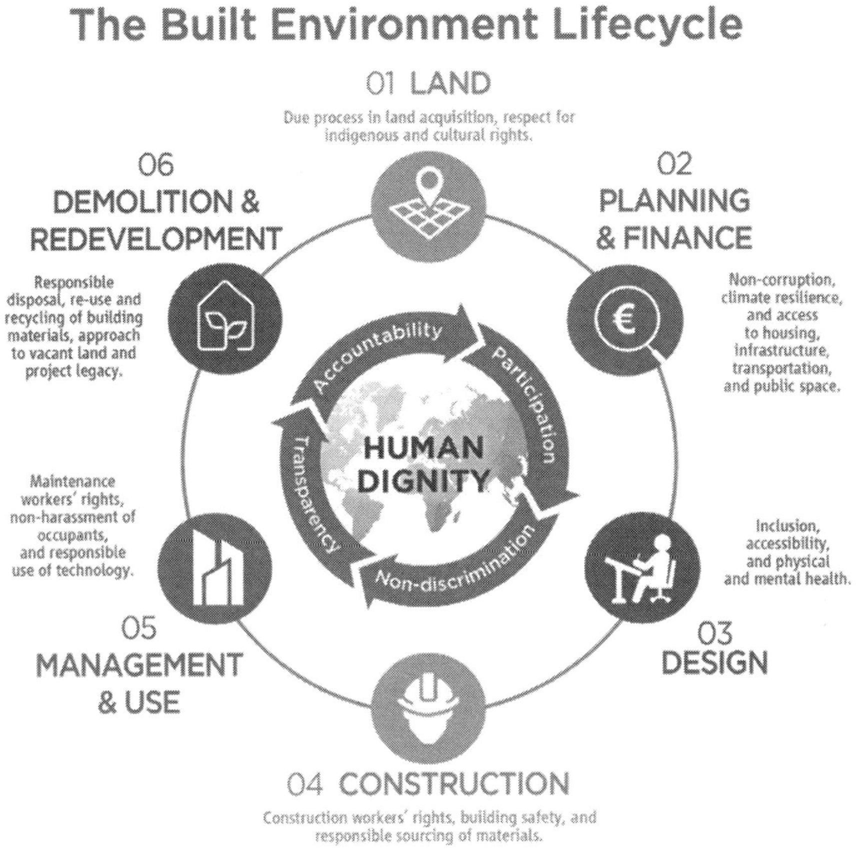

Figure 8.1 The Dignity by Design framework.

Source: © Institute for Human Rights and Business.

Dignity by Design—A Human Rights-Based Tool

These elements resonate with the Dignity by Design framework (see Figure 8.1), developed by IHRB, the Rafto Human Rights Foundation, the Raoul Wallenberg Institute of Human Rights and Humanitarian Law, and the University of Melbourne School of Design (IHRB 2019).

Grounded in the human rights frameworks, the Sustainable Development Goals, and other international standards, the Dignity by Design framework aims to guide decision-making throughout the built environment lifecycle to minimise human rights risks and maximise social outcomes. Its four overarching principles are:

- Accountability: Governments must create mechanisms of accountability to ensure the enforcement of rights. Rights must be recognised in law and policy, and there must also be effective measures in place to hold governments and other parties—including the private sector—accountable if the standards are not met.

- Participation: People have a right to participate in how decisions are made regarding protection of their rights. Governments, local authorities, and businesses must engage and support individual residents and communities to ensure they have clear avenues to have a say over the present and future of their neighbourhoods.
- Non-discrimination: Human rights are universal. They must be afforded to everyone and guaranteed without discrimination of any kind. This includes not only purposeful discrimination but also protection from policies and practices that may have a discriminatory effect. Within the real estate, design, and construction industries, non-discrimination applies to the context of their operations and also to the recruitment, retention, and advancement of employees.
- Transparency: Transparency means providing information about decision-making processes related to rights so that people know and understand how major decisions affecting rights are made.

The Dignity by Design framework has been applied in Bergen, Norway (IHRB 2024g) and Cartagena, Colombia (IHRB 2022), where it has played a crucial step in acknowledging the power dynamics, building dialogue, and aligning the various stakeholders: landowners, planners, architects, builders, financiers, managers, and tenants.

Despite these successes, misalignment remains common. Bounded rationality—where individuals operate with limited information and diverse agendas—complicates consensus-building. High-emitting cities with high rents face trade-offs between increasing supply and meeting carbon budgets. Businesses focus on short-term financial returns, particularly when trying to attract capital in an increasingly competitive global market, pension funds feel constrained by fiduciary duties, and residents often have little insight into the complexities of embodied carbon in urban infrastructure. While some may be aware of climate change, they may lack the tools to make informed decisions about material sourcing or lifestyle choices that reduce their carbon footprints. Economic constraints can further limit their options for sustainable living.

Tenants and homeowners are largely excluded from decisions regarding building design and construction, limiting their influence over carbon emissions and social outcomes. Once they occupy a residence, their energy consumption patterns are often predetermined, and the financial burden of high energy costs can stifle their efforts to adopt more sustainable practices. When local campaigns result in investment and improvement, these may result in gentrification and displacement of individuals who are renting or living informally, the reality of most residents in many rapidly growing, unequal cities.

Many urban dwellers desire a sense of agency regarding their cities, yearning for recognition as stakeholders rather than mere commodities. Yet often their views are less influential than the behaviour of asset managers and institutional investors who are disengaged from the neighbourhoods they invest in but whose actions can drive up housing costs, further marginalising vulnerable people.

The potential for maladaptive outcomes, such as "green gentrification", underscores the importance of inclusive decision-making. Middle-class residents, who are more resilient to change, often possess louder voices and better political connections than their lower-income counterparts. The circular economy, while beneficial in many respects, can inadvertently prioritise middle-class interests over those of working-class communities, rendering social justice an afterthought.

Scotland provides an illuminating case study for a just transition in the public sector. In 2023, the Scottish Government released a discussion paper outlining a just transition approach for the built environment, emphasising the role of public procurement in promoting sustainable practices. This strategy aims to catalyse broader societal change by fostering collaboration between industry and educational institutions, ultimately addressing skill shortages and promoting innovation in construction technologies (Scottish Government 2023).

Land and buildings have become pivotal asset classes in urban finance, compelling mayors and city councils to reconsider traditional taxation methods to fund necessary transitions. While many wealthy individuals reside in cities, much of their tax contributions flow to national governments, often leaving local governments under-resourced. The debate surrounding local income taxes and their implications for various stakeholders—including tourists and temporary residents—illustrates the complexities of urban financing.

Cities function as microcosms of broader financial systems, requiring adept management of spending, taxation, and liabilities. Maintaining favourable credit ratings is vital for attracting investment, necessitating an ability to plan and execute large-scale projects while navigating financial uncertainties. Public-private partnerships can mobilise private capital for public goods but often socialise risk while privatising profit, reinforcing the need for transparency and accountability to gain stakeholder trust and ensure equitable outcomes.

Conclusions

Cities stand at the forefront of the global effort to address climate change while advancing social equity. As hubs of economic, social, and cultural activity, they encapsulate the challenges and opportunities inherent in achieving a sustainable future. The transition to low-carbon urban environments is more than a technical endeavour—it is a moral and systemic transformation that must place human rights at its core.

Central to this effort are four foundational principles embedded in the internationally agreed human rights framework: risk and adverse impact prevention, equal access to opportunities and benefits, accountability to and agency of affected groups, and transformational systems change. Together, these elements provide a framework for cities to balance the dual imperatives of climate action and social justice.

Decarbonising the built environment entails significant risks, particularly resident displacement and labour exploitation. Preventing these adverse impacts requires proactive planning and robust safeguards, both in upholding the right to housing and in increasing transparency and accountability in supply chains. Without deliberate efforts to mitigate these risks, the promise of sustainability could deepen existing inequalities.

The benefits of a green transition, such as energy efficiency, improved housing, and jobs, must be distributed equitably. Marginalised communities, which are often the most vulnerable to climate impacts, must therefore be prioritised in receiving these benefits. This requires embedding redistributive principles in budget allocations and taking an equity-led approach to policy development, ensuring the tenants and vulnerable workers can see and feel the positive impacts of decarbonisation.

The voices of residents, particularly those in historically marginalised communities, are essential to shaping sustainable cities. Transparent decision-making and participatory planning processes are critical to fostering trust and legitimacy. Policies must not only consult but actively empower these groups to influence the trajectory of their neighbourhoods. Providing clear and accessible information, as well as platforms for meaningful engagement, ensures that transitions are driven by local priorities.

Incremental approaches will not suffice. The scale of transformation required to meet climate goals demands systemic change across governance, finance, and urban design. Cities must adopt circular economy models, embrace innovative financing mechanisms, and embed human rights into every layer of their operations. This includes redefining success beyond economic growth to include social and environmental well-being and embedding collaboration across sectors and scales, breaking down silos to create cohesive, impactful strategies.

By aligning climate action with these four principles, cities can lead the way in fostering an equitable transition to sustainability. This approach acknowledges that human rights and decarbonisation are not competing priorities but complementary imperatives. A truly just urban transition ensures that no community is left behind, risks are mitigated, opportunities expanded, and transformative change uplifts all.

As urban centres evolve in response to climate imperatives, their success will be measured not only by their carbon reductions but by their ability to deliver justice and dignity for all. The path forward requires intentionality, collaboration, and a steadfast commitment to these guiding principles. With these elements in place, cities can chart a course towards a more equitable and resilient future.

Bibliography

BBC News. 2018. "France Protests Carbon Tax on Fuel." December 6. Accessed January 6, 2025. https://www.bbc.com/news/world-europe-46424267

Bristol City Council. 2023. *Bristol Just Transition Declaration*. Accessed January 6, 2025. https://democracy.bristol.gov.uk/documents/s90509/App%20A%20-%20Bristol%20Just%20Transition%20Declaration.pdf

C40 Cities. 2018. *The Future We Don't Want: Sea-Level Rise*. Accessed January 6, 2025. https://www.c40.org/what-we-do/scaling-up-climate-action/water-heat-nature/the-future-we-dont-want/sea-level-rise/

Carolan, C. 2024. "Brussels-Capital Region Takes Over Vacant Family Home in Legal First." *The Brussels Times*. October 16. Accessed January 6, 2025. https://www.brusselstimes.com/1270626/brussels-capital-region-takes-over-vacant-family-home-in-legal-first

Catalonia, Government of. 2022. *RIS3CAT 2030 Strategy*. Accessed January 6, 2025. https://fonseuropeus.gencat.cat/ca/ris3cat/2030/

DW News. 2023. "Germany: Thousands in Bavaria Protest Greens' Heating Law." October 6. Accessed January 6, 2025. https://www.dw.com/en/germany-thousands-in-bavaria-protest-greens-heating-law/a-65879493

ECR (European Committee of the Regions). 2024. *State of the Regions and Cities 2024*. Accessed January 6, 2025. https://cor.europa.eu/sites/default/files/2024-09/Report-state-regions-and-cities-EN.pdf

Eurostat. 2011. "Cited in European Commission." *Filing Vacancies*. 2016. Accessed January 6, 2025. https://ec.europa.eu/futurium/sites/futurium/files/long_version_en.pdf.pdf

FEANTSA (European Federation of National Organisations Working with the Homeless). 2023. *Overview of Homelessness in Europe 2023*. Accessed January 6, 2025. https://www.feantsa.org/public/user/Resources/reports/2023/OVERVIEW/Rapport_EN.pdf

GlobalABC (Global Alliance for Buildings and Construction). 2024. *Sufficiency Action Hub Position Paper*. Accessed January 6, 2025. https://globalabc.org/sites/default/files/2024-11/241002_Sufficiency%20Action%20Hub_Position%20Paper_Final%20version.pdf

IHRB (Institute for Human Rights and Business). 2019. *Dignity by Design*. Accessed January 6, 2025. https://www.dignitybydesign.org/

IHRB (Institute for Human Rights and Business). 2022. *Advancing Human Rights in the Built Environment in Cartagena de Indias and Insights for Other Cities*. Accessed January 6, 2025. https://www.ihrb.org/resources/advancing-human-rights-in-the-built-environment-in-cartagena-de-indias-and-insights-for-other-cities

IHRB (Institute for Human Rights and Business). 2022a. *Just Transitions: Exploring the Need for International Rules Based on Local Realities*. Accessed January 6, 2025. https://www.ihrb.org/latest/just-transitions-exploring-the-need-for-international-rules-based-on-local-realities

IHRB (Institute for Human Rights and Business). 2023a. *Building for Today City Toolkit*. Accessed January 6, 2025. https://ihrb-org.files.svdcdn.com/production/assets/uploads/reports/IHRB_Building_for_Today_City_Toolkit.pdf?dm=1726490059

IHRB (Institute for Human Rights and Business). 2023b. *Behind the Green Curtain: An Exploration of Social Justice – Pathways for a Just Transition in Copenhagen*. Accessed January 6, 2025. https://ihrb-org.files.svdcdn.com/production/assets/uploads/reports/Behind_the_green_curtain_-_an_exploration_of_social_justice_-_pathways_for_a_just_transition_in_copenhagen.pdf

IHRB (Institute for Human Rights and Business). 2024a. *Building for Today and the Future*. Accessed January 6, 2025. https://www.ihrb.org/projects/building-for-today-and-the-future

IHRB (Institute for Human Rights and Business). 2024b. *Advancing Just Transitions in the Built Environment. Human Rights Risks and Opportunities in Just Transitions*. Accessed January 6, 2025. https://justtransitionsbuiltenvironment.ihrb.org/human-rights-risks-and-opportunities

IHRB (Institute for Human Rights and Business). 2024c. *Making the Case for Green and Affordable Housing Investment in Europe*. Accessed January 6, 2025. https://www.ihrb.org/resources/toolkit-making-the-case-for-green-and-affordable-housing-investment-in-europe

IHRB (Institute for Human Rights and Business). 2024d. *Future Green Construction Jobs Report*. June 2024. Accessed January 6, 2025. https://ihrb-org.files.svdcdn.com/production/assets/uploads/reports/Future_Green_Contruction_Jobs_June2024.pdf?dm=1726490051

IHRB (Institute for Human Rights and Business). 2024e. *Health and Sustainability in the Megacity: Pathways to a Just Transition in Jakarta Built Environment*. Accessed January 6, 2025. https://ihrb-org.files.svdcdn.com/production/assets/uploads/reports/health_and_sustainability_in_the_megacity_pathways_to_a_just_transition_in_jakarta_built_environment.pdf

IHRB (Institute for Human Rights and Business). 2024f. *From Ancient Roots to Future Resilience: Pathways for a Just Transition in Athens*. Accessed January 6, 2025. https://ihrb-org.files.svdcdn.com/production/assets/uploads/reports/from_ancient_roots_to_-_future_resilience_-_pathways_for_a_just_transition_in_athens.pdf?dm=1727258697

IHRB (Institute for Human Rights and Business). 2024g. *Bergen Inclusion Centre*. Accessed January 6, 2025. https://www.ihrb.org/projects/bergen-inclusion-centre

IHRB (Institute for Human Rights and Business). 2024h. *Just Stories*. https://www.ihrb.org/projects/stakeholder-led-transitions

IPCC (Intergovernmental Panel on Climate Change). 2022. *AR6 WGII Fact Sheet: Human Settlements*. Accessed January 6, 2025. https://www.ipcc.ch/report/ar6/wg2/downloads/outreach/IPCC_AR6_WGII_FactSheet_HumanSettlements.pdf

Lindahl, B. 2018. "A Properly Regulated Labour Market." *Nordic Labour Journal*. September 5. Accessed January 6, 2025. http://www.nordiclabourjournal.org/i-fokus/in-focus-2018/a-properly-regulated-labour-market/article.2018-09-05.9215100414

Lugman, M., P. J. Rayner, and K. R. Gurney. 2023. "Sufficiency Action in Climate Change Mitigation." *Nature Sustainability*. Accessed January 6, 2025. https://www.nature.com/articles/s42949-023-00084-2

Maier, S., and I. Dreoni. 2024. *Who is "energy poor" in the EU*. European Commission. Accessed January 6, 2025. https://publications.jrc.ec.europa.eu/repository/handle/JRC138418

Milman, O. 2023. "Gas Stoves and the Culture War in the United States." *The Guardian*. January 19. Accessed January 6, 2025. https://www.theguardian.com/environment/2023/jan/19/gas-stove-culture-war-united-states

Morrison, J. 2024. *The Just Transition: A Systems-Thinking Approach to Climate Action*. New York: Macmillan/Palgrave, Springer.

Oakland, City of. 2018. *Oakland Equity Indicators*. Accessed January 6, 2025. https://www.oaklandca.gov/projects/oakland-equity-indicators

Scottish Government. 2023. *Transition Built Environment Construction Sector Discussion Paper*. Accessed January 6, 2025. https://www.gov.scot/publications/transition-built-environment-construction-sector-discussion-paper/pages/5/

UN (United Nations). 2021. *Fact Sheet: Climate Change*. Accessed January 6, 2025. https://www.un.org/sites/un2.un.org/files/media_gstc/FACT_SHEET_Climate_Change.pdf

UNEP (United Nations Environment Programme). 2023. *Building Materials and Climate: Constructing a New Future*. Accessed January 6, 2025. https://www.unep.org/resources/report/building-materials-and-climate-constructing-new-future

UNFCCC (United Nations Framework Convention on Climate Change). 2015. *The Paris Agreement*. Accessed January 6, 2025. https://unfccc.int/files/meetings/paris_nov_2015/application/pdf/paris_agreement_english_.pdf

UNFCCC (United Nations Framework Convention on Climate Change). 2022. *Just Transition and the Future of Work*. Accessed January 6, 2025. https://unfccc.int/sites/default/files/resource/MPGCA_COP27_FL_OD_Just%20Transition%20and%20the%20Future%20of%20Work.pdf

UNFCCC (United Nations Framework Convention on Climate Change). 2023. *Loss and Damage Fund: Joint Interim Secretariat*. Accessed January 6, 2025. https://unfccc.int/loss-and-damage-fund-joint-interim-secretariat

UNOHCHR (United Nations Office of the High Commissioner for Human Rights). 2011. *Guiding Principles on Business and Human Rights*. Accessed January 6, 2025. https://www.ohchr.org/sites/default/files/documents/publications/guidingprinciplesbusinesshr_en.pdf

UNOHCHR (United Nations Office of the High Commissioner for Human Rights). 2021. *Ukraine Social Housing Report*. Accessed January 6, 2025. https://www.ohchr.org/sites/default/files/2021-11/UkraineSocialHousing.pdf

UNOHCHR (United Nations Office of the High Commissioner for Human Rights). 2025. *The Human Right to Adequate Housing*. Accessed January 6, 2025. https://www.ohchr.org/en/special-procedures/sr-housing/human-right-adequate-housing

Wilton Park. 2022. *Report: Just Transition and Climate Action*. January 2023. Accessed January 6, 2025. https://www.wiltonpark.org.uk/app/uploads/2023/01/WP3012-Report.pdf

Woetzel, L., J. Mischke, A. Magdavkar, et al. 2021. *The Rise and Rise of the Global Balance Sheet*. McKinsey & Company. Accessed January 6, 2025. https://www.mckinsey.com/industries/financial-services/our-insights/the-rise-and-rise-of-the-global-balance-sheet-how-productively-are-we-using-our-wealth

Zucman, G. 2024. *Report to the G20: Redefining Global Wealth Distribution*. Accessed January 6, 2025. https://gabriel-zucman.eu/files/report-g20.pdf

9 Human Rights and Spatial Planning

Addressing the Increasing Tensions over Access to Land and Resources

Michael Windfuhr

Introduction

The implementation of the International Covenant on Economic, Social and Cultural Rights (ICESCR), and in particular Art. 11 (right to an adequate standard of living), requires governments to take dedicated action to respect, protect, and fulfil access to productive resources. Long-term trends in the demand for land and rapid urbanization have significant impacts on individuals and groups living in situations of vulnerability and poverty. Land plays an essential role in the realization of several Covenant rights. Secure access to, use of, and control over land by individuals and communities play a key role in the realization of the right to an adequate standard of living. The processes of land registrations itself need to be done human rights based, in order to make sure that individuals or groups with legitimate tenure rights to land are not discriminated against in the registration process.

Transparent and reliable spatial planning processes at local, regional, and national levels are first and foremost an extremely helpful precondition for rural and urban development processes. Such planning can foster investments, because security of tenure is useful for it; it allows those who have secure tenure rights to get access to credits and allows them to plan for long-term investments into their land, investments from building infrastructure up to the investments in the protection of soil fertility. Overall stability and security created by transparent planning processes are part of the governance needed to support successful development processes and with that also the fulfilment of economic, social, and cultural rights.

Planning processes for governance of land and other natural resources are typically organized at the regional and local levels of city planning or rural area planning. The implementation of human rights therefore requires dedicated action by all levels of governments, including the local and communal levels. Art. 11 of the ICESCR covers the right to adequate food, the right to housing, the right to clothing, the right to water, and in more recent understanding also energy. The Committee on Economic, Social and Cultural Rights (CESCR) has developed several General Comments (GCs) to clarify the content of these rights, such as GC No. 12 on the right to adequate food adopted

DOI: 10.4324/9781003474845-12

by the CESCR in 1999 (CESCR, 1999). Based on that GC the specialized agency FAO (Food and Agricultural Organisation of the United Nations) developed between 2002 and 2004 "Voluntary Guidelines for the progressive realization of the right to food in the context of national food security". This was adopted unanimously in the FAO Council in 2004.

They were written to concretely inform the implementation of the right to adequate food based on the standards developed in the GC No. 12. The Voluntary Guidelines have a section, "Access to resources and assets", which discusses access to resources such as seeds and water. Land is addressed in Guideline 8.10 (FAO 2004, para 8.10). The text of paragraph 810 calls on States to take measures to promote and protect tenure security, in particular for women, poor, and other disadvantaged segments of society. It also calls for measures to improve access to land, for example through land reform, a provision also contained in Art. 11(2) of the ICESCR. Secure tenure rights are important to protect people's access to land as a means of securing their livelihoods and to avoid or regulate disputes over different user interests in land.

GC No. 26 on land (2023) begins by recognizing the increasing competition for different uses of, and the access to, land worldwide (CESCR 2023, para 2). Several long-term trends of high demand for land are converging, overlapping, and increasing. They will create tensions between different land-use demands. The most important factors include: (a) the situation in cities, where processes such as the financialization of housing markets, speculation, and inflation lead to increased competition between different groups, with negative consequences for those left behind; and (b) in rural areas, where the competition for arable land is fuelled by factors such as the impact of large-scale development projects, large national or foreign investments, tourism, and demographic growth. One important factor is the rapid process of urbanization, which requires space in the rural areas surrounding cities or agglomerations for the construction of houses, roads, industrial zones, shopping areas, and parking lots. As land becomes scarce and expensive, land resources are also used as collateral for financial assets. These developments are further exacerbated by changing environmental conditions such as: (c) land degradation caused by overuse, poor management, and unsustainable agricultural practices, some of which are irreversible; and (d) global environmental trends such as climate change altering water availability, shifting the ecological zones favourable to agriculture, and contributing to sea level rise, affecting many fertile agricultural areas in coastal plains. Rising sea levels will also affect the megacities located on coastlines.

These trends reduce the availability of land and change land-use patterns. Certain areas will become uninhabitable, and people may have to move, first within their own countries, and perhaps in a second process by migrating to other regions or countries. Another trend (e) is that the measures chosen to mitigate climate change, such as the production of biomass for carbon offsetting (e.g., for ethanol or biodiesel), reforestation projects, and large-scale renewable energy projects, have their own land requirements and will contribute to conflicts if not properly managed.

These trends are supported or facilitated by weak or non-existent legal institutional frameworks for land tenure governance. Such institutions are often compromised by mismanagement, by a discriminatory bias, for example, against land tenure for women-headed households or minorities and, not infrequently, influenced by corruption. In particular, many rural areas worldwide lack good and well-developed spatial planning processes as one of the key foundations for a functioning framework for land and natural resource governance. Spatial planning would make it possible to plan in advance which areas of land can and should be reserved for agriculture, for example, because they are suitable for agricultural production, because the soils are fertile, because irrigation water is available, or because rain-fed agriculture is regularly possible. Other areas should be set aside as nature reserves, or may need to be protected as heritage areas, or because they are part of territories reserved for indigenous peoples. Spatial planning also has to take into account which areas should be occupied by cities or industrial areas, and which can and should be used for car transport, railways, and electricity grids.

Background: Access to Land Is Essential for the Realization of Covenant Rights

In response to these challenges, the Rome-based Committee on World Food Security (CFS 2012) negotiated and adopted a legal instrument to provide guidance to States wishing to implement their land-related obligations under the right to adequate food. The Voluntary Guidelines on the Responsible Governance of Tenure of Land, Fisheries and Forests in the Context of National Food Security (VGGT 2012) were adopted by the CFS on 11 May 2012. The Guidelines describe policy choices and measures that States should take to respect, protect, and fulfil tenure security as a key step to contribute to: (1) achieving sustainable livelihoods, through access to land for rural producers as an important first step for rural development; and (2) housing security as well as sustainable social and economic development and social stability.

The VGGT was negotiated in response to the increasing pressure on land during the global food crises of 2008–2010, which led to a rapidly growing number of investments in land, whether for agricultural investment or asset security. The format of the document allowed for a detailed description of how land governance should be set up, from land registration to land administration and land transfers, to avoid violations of the right to adequate food.

The text begins by recognizing that tenure security should be based on the concept of "legitimate user rights" of individuals and groups. States must ensure that all existing user relationships to land are identified and attempted to be registered. Land cadastres cannot and should not legally recognize and allocate only those lands that are already recognized by property rights but should also include a register of all legitimate forms of use. User forms can be, among others, firm guarantees for indigenous communities, collective land titles for families or groups of families, user rights for grazing, or fishing resources. It should likewise cover customary rights to collect fruits, nuts, or herbs. Land registration must be carried out in a fair and responsive manner.

The VGGT also contains a clear description of how land administration should be organized and developed. States should avoid overlapping or competing registries but have a single record for each defined area to avoid conflicts created by administrative systems. Land administration should be based on a fair valuation and taxation of land. A good land administration system should be based on spatial planning and should have facilities for resolving disputes over tenure rights. Spatial planning should facilitate policy decisions on the development of rural or urban areas.[1] A third pillar focuses on the process of land transfer. These should be implemented in such a way that legitimate land-user rights are not overlooked or neglected when land transfers are initiated or processed.

For each of the three pillars (land registration, land administration, and land transfers), the VGGT describes the elements of good governance. The text calls for a human rights-based approach to governance, respecting the human rights principles relevant to the implementation of all human rights, i.e. non-discrimination, transparency, and participation. Transparency is important because people whose property is being registered should know about the process, how the land valuation process is organized, what prices are set, etc. Participation means that they should be heard and involved in the design of all policies that affect their tenure rights.

The VGGT and GC No. 26 already recognize the important influence that climate change will have on, inter alia, land-use patterns and the availability of usable land. The effects of climate change may also be a cause for the resettlement of individuals and groups. Climate change will increase the incidence of emergencies and natural disasters. States must have the capacity to properly assess the potential risks, especially to individuals, communities, or people likely to be affected. These individuals or groups need to be respected and protected by laws, policies, strategies, and actions to avoid or adapt to the impacts of climate change, in accordance with their human rights obligations. Where people need to be resettled or evacuated as a result of natural disasters such as floods or droughts, any provision of alternative land, fisheries, or forests should be prepared and implemented in consultation with the participation of all those affected by the resettlement processes. Adaptation policies to climate change must be based on human rights.

It is therefore important for States to address tenure in disaster prevention and preparedness programmes. Systems for recording legitimate tenure rights should be resilient to natural disasters so that rights holders can prove their rights and livelihoods. In August 2022, Pakistan experienced one of the deadliest floods in its history. Almost a third of the country was inundated. The Indus flood killed 1,739 people. More than 33 million people were directly affected by the floods and around 2.1 million people were made homeless and/or lost access to their farmland (Islamic Relief 2022). Many of the affected individuals, families, or groups affected did not have formal land titles registered. This is a typical situation that shows how difficult it is to respond properly to the challenges posed by disasters when legitimate land titles are not properly registered, when affected people are unlikely to receive compensation, and when resettlement may be too complicated.[2]

GC No. 26 on land and ESC rights is an interpretative description of the obligations of States parties to the ICESCR have in relation to land. The GC clarifies that the Covenant requires States parties not to interfere, directly or indirectly, with the rights to land set out in the Covenant, including access to, use of, and control over land. States shall not interfere with the legitimate tenure rights of land users by not evicting them by force, by not engaging in discrimination in land registration and administration, and by not engaging in corruption in land-related administrative processes (CESCR 2023, para 22–25). In any land tenure system, States must ensure that all persons enjoy a reasonable degree of security in their land tenure (CESCR 2023b, para 26ff). The GC reiterates the key processes of land registration, administration, and transfers already described by the VGGT. The obligations of the State are clearly set out: "Land administration shall be based on accessible and non-discriminatory services implemented by accountable agencies whose actions are reviewed by judicial bodies" (CESCR 2023, para 34).

Spatial Planning and Human Rights

Spatial planning, traditionally a technical and administrative process, can be seen as an important instrument for the realization of human rights related to land. It can serve as a powerful tool to resolve user conflicts over land in rural and urban areas. It has been recognized in several policy instruments such as the 2030 Agenda for Sustainable Development, particularly in the context of sustainable urbanization. During the Habitat III conference in Quito in 2016, a New Urban Agenda was adopted, focusing on well-planned and well-managed urbanization processes.[3] The Urban Agenda specifically recognizes the role of urban and spatial planning, "[r]einvigorating long-term and integrated urban and territorial planning and design in order to optimize the spatial dimension of the urban form and deliver the positive outcomes of urbanisation" (New Urban Agenda 2016, para 15 ii). This is a recognition that urban governance requires "sound institutions and mechanisms that empower and include urban stakeholders" to achieve predictability and coherence in urban development plans, with the aim of enabling social inclusion, inclusive and sustainable economic growth, and environmental protection.

The demand for a right to the city has been constructed from the elements of equitable access to resources and services relevant to the development of urban areas and a demand for people-centred urban planning. Social movements launched the "Right to the City Alliance" in 2007 as a network against forced evictions in many urban contexts worldwide.[4] In 2014, the Global Platform on the Right to the City was launched at an International Meeting on the Right to the City in Brazil. The founding members[5] saw the need for an international and strong platform where social movements and organizations could join efforts to strengthen the demand for the right to the city worldwide.[6]

The roles of regional, land use and spatial planning are also recognized in GC26 and the VGGT. The GC emphasizes the importance of long-term regional planning as a key tool (CESCR 2023, para 38) and encourages international cooperation and assistance to support efforts to ensure that land policies are sustainable and become "an integral part of official land use planning and States' broader spatial planning" (CESCR 2023, para 47).

The VGGT has a separate guideline devoted to spatial planning (Guideline 20), because it considers spatial planning as an essential tool for reconciling different objectives in land use and a necessary instrument for harmonizing different objectives (VGGT 2012, Guideline 20.1). The Guideline calls for States to link the recognition, administration, and transfer of legitimate tenure rights to spatial planning. Guideline 20 describes the quality standards that spatial planning processes must meet if they are to achieve reconciliatory outcomes and be one of the key governance instruments for avoiding potential user conflicts, as they regulate the future use of the resources. It notes that spatial planning processes (1) need to be organized in a way that is sensitive to the user rights of more marginalized groups. To fulfil this role, the planning process itself must be inclusive, i.e. non-discriminatory, and allow for the participation of all relevant individuals and groups. Such planning must be carried out (2) with broad public participation in the development of planning proposals and the review of draft spatial plans to ensure that the priorities and interests of communities, including indigenous peoples and food-producing communities, are reflected. Communities must also receive the support they need to actively participate in planning processes, and the process must ensure (3) diversity of representation. States must ensure (4) that such planning processes are transparent and free from corruption by establishing safeguards against the abuse of spatial planning powers, particularly when existing plans are to be updated (VGGT 2012, Guideline 20.4). The VGGT emphasizes that all information must be available in advance to all participants and that the process itself should follow clear rules and regulations. In addition, the processes (5) must allow for redress if things go wrong. Access to complaint mechanisms at all levels during land registration, administration, and transfers must be established, functioning, and transparent. All decisions of institutions involved in land administration should also be subject to judicial review.

The VGGT reflects the need for spatial planning to promote a diversified and sustainable management of land, fisheries, and forests to meet the long-term challenges of climate change and food security. Given the planetary environmental crises of climate change, biodiversity loss, pollution, and other challenges such as desertification and soil degradation, there is a strong need to focus on the sustainable management of land, fisheries, and forests. The Club of Rome report "Earth for all" identifies agriculture and land use as one of the key areas in which a transition to sustainability is needed (Club of Rome (ed.) 2022).

Both the VGGT and the GC describe the continuing and even increasing tensions around the different uses of land. The IPCC produced a report in 2020 describing the combined challenges for land use in terrestrial ecosystems (IPCC 2020). The report examines the challenges posed by climate change, desertification, land degradation, sustainable land management, and food security. To address these challenges, land-use planning requires careful and well-managed spatial planning to provide the necessary transparency in the flow of information to make informed decisions at local, regional, and national levels on how land can and should be used, while respecting planetary boundaries.

As highlighted in the GC, different groups have uneven opportunities to influence land-use planning decisions. It is therefore of paramount importance to overcome historical and practical disadvantages in the planning process to ensure that all relevant societal interests can be reflected (FAO 2020). Spatial planning processes can be sensitive to overcoming discrimination, or they can reinforce and contribute to inequitable resource allocation. It is therefore the place for informed and human rights-based decision-making for regions and cities to bring together environmental and equity concerns. The CESCR has dealt with many situations in which it was evident that particularly marginalized groups are often discriminated against in administrative procedures and not invited to participate in urban or rural planning processes. Examples are related to Sinti and Roma in Europe (Vuksanović-Macura et al. 2021), for scheduled caste and scheduled tribes in India (E/C.12/IND/CO/5, 2008, para 13 and 31), Indigenous Peoples in Cameroon (E/C.12/CMR/CO/4, Concluding Observations 2019, para 12 and 13), Indigenous Quilombolas in Brazil (E/C.12/BRA/CO/3, Concluding observations 2023, para 12b and 20), as well as minorities in many countries. The Committee is asking in all cases for a proper participation of marginalized groups in administrative procedures affecting them.

Spatial Planning: Importance for Rural Areas

The key challenges with respect to land use in rural areas are well described in the IPCC Special Report on Climate Change and Land. Demand for land has increased since 1961, the reference period of the report. Population growth and the changes in per capita consumption of food, feed, fibre, timber, and energy have increased at high rates. Agriculture currently uses about 70 per cent of the world's fresh water. At the same time, there has been a tremendous expansion of area used for agriculture and forest. "With large regional variation, these changes have contributed to increasing net GHG emissions (very high confidence), loss of natural ecosystems, e.g., forests, savannahs, natural grasslands and wetlands, and declining biodiversity (high confidence)" (IPCC 2020, A 1.3, page 5).

In parallel, several processes are increasing the pressure on land use. A first set of developments is reducing land availability worldwide, with regional variations. About a quarter of ice-free land is subject to human-induced degradation, according to the IPCC report. Climate change further exacerbates the degradation process in permafrost areas, but also in low-lying coastal areas. Desertification is increasing in many drylands.

A second set of processes is related to the increasing demands on land. Increased consumption of animal feed has led to an expansion in the production of feed crops, such as soya. Agricultural biomass can also be used to produce bioenergy or biofuels. The use of biomass for biodiesel or ethanol as an additive to diesel or gasoline is intended to reduce greenhouse gas emissions from car fuel. It has led to an increase in the production of palm oil and corn. Following the global financial crisis of 2007/8, land was also increasingly used as an asset for financial security and large-scale land investment. Currently, land is also being used for carbon offsetting projects, and this demand will increase as the price of CO2 rises in line with climate change policies. In addition, trends such as the rising surface temperatures will affect land-use areas, the growth of cities, and the areas needed for roads, industrial areas, housing, tourism, etc.

To respond to these developments, standards have been developed to guide land investment processes. In addition to the VGGT, in 2012, the International Finance Corporation (IFC) adopted its standards for investments by private actors in other countries: the IFC Performance Standards. They are applied basically by all public development banks. The World Bank has revised its Environmental and Social Safeguards, which are binding on public investments. Both standards have a separate chapter on the treatment of land-related investments and provisions for transparency and participation (Windfuhr, 2017). These standards, together with the VGGT and the GC, can guide land-related policies if they are systematically applied to all land-use changes and transactions. Spatial planning processes can and should be the place where standards can be effectively implemented. They can also be used to integrate sustainability concerns into rural as well as urban spatial planning, which is also important for ensuring human rights in the long term (Knaps et al. 2020). In parallel, there is increasing research on how rural development and spatial planning can and should be combined.[7]

Spatial Planning: Importance for Urban Areas

Tenure security is also a key objective in urban areas from a human rights perspective. In rural areas, tenure security covers two human rights concerns: (a) the right to housing, by ensuring a place to live; and (b) the right to adequate food, because land is also used for agricultural production, allowing peasants to produce and earn an income from their own production. In urban areas, tenure security is more directly linked to the right to housing. However, even in urban areas, families often use their homes for income-generating activities, micro and small enterprises and, where possible, forms of urban agriculture.

In fast-growing megacities, as well as in other fast-growing smaller or medium-sized cities in more remote areas, the processes of urban development can lead to user conflicts. Space for roads or other transport corridors, power grids, urban development zones for industry and commerce, and also the increasing demand of wealthier individuals for newly constructed housing often lead to forced evictions or demolitions of residential areas. Cities are growing and will be the places where most people will live in the future. The world's population reached 8 billion in 2022, more than half of whom live in urban areas. This number will further increase, with the urban population more than doubling its current size by 2050, at which point seven of ten people will live in cities. The SDG Report estimates that by 2050, 70 per cent of all people will live in cities. Currently, around 1.12 billion people live in slums or slum-like conditions in cities, with 2 billion more expected in the next 30 years.[8] Most people living in informal settlements have no security of tenure. They are at risk of being displaced by urban development. They lack the security to invest in their homes and small businesses.

Spatial planning can play a key role in dealing with this tension in urban development. It makes it possible to plan which areas and zones will be used for which functions. At the same time, it is the most reliable tool for enabling participation in urban development. Participation must always include those who do not yet have security of tenure, but who are legitimate land users. Spatial planning is particularly important because urban development trends are often rapid and driven by more powerful economic actors: The UN Special Rapporteur on Housing at that time, Leilani Farha, published a report in 2017 describing the economic development of urban housing markets through the financialization of housing. It describes the structural changes that have taken place in housing markets since the financial crisis of 2007/8. Large amounts of global capital have been invested in housing as a commodity, as collateral for financial instruments traded on global markets. Farha's report (Farha, L. 2017) and a later publication (Farha and Schwan, 2021) document the impact of this trend on the housing market and on the enjoyment of the right to adequate housing, and outline an appropriate human rights framework for States to address it. Urban planning must respect and be based on human rights standards.

Urban development and growth are also under pressure from environmental trends. Cities need to be green, including in terms of adequate sanitation, a functioning waste management system, and the ability to cope with pollution. Cities need to be sensitive to climate change, such as heat waves, planning needs to integrate green areas for cooling, and to cope with heavy rainfall and other extreme weather events.[9] These trends can only be recognized and integrated in urban planning when they are integrated in spatial planning. Only at that level it is possible to identify and coordinate competing interests. Spatial planning makes it possible to share information on decisions to be taken in advance to all involved parties and would potentially allow all stakeholders to be involved in the decision-making process on an informed basis.

Conclusion

Keys to Spatial Planning Processes Based on Responsible Tenure Governance: Governments' Human Rights Obligations, Responsible Institutions, and Accountability

This chapter argues that long-term spatial planning is a key policy process for both rural and urban development, which can help to use a human rights framework to guide planning processes. Within the human rights implementation system, important guidance and standards have been developed that provide clarity on the relevant human rights norms that can be used in planning processes, such as CESCR GC No. 26 and the VGGTs. At the same time, a human rights framework requires the recognition of procedural rights that must be respected and protected in all processes of planning and tenure registration, including the transfer of tenure. All processes of registration, and tenure administration and transfers must be open to the participation of those affected by the planning. A transparent and participatory process is the best guarantee for conflict prevention, as concerns can be addressed. Participation is only possible if the people or groups who attend and participate are respected and not persecuted. They need to be protected in the same way as other human rights defenders. Such processes will create or increase the stability and security for decisions in rural and urban planning, a key condition of positive economic development. It will foster investments into its own assets, such as buildings, in agriculture, and also into the sustainable use of such resources, by making it reasonable to improve water management and invest in long-term soil fertility, among other measures.

There needs to be a de facto link between urban and rural planning. It needs to be seen as a continuum because dynamic processes such as climate change, migration, urban expansion into rural areas, and financialization of land and housing markets need to be managed and planned together. Similarly, environmental concerns can often only be adequately addressed if all these trends are considered together. Governments need to make informed decisions about how to prioritize the use of resources, for example, water, whether for drinking and personal hygiene or for industrial use or agricultural production (Windfuhr, 2013). These decisions are mostly taken by regional or local government institutions for registration of land and spatial planning. The standards and legal frameworks at the national level should incorporate the human rights standards, and the application needs to be human rights based. The same applies to the protection of biodiversity, which requires protected areas, waste management, including the siting of landfills, etc.

Functioning and reliable spatial planning processes require institutions that are independent, adequately funded, and include accountability mechanisms in case decisions taken may violate the rights of certain individuals or groups. Institutions need to be open and accessible, especially to marginalized groups, minorities, or other marginalized communities. Planning institutions are potentially vulnerable to corruption. It is therefore of paramount importance that States establish and ensure the independence and functioning of planning institutions at the relevant levels of government, mostly at local levels.

In conclusion, human rights-based spatial planning can be used as a tool to deal with the increasing tensions of land-use demands. It can help to prevent and manage conflicts by allowing affected individuals and communities to be heard and by providing accountability for decisions taken on land use that affect legitimate tenure rights.

Notes

1 Details will be introduced in the next section.
2 See longer report on the Flood by Islamic Relief Pakistan, Islamic Relief Pakistan (2022) file:///C:/Users/windfuhr/Downloads/Floods%20Emergency%20Sitrep%20 28%20Pakistan%2012.10.22-1.pdf.
3 The Quito Declaration was later endorsed by the UN-General Assembly at its 71st session on December 23, 2016. UN-Doc: A/RES/71/256, https://habitat3.org/wp-content/uploads/New-Urban-Agenda-GA-Adopted-68th-Plenary-N1 646655-E.pdf.
4 Right to the City Alliance was created in 2007 with participation from 45 cities in 26 countries. https://www.righttothecity.org/who-we-are.
5 Habitat International Coalition and the Polis Institute in Brazil.
6 See the website of the Platform for more details: https://www.right2city.org/ the-platform/#.
7 For example, Cora van Oosten and Kimberly Merten, 2021. Securing Rights in Landscapes: Towards a Rights Based Landscape Approach. Wageningen Centre for Development Innovation, Wageningen University & Research. Report WCDI-21-135. Wageningen. https://doi.org/10.18174/543254 r at www.wur.eu/cdi.
8 See https://www.statista.com/statistics/267714/urban-population-in-slums/ February 2025 + SDG reporting under SDG Goal 11: Make cities inclusive, safe, resilient and sustainable. https://www.un.org/sustainabledevelopment/cities/.
9 Research is underway on what an urban sustainability planning framework could look like and how it could work (Puchol-Sulort, P., O'Keeffe, J. et al. 2021).

Bibliography

Club of Rome, ed. 2022. *Earth for All*.

Committee on Economic, Social and Cultural Rights. 1999. *General Comment No. 12: The right to adequate food (Art. 11)*. E/C.12/1999/5, May 12, 1999.

Committee on Economic, Social and Cultural Rights. 2008. *Concluding Observations India*. E/C.12/IND/CO/5, August 8, 2008.

Committee on Economic, Social and Cultural Rights. 2019. *Concluding Observations Cameroon*. E/C.12/CMR/CO/4, March 25, 2019.

Committee on Economic, Social and Cultural Rights. 2023. *Concluding Observations Brazil*. E/C.12/BRA/CO/3, November 11, 2023.

Committee on Economic, Social and Cultural Rights. 2023b. *General Comment No. 26: Land and Economic, Social and Cultural Rights*. C/C.12/GC/26, January 24, 2023, para 2.

Committee on World Food Security (CFS). 2012. *Voluntary Guidelines on the Responsible Governance of Tenure of Land, Fisheries and Forests in the Context of National Food Security*. https://www.fao.org/tenure/voluntary-guidelines/en/

FAO. 2004. *Voluntary Guidelines to Support the Progressive Realization of The Right to Adequate Food in The Context of National Food Security*. Adopted at the 127th session of the FAO Council in November 2004. Para 8.10.

FAO. 2020. *Strengthening Civic Spaces in Spatial Planning Processes*. Rome: Governance of Tenure Technical Guide No. 12. https://doi.org/10.4060/cb0422en

Farha, L., and K. Schwan. 2021. "The Human Right to Housing in The Age of Financialization." In M. F. Davis, M. Kjaerum, and A. Lyons (eds.), *Research Handbook on Human Rights and Poverty*, 386–401.

IPCC. 2020. *Special Report: Climate Change and Land*. An IPCC Special Report on climate change, desertification, land degradation, sustainable land management, food security, and greenhouse gas fluxes in terrestrial ecosystems.

Islamic Relief Pakistan. 2022. *Pakistan Monsoon Floods 2022*. October 12, 2022. *Reliefweb*. https://reliefweb.int/report/pakistan/pakistan-monsoon-floods-2022-islamic-relief-pakistan-12-october-2022

Knaps, F., T. Mölders, and S. Herrmann. 2020. Sustainable Spatial Development – Landscape Identity as Theoretical and Practical Challenge for Spatial Planning. *RuR [Internet]* 78(3): 289–304. https://rur.oekom.de/index.php/rur/article/view/269

Leilani Farha, L. 2017. *Report of the UN-Special Rapporteur on Housing to the Human Rights Council on financialisation of housing: A/HRC/34/51*. January 18, 2017. https://documents.un.org/doc/undoc/gen/g17/009/56/pdf/g1700956.pdf7

Pepe Puchol-Salort, J., J. O'Keeffe, M. van Reeuwijk, and A. Mijic. 2021. "An Urban Planning Sustainability Framework: Systems Approach to Blue Green Urban Design." *Sustainable Cities and Society*, 66: 102677. https://www.sciencedirect.com/science/article/pii/S2210670720308921

van Oosten, Cora and Kimberly Merten, 2021. "Securing Rights in Landscapes: Towards a Rights Based Landscape Approach." Wageningen Centre for Development Innovation, Wageningen University & Research. Report WCDI-21-135. Wageningen. https://doi.org/10.18174/543254 r at www.wur.eu/cdi.

VGGT. 2012. *Voluntary Guidelines on the Responsible Governance of Tenure of Land, Fisheries and Forests in the Context of National Food Security*. Rome: CFS. https://www.fao.org/tenure/voluntary-guidelines/en/

Vuksanović-Macura, Z., and I. Miščević. 2021. "Excluded communities and participatory land-use planning: Experience from informal Roma settlements in Serbia." *Environment & Urbanization* 33(2): 456–477. https://doi.org/10.1177/09562478211024095

Windfuhr, M. 2013. *Water for Food: a Human Rights Obligation. How States can Manage Conflicts Between the Human Right to Water and the Human Right to Adequate Food*. Berlin: DIMR. https://www.institut-fuer-menschenrechte.de/publikationen/detail/water-for-food-a-human-rights-obligation

Windfuhr, M. 2017. *Safeguarding Human Rights in Land Related Investments: Comparison of the Voluntary Guidelines Land with the IFC Performance Standards and the World Bank Environmental and Social Safeguard Framework*. Berlin: German Institute for Human Rights.

Part 3

Subnational Implementation of Human Rights Economy

10 Towards the Realisation of a Human Rights Economy through Human Rights Budgeting at Local Level

Markus Möstl, Gerd Oberleitner, and Klaus Starl

Introduction: The Role of Local Budgets in the Human Rights Economy

In 2023, the United Nations High Commissioner for Human Rights (OHCHR 2023) issued his landmark call to build economies that advance human rights for all. His vision of a human rights economy implies no less than that budgets, taxes, trade policy, consumption and production patterns, investment decisions, and business models need to be redesigned in such a way that all countries can better and fully comply with their human rights obligations. The High Commissioner emphasised that the (national) budget is one of the most important economic policy tools to advance human rights and progress on the Sustainable Development Goals. A human rights economy should therefore invest maximum available resources in the promotion of human rights, in particular in social protection, universal education and healthcare, food, housing, and in ensuring a decent standard of living for all. Since as of now many budget documents do not reflect human rights standards and obligations, the High Commissioner called for taking a deeper look at "human rights budgeting" so that policy makers can design policies and institutional practices that uphold human rights.

While many of the proposals brought forward by the High Commissioner require action by global and national actors, fresh thinking and political leadership is also required at the local level to ensure that public resources are allocated in ways that advance human rights. Local governments play a central role in managing key civic, political, social, economic, and cultural aspects of daily life of millions of people around the world. Being the administrative units closest to the citizens, they bear a significant responsibility for addressing local inequalities and ensuring that the most marginalised populations receive the support they need to realise their rights. This proximity to the constituents puts municipalities, cities, and regions in a unique position to directly influence the living conditions of people and communities.

Local governments leverage their budgetary powers in manifold ways to strategically generate, allocate, and spend resources to deliver public services, promote infrastructure development, support economic growth, ensure public safety, provide social services, improve the overall quality of life, and maintain

DOI: 10.4324/9781003474845-14

their functionality. In doing so, local governments must observe budgetary laws in order to ensure solvency and prevent imprudent spending. Moreover, they must comply with general legislation applicable at the local level, including human rights obligations. The way in which local governments prioritise and allocate their public resources will thus determine whether the realisation of rights is either promoted or hindered.

To date, the role that local governments play in the realisation of a human rights economy is largely unexplored. The implications of thinking in terms of a human rights economy still need to be contextualised for the local level. In this process, human rights budgeting emerged as a crucial idea for achieving better outcomes for people and the planet. Although a wide range of spending by local authorities is related to and can have an impact on human rights, there is no common understanding or practically accepted definition of the term human rights budgeting. As convincingly argued by the OHCHR:

> […] almost all government allocations and expenditure are human rights-related, if they are intended to ensure a stable, functioning society, as this is a sine qua non for the realization of rights. However, such a broad understanding of the term would fail to acknowledge that, while it can sometimes be difficult to draw a hard and fast line separating "human rights-related" allocations and expenditure from other allocations and expenditure, certain types of spending are more directly conducive to the realization of people's rights.
>
> (OHCHR 2017)

In the absence of a fully fledged concept, we may understand human rights budgeting at the local level tentatively as an approach by which a local government seeks to ensure that its budgets meet human rights standards, rather than privileging economic considerations. It would thus take into account the planning, allocation, spending, and monitoring of the use of public funds and be deliberately designed to ensure that the results of budgetary measures contribute to the respect, protection, and fulfilment of human rights obligations. For a human rights economy, however, not only the outcomes but also the process leading to the outcomes must be in conformity with human rights.

To better cover this procedural aspect, one could adopt the phrase "human rights-based approach to budgeting". Such an approach would require that public funds are allocated in a way that is compliant with human rights principles such as equality, non-discrimination, participation, transparency, and accountability. By integrating these principles into budgetary processes, local governments need to ensure that their financial decisions address the rights-based needs of the population, particularly those that experience multiple and persistent discrimination and are the most marginalised populations. Specifically, a human rights-based approach to budgeting would seek to prevent direct and indirect discrimination and instead help to ensure that public services are accessible and available to all constituents regardless of their background or identity. Furthermore, it would recognise the fact that local governments are responsible for the use of public funds and accountable to their citizens for their decisions and their impact on the people's lives. Local budgets informed by a human-rights based approach would therefore need to be open to public scrutiny, allowing residents to hold their governments accountable for how resources are utilised to promote human rights. Providing access to information on the content and process of the local budget would further serve transparency and thus reduce the risk of corruption and abuse of power. Finally, the participation of stakeholders in decision-making processes would be a key element of a human rights-based approach to budgeting, which calls on local governments to involve constituents in budget planning and implementation to ensure that their needs and concerns are taken into account.

But what do these terminological and conceptual reflections mean for the budgetary practice of local governments? Since this is a question where much is still in its infancy, this chapter attempts to lay the groundwork for a more in-depth examination of the realisation of a human rights economy through human rights budgeting or a human rights-based approach to budgeting at the local level. We are examining the question of what theoretical and practical guidance there is for the implementation of such approaches at local level. In Section 1, we address this question by briefly reviewing conceptual works and models that deal with this topic. In Section 2, we map related practices of local governments and derive some key observations. We then synthesise the findings from theory and practice to determine some first conceptual contours for human rights budgeting and a human rights-based approach to budgeting at the local level (Section 3). This is followed by some final conclusions to support further research into how local governments can meet the requirements of a human rights economy (Section 4).

Overview of Conceptual Works and Models

In the absence of a specialised academic field focusing on human rights and budgeting, there exists a small body of work exploring the nexus between public budgets and human rights that could provide methodological and conceptual guidance for human rights budgeting or a human rights-based approach to budgeting at the local level.

The OHCHR pointed out in 2012 that human rights budgeting requires that the entire budget cycle must be participatory, transparent, objective, and characterised by accountability. The OHCHR further highlighted that appropriate indicators make it easier to align the State's budget with its human rights obligations (OHCHR 2012). Building on the conviction that a "government's budget is the most important economic policy and planning document, and is an essential means by which to assess government's efforts for the realization of human rights", the OHCHR discussed the manifold points of intersection between human rights law and public budgets in its guide for states on how to realise human rights through government budgets in 2017 (OHCHR 2017). In a handbook for civil servants, the United Nations OHCHR in Mexico explains to practitioners how the human rights perspective can be integrated into public policy and budgets in all phases of the budget cycle (OHCHR 2010). The European Union Agency for Fundamental Rights has identified human rights budgeting as a key element of a Human Rights City (European Union Agency for Fundamental Rights 2022). The Agency specifically suggested including "robust data in budget information to identify areas requiring public action" and "provisions on respect for and fulfilment of human rights standards in public procurement rules". The idea of linking local budgets to human rights has further been identified by the International Centre for the Promotion of Human Rights at the Local and Regional Levels as a promising management tool for implementing human rights with a specific focus on accountability at the local level (Centre for the Promotion of Human Rights at the Local and Regional Levels 2023).

The Scottish Human Rights Commission has developed a sophisticated system called "Human Rights Budget Work" to use human rights to create and scrutinise Scotland's national budget. It is based on the simple, but conclusive conviction that "if human rights are not in the budget, they are not a value worth counting" (Scottish Human Rights Commission n.d.). Their briefing papers explain in detail the application of human rights in the preparation and scrutiny of the Scottish national budget. Ann Blyberg wrote a very insightful account of the issue for the Scottish Human Rights Commission (Blyberg n.d.).

Non-state actors also use human rights as a yardstick for assessing public budgets. As early as 2004, Fundar and others pointed at budget analysis as a strategy to protect and promote the enjoyment of human rights, including economic, social, and cultural rights, and provided a guide to using budget analysis to advance human rights (Fundar et al. 2004). The globally active International Budget Partnership focuses on the generation of relevant data to advocate for reform (International Budget Partnership n.d.). Their Open Budget Survey ranks countries according to their performance across three dimensions of accountability, namely public participation, budget oversight, and transparency in national budget processes. The Danish Institute for Human Rights addressed the topic of human rights compliant public procurement in a toolkit on human rights for policy makers and public buyers (Danish Institute for Human Rights 2020). There are also relevant initiatives in the area of education and training, as the Swedish International Centre for Local Democracy developed a course on Human Rights Budgeting & Corruption in Local Level Governance for local elected politicians (Swedish International Centre for Local Democracy n.d.).

Several contributions have thus addressed the question of how human rights and public budgets relate to each other, all suggesting that budgets can be a powerful instrument for advancing human rights, and accountability for human rights in particular. Some of the above-mentioned initiatives have attempted to build a first theoretical framework around the topic of human rights budgeting, and some have analysed the topic for a very specific geographical context. However, most initiatives address the budget and its process at national level. The seminal work of the Scottish Human Rights Commission deserves special attention in this respect. Its structured and at the same time comprehensive approach to work with the Scottish budget from a human rights perspective seems to be very close to the thinking of human rights economy. Some of the guidance provided therein is most likely transferrable to subnational budget processes and will thus be taken up in the following section. Nonetheless, we may conclude from the overview of existing work that there is no ready-made concept or model for human rights budgeting or a human rights-based approach to budgeting that can be applied at the local level.

Mapping the Practice of Local Governments

Next, we considered whether a model for human rights budgeting or human rights-based approach to budgeting can be derived from the existing practice of local governments. Given the large number of cities and thus potential research subjects, we had to limit ourselves to an exploratory mapping of the approaches used by local governments. The main purpose of this exercise was to capture the diversity of approaches that exist in practice. We therefore did not attempt to produce a comprehensive account of all practices in use, but rather set out to find illustrative examples that could be informative for the realisation of a human rights economy at the local level. We limited our mapping to desk research and decided to consider only practices currently or recently used by local governments that are sufficiently documented for our purpose and for which relevant information is publicly available online. Our search process focused on city websites and was complemented by a review of reports and documents from international organisations.

It was clear to us from the outset that the choice of search terms would have a significant influence on the results of the mapping. The development of search terms followed an iterative process, resulting in a comprehensive set of keywords. We further expanded our search by using translations of these search terms in different languages.[1] We were fully aware that case studies and consultations with cities and other stakeholders would be necessary to validly identify the concrete outcomes of particular initiatives. However, we have deliberately chosen not to analyse the practices identified in detail, but to examine what cities do in the area of financial management when they themselves claim a link to human rights. Our mapping is therefore based on the information, terms, titles, and assessments used by the local authorities themselves. We therefore also accepted that our primary objective of mapping does not allow us to draw final conclusions as to whether the budgets actually comply with human rights or not.

Although we aimed at achieving geographical diversity, the final mapping results proved to be regionally unbalanced due to factors such as accessibility, language barriers, and even technical limitations related to the accessibility of websites from abroad. Moreover, our attempts to track the application of pertinent practices over a longer period of time often failed due to a lack of sufficient information from the local governments. The result of the mapping must therefore be regarded as a somewhat selective choice of key initiatives that makes no claim to representativeness. We identified the following 34 local and regional practices that in one or another way may inform a model for human rights budgeting or human rights-based approach to budgeting (in alphabetical order): Aberdeen (UK), Austin (US), Bainbridge Island (US), Barcelona (Spain), Battle Creek (US), Batumi (Georgia), Cairo (Egypt), Cascais (Portugal), City of Duluth (US), City of Roanoke (US), Eugene (US), Flanders (Belgium), Fulton County (US), Gdańsk (Poland), Gori (Georgia), Gothenburg (Sweden), Krasnodar (Russia), Lahti (Finland), Las Condes (Chile), Makueni County (Kenya), Mexico City (Mexico), Milwaukee County (US), Montevideo (Uruguay), Naga City (Philippines), Nantes (France), New York City (US), Porto Alegre (Brazil), Rosario (Argentina), Salt Lake City (US), San Francisco (US), Seoul (South Korea), Şişli (Turkey), Vermont (US), Vienna (Austria).

From a practical perspective, the above overview of practices can be a first orientation for local governments wishing to implement their human rights obligations through fiscal mechanisms. From an analytical perspective, however, this inventory of practices allows for 11 key observations.

First, in our mapping we did not come across a single local government that refers to an existing framework or methodology for developing human rights budgeting or human rights-based approach to budgeting. There thus seems to be no ready-made instrument that can claim to be a universally applicable tool for drawing up a local budget that is primarily guided by human rights principles and standards. Rather, all of the methods identified appear to be customised solutions for a certain local context. Perhaps as a result, the practices identified are applied quite selectively and unsystematically.

Second, the extent to which human rights are legally anchored in the budgets of local authorities varies significantly. Constitutional law is used in five cases.[2] In another five cases, budget laws mention human rights, human rights principles, or respective methods for implementation.[3] Other types of legal provisions establishing a human rights context are municipal directives,[4] national equality laws,[5] decentralisation law,[6] and a Voluntary Local Review Ordinance in Naga City.

Third, the spectrum of local budgeting initiatives that are related to human rights budgeting or a human rights-based approach to budgeting at local level is very broad. Local governments name their human rights efforts in budgets very differently. We came across practices termed "participatory budgeting", "people's budget", "gender budgeting", "outcome-orientation", "results-based budgeting", "priority-based budgeting", "human rights impact assessment", "human rights-sensitive procurement", and many initiatives denoting essentially process- or results-oriented methods in budget planning, implementation, and monitoring. The most common method used by the local authorities in our sample is participatory budgeting in various forms, which 19 authorities state to use.[7] The phrase human rights-based approach to budgeting is used in slightly varying ways by five local authorities.[8] "Gender budgeting" is applied by four of the authorities under scrutiny,[9] "equity budgeting" by two authorities.[10] "Priority-based budgeting"[11] and "performance informed budgeting"[12] are further methods frequently used. We came across only one local practice that explicitly referred to "budgeting with a human rights approach".[13] Local governments thus not only focus on very different topics, but also use very different terms for them.

Fourth, local authorities often extend their human rights-related budgetary measures to only some areas of competence. Merely ten local governments taking a more comprehensive human rights-based approach state that they apply human rights principles in all areas of their competence.[14] The other local governments establish links between budgetary measures and selected areas, such as housing (four),[15] education (four),[16] or health (five).[17] Six cities mention to apply human rights principles in particular to their welfare services,[18] while another five apply them to all their services' budgets.[19] Milwaukee County and Gothenburg mention human rights principles in relation to budget allocation for the diversity of their employees. Five local authorities mention, partly in the context of their commitment to the Sustainable Development Goals, the environment and transport and mobility as areas where they apply human rights principles.[20] Las Condes mentions the justice sector as a field of human rights-based budgeting. Further engagement was stated for culture and sports, economic development, labour, or infrastructure.[21]

Fifth, local governments often use human rights terms when allocating budgets for specific groups and for the promotion or guarantee of selected group rights.[22] Women's rights and gender equality are pursued by eight cities and regions of the sample.[23] Indigenous peoples' rights are targeted by the budget of Mexico City, while Aberdeen and Seoul mention most vulnerable and marginalised groups to benefit from their budgets. In the Austin and Milwaukee County budgets, both in the US, specific attention was paid to racial minorities.

Sixth, the practices of local governments can roughly be differentiated according to whether they are primarily concerned with either human rights principles or human rights standards. On the one hand, local authorities refer to human rights principles when developing, implementing, and reviewing their budgets. Participation (31),[24] non-discrimination (34),[25] accountability (29),[26] and transparency (31)[27] are mentioned most frequently. Good governance, democracy, legitimacy, and representation are also mentioned, as are the principles of universality,[28] indivisibility, interdependency, and inalienability[29] in the budget execution.

On the other hand, local authorities also explicitly target specific human rights standards with their budgets. Non-discrimination and equality, as well as participation in society, are the most prominent rights. A total of 25 cities and regions state that they promote, guarantee, and respect participation.[30] According to 21 authorities, budgets must respect and promote equality, inclusion, and non-discrimination.[31] Good governance, understood as the right to an administration that fulfils human rights, is targeted in 18 local budgets.[32] Social, economic, and cultural rights are directly addressed in the budgets of five cities.[33] The right to health is explicitly mentioned in the budgets of four cities.[34] Other cities mention civil rights,[35] the right to information,[36] and the right to the city[37] as important values to be guaranteed through the use of its financial resources. The budgets of Mexico City, Eugene, and Aberdeen are more generally directed to the fulfilment of rights. The right to education is explicitly mentioned as a right to be realised in the Barcelona budget documentation. Finally, collective and community rights and the rights of minorities are addressed in the budgets of Mexico City and Barcelona.

The results of the mapping indicate that local governments usually either explicitly address a specific human rights standard or mention single human rights principles in the context of budget processes, but hardly ever address human rights standards and processes simultaneously.

Seventh, the approaches identified mainly focus on various budgeting processes. Most governments that implement participatory budgeting, for instance, use this tool to collect proposals for action.[38] Nine local authorities have set up councils or committees to advise the government or act as a jury to decide on project funding.[39] The use of management and urban planning systems for human rights-based approaches to budgeting was mentioned by nine authorities.[40] Six governments state that they apply a people-centred perspective to budgeting.[41] Further six local authorities target human rights standards through objective orientation and strategic planning,[42] while another six governments[43] refer to outcome orientation. Vienna applies gender mainstreaming as the most important instrument of human rights-oriented spending. A needs-based allocation was mentioned as a planning approach by five governments.[44] Aberdeen applies the Equality and Human Rights Impact Assessment; Milwaukee County incorporates the Racial Equity Budget Tool into its Balanced Score Card (an objective-oriented new public management system). An indicator-based monitoring has been introduced in five cities.[45] Four authorities state that they regularly review the impact of budgetary decisions on human rights.[46] Naga City conducts a Voluntary Local Review and measures SDG performance. Mexico City and Barcelona state that they maximise the availability, accessibility, acceptability, and adaptability in the provision of public goods, services, and infrastructure. Some of the processes are related to the progressive realisation of human rights and the obligation to use maximum available resources for respecting, protecting, and fulfilling human rights. However, none of the scrutinised approaches mentioned these obligations as standards or goals of their financial policies.

Eighth, in most of the practices identified, human rights standards or principles are included in the budget at the allocation or spending stage. Human rights considerations are taken into account by 29 local authorities during the planning and drafting processes in the form of citizen participation, application of human rights principles, or direct consideration of human rights in the allocation of financial resources.[47] A total of 27 local authorities[48] mention that they consider human rights standards or principles when executing the budget, and 23 governments[49] refer to human rights in their review processes. Mexico City also refers to human rights in the field of debt and asset management. Only Porto Alegre, Mexico City, and Vermont mention human rights-based approaches to revenue raising. Local practices that focus on raising funds with human rights in mind are therefore comparatively rare.

Ninth, monitoring is foreseen for many of the budgetary measures identified. Thirty-two local governments under scrutiny monitor and evaluate their budgets regularly.[50] While ex ante human rights impact assessment is less prominent (14 governments),[51] the performance is monitored by 16 governments.[52] Twenty-four governments review the actual spending of those budgets where they state that they consider human rights, target human rights standards, or base the budget execution on human rights principles.[53]

Tenth, the mapping revealed very different drivers and incentives for local governments to implement practices related to human rights budgeting or a human rights-based approach to budgeting. A key driving force is the legal, sometimes even constitutional, requirements. One example of this is the case of gender budgeting, which is required by law also for the local level in Austria.[54] Further drivers emerged in connection with decentralisation. Local authorities in Georgia, for instance, have been given human rights competences in several aspects as part of the implementation of the Georgian Law on Decentralization. This has led to the introduction of a number of participatory instruments in Georgian cities and municipalities, including participatory budgeting (Meier and Starl 2022). Yet, drivers may also be deeply rooted in the local government's commitment to human rights. In the City of Gothenburg's budget for 2024, for instance, there are seven overarching goals that reflect the challenges and focus areas that the city intends to work on in both the short and long term (Gothenburg 2023). The objectives are closely related to human rights, as they aim to make Gothenburg an equal and safe city where all residents have the opportunity to participate, to overcome segregation, to create a welfare system that meets the needs of citizens, and to provide employees with a good working environment and working conditions.

Eleventh and finally, we noted that additional areas that are relevant to municipal budgets from a human rights perspective may have remained somewhat under the radar in our mapping. Local governments regularly provide important infrastructure and services that are directly related to human rights, such as infrastructure for the provision of clean drinking water and sewage. In practice, however, the costs of maintaining water infrastructure are generally not budgeted or labelled as funds for the realisation of the human right to drinking water and sanitation. The same applies to many other financial allocations and expenditures for basic infrastructure or services provided by local authorities. Having limited ourselves to a keyword search based heavily on human rights terms, many of these de facto human rights expenditures were not necessarily captured in our mapping.

Building Blocks for Implementing the Human Rights Economy at Local Level

When we attempt to synthesise the above findings from theory and practice, still no concrete picture emerges of how a human rights economy can be implemented at local level through human rights budgeting or a human rights-based approach to budgeting. Rather, we must recognise that there is much unexplored territory in this area that requires further theoretical investigation and deeper analysis of practices. We have gained the impression that as of now there are already many relevant elements for a local human rights economy available, but that these are still very disorganised and must first be sorted and put together before they can take the form of concrete tools and be put into practice.

With this somewhat unsatisfactory result in hand, we felt that a framework of key building blocks would be helpful on the way to designing concrete tools for implementing a human rights economy at the local level. We therefore made an effort to develop such a framework in an interdisciplinary team with researchers having backgrounds in law, sociology, economics, and political science. We based our building blocks on relevant human rights considerations, as largely reflected in the work by the Scottish Human Rights Commission (n.d.) and the OHCHR (2017), relevant budgetary considerations, the lessons drawn from practice in our mapping exercise, and in particular the requirements of the human rights economy as outlined by the UN High Commissioner for Human Rights. The resulting framework shall not only serve to better classify existing practices in future analyses, but also represents a first catalogue of requirements for the further development of concrete tools that claim to be capable of implementing a human rights economy at local level. We propose the following five questions as building blocks for measures or tools that seek to implement the human rights economy at local level.

First, which local authorities' functions are covered by the measure or tool? Local authorities act as a democratic institution, a rule-maker, an employer, a service provider, and/or a private law contractor (Lappalainen et al. 2015). The Swedish Association of Local and Regional Authorities similarly stated that municipalities and regions assume the role of social actors, democratic actors, welfare actors, and employers (Swedish Association of Local Authorities and Regions 2019). They must make decisions about their resources in all these functions to address the challenges faced by their constituents. In doing so, local governments have human rights responsibilities in all of these functions. The logic of the human rights economy requires local governments to consciously orient their actions in all their functions towards the respect, protection, and fulfilment of human rights. This claim to comprehensiveness must be taken into account when developing measures or tools aimed at implementing a human rights economy at local level.

Second, does the measure or tool relate to the budget process or the budget content? This needs to be determined because it makes a fundamental difference, if the inclusion of human rights relates to the process or the content of a local budget, or both. In case the measure or tool addresses the budget process, it needs to be clarified, what specific human rights principles are addressed. Budget processes should in principle always be related to non-discrimination and equality, strengthening accountability, increasing transparency, and/or improving constituency participation, if possible (OHCHR 2017). If the measure or tool relates to the content of the budget, it must be clear which specific human rights standards it addresses. From a legal perspective, local governments are obliged to maximise the resources available for the realisation of human rights, to implement the basic minimum obligations, and to refrain from regressive measures. Therefore, practices intending to implement a human rights economy need to demonstrate how they fulfil these obligations in relation to specific human rights standards. This also means that a local government must have or generate relevant data to demonstrate this commitment and the corresponding outcomes. Economy gives preference to economically efficient allocations. Thus, the human rights economy requires a human rights-informed approach to balance competing claims.

Third, at what stages of the budget cycle does the measure or tool bring the human rights considerations into play? This building block is based on the consideration that human rights may be linked to the generation, allocation, or spending of resources, or may even be embedded in all these phases of the budget process. The comprehensive approach suggested by the human rights economy implies that human rights must be consciously considered in the overall conception and thus potentially in each of these phases.

Fourth, does the measure or tool include mechanisms for adequate monitoring? The very subject of monitoring will depend on whether the measure or tool concerns the budget process or the budget content. A human rights economy requires that the people concerned are able to follow the money through transparent financial processes. In relation to the content of the budget, a local government is required to demonstrate how it will monitor the impact of the budget on the realisation of concrete rights. The question of whether and how local and regional authorities monitor the impact of their measures or instruments lies at the heart of key requirements of the human rights economy, namely transparency and accountability.

Fifth, to what extent is the measure or tool structurally anchored in the existing processes and structures of local governments? The rationale behind this question is that thinking in terms of a human rights economy requires that human rights considerations become a permanent practice and thus a structural component of local government budgets, rather than a one-off initiative. This is also due to the fact that long-term efforts are needed to overcome the challenges that the human rights economy is intended to address.

Conclusions

Our review has shown that human rights budgeting and human rights-based approaches to budgeting are still in the early stages of serving a human rights economy at the local level. Neither theory nor practice convincingly suggests a budgeting model or tool that could be adopted by local governments for this purpose. Instead, the human rights-related budgeting practices currently in use vary widely and appear to be applied selectively without following an overall concept.

This is not surprising. Local governments operate under constrained budgets and with limited autonomy and competing financial priorities, balancing fiscal sustainability with the need to deliver basic services and this often with little guidance on how to integrate human rights into budgeting processes. Moreover, cities and other local-level entities depend on national transfers for a significant portion of their budgets or may face statutory limitations on their ability to raise revenues through local taxes or borrowing, all of which limits their autonomy in resource allocation and somehow questions the very idea of local human rights budgeting. The extent to which relevant local infrastructure and services are included in the budget is usually part of a broader political prioritisation, which is always about meeting unlimited needs with limited resources. While many competing interests need to be considered in this process, the setting of priorities is generally not derived from a budget model that is structurally informed by human rights considerations. Instead, such prioritisation is ultimately brought about by a political decision that may or may not be based on human rights deliberations. The challenge is therefore to ensure that human rights aspects are given sufficient priority so that they can adequately be incorporated into budgetary procedures and contents.

Against this background, our analysis confirms that "[t]he case for a human rights economy that is rooted in human rights obligations and principles, in which people and the planet are at the centre of economic policymaking, has become increasingly powerful" (OHCHR 2024). The human rights economy could be taken up by local governments as a forceful narrative to put people at the centre of their local budgets. Adopting a thinking grounded in the human rights economy could assist local governments to structure and inform the prioritisation process for drawing up the local budget. It would ensure that the budget (1) is informed by the normative content of relevant human rights and (2) is based on a balancing of these individual human rights against each other, and (3) the budgeting, spending, and reviewing processes are in line with the human rights principles. It therefore provides fresh thinking and guidance for local governments on how to use their resources efficiently by setting appropriate priorities responding to the needs of their constituents. Such a structured and transparent prioritisation process would help to bridge the alleged divide between economic governance and human rights and particularly strengthen the accountability of local authorities.

Rethinking in terms of a human rights economy brings further benefits for local governments. Many expenditures by local governments are not yet perceived by the constituents as human rights expenditures because they are not explicitly labelled as such. Under the narrative of a human rights economy, local governments could take stock of all the infrastructures and services with which they already contribute to the respect, protection, and fulfilment of human rights. They could make their relevant expenditure visible and show the rights-bearers concerned how local actions implement their rights in manifold sectors such as healthcare, education, social services, transportation, and housing. Such communication to the public will first and foremost help building trust. Moreover, showing such commitment to upholding human rights through budgetary measures could be very helpful for politicians to get re-elected or to attract international funding.

However, even where local governments are committed to promoting social justice, equality, and the realisation of civil and political as well as economic, social, and cultural rights, our review has shown that they may lack the necessary tools to reflect these commitments in their financial planning. The contours of concrete practices for human rights budgeting or a human rights-based approach to budgeting that can operationalise a human rights economy at the local level have not yet been sufficiently outlined. There is still a fundamental gap in understanding the link between respecting, protecting, and fulfilling socio-economic rights and the financial mechanisms that sustain them. Although the five building blocks presented above are initial starting points for further conceptual work, they cannot obscure the fact that human rights budgeting at the local level is currently more of a vision than a reality.

This points at the urgent need for more research on human rights budgeting, particularly at the local level, where the practical aspects of service delivery intersect with the fundamental principles of human dignity, freedoms, equality, and social justice like nowhere else. Implementing the human rights economy requires a sophisticated understanding of both human rights law and fiscal policy, as well as the ability to integrate these fields into concrete budgetary decisions. Law, sociology, economics, and political science all have their relevant and important understanding of these topics. However, human rights budgeting is not an established field of specialisation in any of these disciplines.

The need for further research within this complex field is broad indeed. A critical area for future applied research will certainly be the development of practical tools and adaptable methodologies for implementing human rights budgeting and human rights-based approaches to budgeting in diverse local contexts. More research will also be needed on the long-term outcomes of such practices, exploring whether they indeed lead to measurable improvements in the overall well-being based on human rights fulfilment. To this end, comparative case studies of cities will need to provide insights into the political conditions which facilitate or hinder success in implementing human rights at the local and regional level. Furthermore, the role of national governments in a multi-level governance structure as well as the technical support of international institutions, and particularly international financial institutions, will be areas of concern. Research should explore how these actors can create enabling environments for human rights budgeting at the local level, including through legal reforms, capacity-building programmes, and the promotion of fiscal decentralisation in the framework of strengthened local self-governance. The research findings, even if preliminary, need to be incorporated into capacity building by providing expertise on human rights economy implementation tools to local government staff involved in budget processes.

Notes

1 We conducted keyword searches in English, Arabic, Portuguese, and other languages to capture a broad spectrum of information. Keywords included "human rights budgeting", "human rights-based approach to budgeting", "human rights-focused budgeting", "outcome orientation", "participatory budgeting", "municipal finance", "inclusive budgeting", "transparent budgeting practices", "budgeting for equal rights", "budgeting for human rights", "gender-based budgeting", "gender-responsive budgeting", "effective budgeting", "good governance", "equity in budgeting", and "socially inclusive budgeting".
2 Vienna; Mexico City; Montevideo; San Francisco; Makueni County.
3 Vienna; Porto Alegre; Mexico City; Gothenburg; Naga City.
4 Barcelona; Eugene; Naga City.
5 Flanders; Aberdeen.
6 Batumi; Gori.
7 Rosario; Porto Alegre; Mexico City; Montevideo; New York City; Vermont; Cascais; Nantes; Şişli; Krasnodar Krai; Makueni County; Cairo; Lahti; Gdańsk; Las Condes; Seoul; Naga City; Batumi; Gori.
8 Mexico City; Barcelona; Gothenburg; Eugene; Battle Creek.
9 Vienna; Barcelona; Fulton County; San Francisco.
10 Milwaukee County; Austin.
11 Duluth; Roanoke; Aberdeen; Salt Lake City; Bainbridge Island; Battle Creek.
12 Flanders; Makueni County.
13 Mexico City.
14 Mexico City; Barcelona; Vienna; San Francisco; Flanders; Aberdeen; Battle Creek; Makueni County; Austin; Naga City.
15 Rosario; Porto Alegre; Vermont; Salt Lake City.
16 Rosario; Porto Alegre; Vermont; Las Condes.
17 Rosario; Porto Alegre; Eugene; Vermont; Las Condes.
18 Gothenburg; Montevideo; Eugene; Seoul; Naga City; Gori.
19 Vienna; Porto Alegre; Seoul; Batumi; Gori.
20 Rosario; Porto Alegre; Eugene; Vermont; Naga City.
21 Porto Alegre; Las Condes (culture and sports), Porto Alegre; Eugene; Gori (economic development), Porto Alegre; Salt Lake City (labour), Montevideo; Gori (infrastructure).
22 Budgets are more often used to achieve something and therefore use promoting or guaranteeing a right instead of respecting or protecting it.
23 Rosario; Vienna; Mexico City; Barcelona; Gothenburg; Fulton County; San Francisco; Flanders.
24 Rosario; Vienna; Porto Alegre; Mexico City; Barcelona; Gothenburg; Montevideo; Eugene; New York City; San Francisco; Vermont; Cascais; Nantes; Şişli; Duluth;

Roanoke; Flanders; Aberdeen; Milwaukee County; Battle Creek; Krasnodar Krai; Makueni County; Austin; Cairo; Lahti; Gdańsk; Las Condes; Seoul; Naga City; Batumi; Gori.

25 Rosario; Vienna; Porto Alegre; Mexico City; Barcelona; Gothenburg; Montevideo; Fulton County; Eugene; New York City; San Francisco; Vermont; Cascais; Nantes; Şişli; Duluth; Roanoke; Flanders; Aberdeen; Salt Lake City; Bainbridge Island; Milwaukee County; Battle Creek; Krasnodar Krai; Makueni County; Austin; Cairo; Lahti; Gdańsk; Las Condes; Seoul; Naga City; Batumi; Gori.

26 Rosario; Porto Alegre; Mexico City; Barcelona; Gothenburg; San Francisco; Montevideo; Cascais; Nantes; Şişli; Duluth; Roanoke; Flanders; Aberdeen; Salt Lake City; Bainbridge Island; Milwaukee County; Battle Creek; Krasnodar Krai; Makueni County; Austin; Cairo; Lahti; Gdańsk; Las Condes; Seoul; Naga City; Batumi; Gori.

27 Rosario; Porto Alegre; Mexico City; Barcelona; Montevideo; Fulton County; New York City; San Francisco; Vermont; Cascais; Nantes; Şişli; Duluth; Roanoke; Flanders; Aberdeen; Salt Lake City; Bainbridge Island; Milwaukee County; Battle Creek; Krasnodar Krai; Makueni County; Austin; Cairo; Lahti; Gdańsk; Las Condes; Seoul; Naga City; Batumi; Gori.

28 Mexico City; Barcelona; Vermont.

29 Barcelona.

30 Rosario; Vienna; Porto Alegre; Mexico City; Barcelona; Montevideo; Fulton County; New York City; Vermont; Cascais; Nantes; Şişli; Aberdeen; Milwaukee County; Krasnodar Krai; Makueni County; Cairo; Lahti; Gdańsk; Las Condes; Seoul; Naga City; Batumi; Gori.

31 Rosario; Vienna; Porto Alegre; Barcelona; Gothenburg; Montevideo; Fulton County; Eugene; New York City; San Francisco; Vermont; Duluth; Flanders; Aberdeen; Salt Lake City; Milwaukee County; Battle Creek; Makueni County; Austin; Lahti; Gdańsk.

32 Rosario; Porto Alegre; Mexico City; Barcelona; Fulton County; Cascais; Duluth; Roanoke; Montevideo; Bainbridge Island; Milwaukee County; Krasnodar Krai; Makueni County; Cairo; Gdańsk; Naga City; Batumi; Gori.

33 Mexico City; Gothenburg; Eugene; Vermont; Aberdeen.

34 Eugene; Vermont; Bainbridge Island; Las Condes.

35 Fulton County; Eugene.

36 Montevideo; Cairo.

37 Barcelona.

38 Rosario; Montevideo; Cascais; Nantes; Şişli; Krasnodar Krai; Makueni County; Batumi; Gori.

39 Rosario; Porto Alegre; Gothenburg; Montevideo; Makueni County; Lahti; Seoul; Batumi; Gori.

40 Mexico City; Barcelona; Gothenburg; Eugene; Duluth; Roanoke; Flanders; Aberdeen; Milwaukee County.

41 Gothenburg, Barcelona, Vermont, Roanoke, Aberdeen and Makueni County.

42 Gothenburg; Eugene; Duluth; Roanoke; Flanders; Aberdeen.

43 Vienna; Mexico City; Roanoke; Flanders; Aberdeen; Naga City.

44 Vermont; Flanders; Aberdeen; Krasnodar Krai; Makueni County; Seoul.

45 Mexico City; Barcelona; Eugene; Aberdeen; Naga City.

46 San Francisco; Flanders; Aberdeen; Makueni County.

47 Rosario; Vienna; Porto Alegre; Mexico City; Barcelona; Gothenburg; Montevideo; San Francisco; Vermont; Cascais; Nantes; Şişli; Duluth; Roanoke; Flanders; Aberdeen; Salt Lake City; Milwaukee County; Battle Creek; Krasnodar Krai; Makueni County; Cairo; Lahti; Gdańsk ; Las Condes; Seoul; Naga City; Batumi; Gori.

48 Rosario; Vienna; Porto Alegre; Mexico City; Barcelona; Gothenburg; Montevideo; Eugene; New York City; San Francisco; Vermont; Cascais; Duluth; Roanoke; Aberdeen; Salt Lake City; Milwaukee County; Battle Creek; Krasnodar Krai; Makueni County; Austin; Lahti; Gdańsk ; Las Condes; Seoul; Naga City; Gori.
49 Rosario; Vienna; Porto Alegre; Mexico City; Barcelona; Gothenburg; Eugene; San Francisco; Vermont; Cascais; Duluth; Roanoke; Flanders; Aberdeen; Salt Lake City; Battle Creek; Krasnodar Krai; Makueni County; Lahti; Gdańsk ; Las Condes; Seoul; Naga City; Gori.
50 Rosario; Vienna; Porto Alegre; Mexico City; Gothenburg; Montevideo; Fulton County; Eugene; New York City; San Francisco; Vermont; Cascais; Nantes; Şişli; Duluth; Roanoke; Flanders; Aberdeen; Salt Lake City; Bainbridge Island; Milwaukee County; Battle Creek; Krasnodar Krai; Makueni County; Austin; Cairo; Lahti; Gdańsk ; Las Condes; Seoul; Naga City; Batumi; Gori.
51 Rosario; Vienna; Mexico City; Barcelona; Montevideo; Fulton County; Eugene; San Francisco; Vermont; Aberdeen; Las Condes; Seoul; Naga City; Gori.
52 Rosario; Porto Alegre; Montevideo; Fulton County; Eugene; New York City; Vermont; Flanders; Salt Lake City; Krasnodar Krai; Makueni County; Gdańsk ; Las Condes; Seoul; Naga City; Gori.
53 Rosario; Vienna; Porto Alegre; Mexico City; Barcelona; Gothenburg; Montevideo; Fulton County; Eugene; New York City; San Francisco; Nantes; Roanoke; Flanders; Aberdeen; Milwaukee County; Battle Creek; Austin; Cairo; Gdańsk ; Las Condes; Seoul; Naga City; Gori.
54 Gender budgeting has been enshrined in the Austrian Federal Constitution since 1 September 2009. Accordingly, the federal government, federal states, and municipalities must endeavour to achieve equality between women and men in budget management.

Bibliography

Blyberg, Ann. n.d. "Human Rights Budgeting and Budget Analysis." *Report authored for the Scottish Human Rights Commission*. Accessed September 3, 2024. https://www.scottishhumanrights.com/media/1706/human-rights-budgeting-and-budget-analysis-oct-2015-vfinal.doc

Centre for the Promotion of Human Rights at the Local and Regional Levels. 2023. "Governing the City by Human Rights Objectives: Embedding Human Rights in Public Management Instruments." In Gerd Oberleitner and Klaus Starl (eds.), *Human Rights Go Local Publication Series*, Vol. 4. HRGL Publishing.

Danish Institute for Human Rights. 2020. *Driving Change Through Public Procurement: A Toolkit on Human Rights for Policy Makers and Public Buyers*. https://www.humanrights.dk/files/media/document/dihr_toolkit_public_procurement_2020_webaccessible.pdf

European Union Agency for Fundamental Rights. 2022. *Human Rights Cities in the European Union: A Guide to Support Local Authorities in Making Human Rights Part of People's Daily Life*. https://fra.europa.eu/sites/default/files/fra_uploads/fra-2022-guide-human-rights-cities_en.pdf

Fundar, International Human Rights Internship Program, and International Budget Project. 2004. *Dignity Counts: A Guide to Using Budget Analysis to Advance Human Rights*. https://internationalbudget.org/wp-content/uploads/Dignity-Counts-A-Guide-to-Using-Budget-Analysis-to-Advance-Human-Rights-English.pdf

Gothenburg. 2023. *Budget 2024 Göteborgs Stad*. https://goteborg.se/wps/wcm/connect/a485e679-38a2-4ad1-814c-30fb9d33eb9f/Beslutad+budget+f%C3%B6r+G%C3%B6teborgs+Stad+2024%2C+S%2C+V%2C+MP.pdf?MOD=AJPERES

International Budget Partnership. n.d. "Open Budget Survey." Accessed September 3, 2024. https://internationalbudget.org/network/

Lappalainen, Paul, Isabella Meier, Ingrid Nicoletti, and Klaus Starl. 2015. "Toolkit for Equality: The Local Level - Mapping and Clustering of Policy Approaches." https://www.etc-graz.eu/wp-content/uploads/2020/09/TOOLKIT_Survey-Report.pdf

Meier, Isabella, and Klaus Starl. 2022. "Strengthening human rights at the local level in Georgia: A Case Study Based on the European Charter of Local Self-Government." In Philip Czech, Lisa Heschl, Karin Lukas, Manfred Nowak, and Gerd Oberleitner (eds.), *European Yearbook on Human Rights 2022*, 567–585. Intersentia.

Scottish Human Rights Commission. n.d. "What is Human Rights Budget Work?" Accessed September 3, 2024. https://www.scottishhumanrights.com/projects-and-programmes/human-rights-budget-work/

Swedish Association of Local Authorities and Regions. 2019. "Human Rights on The Local and Regional Level – A Platform for Policy and Operational Development." https://skr.se/download/18.45167e4317e2b341b24ae41c/1642689849507/5509.pdf

Swedish International Centre for Local Democracy. n.d. "Human Rights Budgeting & Corruption in Local Level Governance." Accessed September 3, 2024. https://learn.icld.se/course/human-rights-budgeting-corruption-in-local-level-governance/

United Nations High Commissioner for Human Rights. 2023. "Vision of the Office of the United Nations High Commissioner for Human Rights for Reinforcing its Work in Promoting and Protecting Economic, Social and Cultural Rights within the Context of Addressing Inequalities in the Recovery from the COVID-19 Pandemic." *Report of the United Nations High Commissioner for Human Rights*, A/HRC/54/35. https://documents.un.org/doc/un.oc/gen/g23/145/44/pdf/g2314544.pdf

United Nations Office of the High Commissioner for Human Rights in Mexico. 2010. *Latin American Faculty of Social Sciences-Mexico, Fundar, Gesoc, Políticas Públicas y Presupuestos con Perspectiva de Derechos Humanos. Manual Operativo para Servidoras y Servidores Públicos*. UNOHCHR-Mexico.

United Nations Office of the High Commissioner for Human Rights. 2024. *Management Plan for 2024–2027*. https://www.ohchr.org/sites/default/files/documents/aboutus/OHCHR-OMP-2024-2027.pdf

United Nations Office of the High Commissioner for Human Rights. 2012. *Human Rights Indicators: A Guide to Measurement and Implementation*. United Nations. https://www.ohchr.org/en/instruments-and-mechanisms/human-rights-indicators

United Nations Office of the High Commissioner for Human Rights. 2017. *Realizing Human Rights through Government Budgets*. United Nations. https://www.ohchr.org/Documents/Publications/RealizingHRThroughGovernmentBudgets.pdf

11 Devolution and the Right to Budgetary Participation

Insights from Subnational Governments in Midlands Province, Zimbabwe

Edson Paul Mutema, Zvimekria Clive Mukushwa, and Amos Zevure

Introduction and Background of Study

This chapter contributes to current discussions among scholars, policy makers, human rights advocates on the relationship between participatory budgeting (PB) and the concept of human rights economy. The term "human rights economy" means using human rights obligations to guide budget decisions and to invest sufficiently in public education, health, social protection and other rights to make meaningful action to reduce inequalities, and to refrain from austerity measures, social cuts and retrogressions (Office of the High Commissioner for Human Rights, 2024). The approach emphasises that economic development should not only focus on growth metrics such as Gross National Product and Gross Domestic Product but also on ensuring that all individuals can enjoy their fundamental rights and freedoms (United Nations Pact for the Future Action 53). A number of scholars of local governance tend to concur that there is minimum citizen participation in local authorities' budgetary planning process in Zimbabwe (Munyede & Machengete, 2020). Their findings largely cite citizen apathy in budgetary planning processes, a high level of exclusion and poor budget consultation. The chapter examines the low uptake in the face of a devolution policy. It examines the extent to which citizens are engaged in the budgetary formulation process, focusing on selected subnational authorities in Zimbabwe's Midlands Province. The chapter will argue that PB serves as a vibrant machinery for advancing the principles of a human rights economy by cultivating citizen engagement, promoting accountability, addressing social inequalities and backing up democratic governance.

Citizen participation, which is one of the principles that anchors on the human rights economy approach, entails the redistribution of decision-making powers which enabled the *have-not* citizens, currently excluded in the political and economic processes, to be deliberately included (Arnstein, 1969). The United Nations Economic Commission for Africa Executive Secretary, as cited in Makumbe (1996), observed that "the democratisation of the development process, by which we mean the empowerment of the people, their involvement

DOI: 10.4324/9781003474845-15

in decision making, in the implementation process is a *sine qua non* for socio-economic recovery and transformation."

The Universal Declaration of Human Rights (UDHR) of 1948 recognises, promotes and respects rights for every citizen to participate in the conduct of public affairs (Brown, 2016). The Universal Declaration was a giant leap towards promoting the concept of participatory governance which broadens the democratic space for historically marginalised citizens to have a voice in the administration of public affairs intended to improve their livelihoods (Brown, 2016). Additionally, it positions citizens at the epicentre of policy planning by giving them the right to participate. Article 21(1) states that "everyone has the right to take part in the government of his/her country, directly or through freely chosen representatives" (United Nations, 1948). Devolution policy is highly expected to be delivering what is espoused in the UDHR.

As one of the several approaches of participatory governance or democratic innovations, PB is described by Goldfrank (2012) as a direct-democracy model of budgeting where citizens at large are offered an opportunity to learn about government operations, deliberate, debate and influence the allocation of public resources. It is in this context that this chapter explores how citizens and other community-level stakeholders are practically participating in budgeting planning processes in selected subnational governments in Midlands Province.

History of Subnational Governance in Zimbabwe since 1890

Before the arrival of the European colonialists in the late 1880s, community affairs were administered by traditional leaders such as the traditional chiefs, headmen and village heads (Kurebwa, 2015). The Africans were engaged in community governance through *matare/bahlezi idale* (Chiefs' or headmen's meetings) (Marango et al., 2020). This traditional participatory space was largely dominated by male participants by virtue of the patriarchal nature of the society. Walby (1990) indicates that the practice reinforced gender inequality which in turn strengthened male dominance in society and impeded women's engagement in community initiatives. The 1890 British colonial rule saw the establishment of a western local governance system which replaced the traditional practices of community governance.

The British South African Company entrenched colonial rule by introducing repressive legislation which included, among others, the Board of Management Act of 1892, the Town Management Ordinance of 1894, the Municipal Law of 1897 and the Urban Councils Act of 1973 (formerly the Municipal Act of 1930) (Madhekeni & Zhou, 2012). These discriminatory laws saw urban residential areas being divided along racial lines. The townships (urban) characterised by poor service delivery were reserved for black urban dwellers while the white community resided in affluent urban areas where service delivery was efficient and prioritised. In agreement, Paradza (2010), Ranger (2007) and Wekwete (1991) state that the urbanised areas were reserved for the white minority while the black majority were merely employees who were required to be registered through the municipalities in accordance with the Vagrancy Act (Chapter 10), 1960 and the Natives (Urban Areas) Accommodation and Registration Act of 1922. The colonial regime established two unequal nations in a single country which was the European nation and that of Africans. The right to strike against poor service delivery and working conditions, and inadequate wages, as well as to participate in governance processes, was outlawed by the Law-and-Order Maintenance Act of 1960. In addition to this, the Native Affairs Amendment Act of 1959 also abolished public meetings of 12 or more people without the authority of the Native Commissioner (Native Affairs Amendment, 1959).

Colonial laws were largely designed to consolidate the colonial hegemony over urban African residents (Jonga, 2014). Subsequently, African dwellers were segregated from participating in the processes of urban local governance (Yoshikuni, 2006). Only the male Africans aged 21 years of age and above who occupied a property valued £75 and an annual income of £50 were permitted to vote in terms of the 1898 Reform Proclamation (Muchanyuka & Jeranyama, 2016). All the qualifications were far beyond the reach of many Africans (Muchanyuka & Jeranyama, 2016). As a result, very few Africans qualified to vote under these stringent conditions because property rights and better wages were exclusively reserved for the white settler minority. The colonial system of governance continued up to 1980 when an independent black majority government came in.

The post-colonial government inherited a highly centralised administrative bureaucracy which (in size, composition, operation and orientation) was heavily segregated (Chigudu, 2014). The local authorities continued to derive their legal existence from the Urban Councils Act as the Lancaster House Constitution of 1979 was silent on their legal status. This administrative structure lacked compatibility with the socio-economic political imperatives of nation building, reconciliation and transformation of the economy along equity lines advanced by the new administration (Zhou, 2012; Agere, 1998).

After realising these shortcomings, the government gradually reformed the inherited local government systems to match the ethos that inspired the armed liberation struggle. The Robert Mugabe administration pursued a number of legal, institutional and policy reforms to redress the legacy of colonial rule (Mapuva and Muyengwa-Mapuva, 2015). The government also issued a Policy Directive on Decentralisation and Development in 1984 which gave the previously marginalised Africans the latitude to participate in local development planning processes. A 1984 Prime Minister's Directive guided the establishment of grassroots participation structures and provided a framework for coordination of government institutions' participation in rural development (Chakaipa, 2010). However, limited administrative authority and political power were transferred to local government authorities and nothing much was realised from these policies in terms of promoting citizen participation (Munzwa and Jonga, 2010; Government of Zimbabwe, 2004).

In the early 1990s, Zimbabwe started to experience massive demand for democratic reforms and respect of human rights by civil society movements (Sachikonye, 2017). As observed by Zhou, Mukonza and Zvoushe (2016) as well as Moyo (1993), budgetary practice of early post-independence was state centrist and marked by pervasive state interventionism which surrenders more policy decision-making powers to the executive. Due to pressure in 2000, a PB model was adopted. This PB model derived its legal implementation from the Decentralisation and Development Policy of 1984, the Urban Councils Act (29:15) and Ministerial directives (issued from 2012) (Jonga, 2014). The PB model provides an opportunity for direct-democratic participation of citizens in the use of public funds to ensure efficient service delivery, equality, transparency and accountability (Marumahoko, Chigwata & Nhede, 2018). Later, this PB model was mandatorily adopted by all urban local councils to allow urban dwellers to take part in city budget planning process through ward development committee systems. Nevertheless, citizen participation remained low despite cosmetic efforts put by the government since there was no political will to fully implement the policy.

In 2013, the government adopted a constitution that breathed new democratic features to the local government system through the introduction of a devolution policy (Chigwata, Marumahoko & Madhekeni, 2019). It promotes citizen participation through devolution as provided for in Chapter 14 of the Constitution of Zimbabwe Amendment Number 20 of 2013. This constitutional development saw the establishment of the three-tier system of government in line with Section 264(1) of the Zimbabwean 2013 Constitution which recognises the multi-tier system of government that includes provincial and metropolitan councils and local municipalities (urban and rural) (Constitution of Zimbabwe, 2013). The Emmerson Mnangagwa administration, which assumed office in November 2017, started to implement the devolution framework in 2019 through the disbursement of devolution funds by the national treasury. The Constitution provides that the intergovernmental fiscal transfer targets at least 5 per cent of national revenue in any financial year to be given to lower tiers of government in order to finance the devolution agenda in terms of Section 301(3) of the Constitution. Devolution, which opens the democratic space for citizen participation in development programmes, has been regarded as the key pillar for spearheading the development agenda by the government (Zimbabwe Economic Policy Analysis and Research Unit, 2020).

In 2021, the government launched the National Development Strategy (NDS1) 1 (2021–2025) to promote inclusive participatory development under the country's Vision 2030. It is anchored on the global aspirations espoused in the Sustainable Development Goals and Agenda 2030 of ensuring inclusive and transformative development, aiming to leave no one and no place behind which is at the heart of attaining sustainable development. In the NDS1 document, the government provides the organisational structures that allow citizens to take part in development planning processes in line with the devolution agenda (Government of Zimbabwe, 2020).

The Second Republic has made tremendous efforts to position the citizens at the epicentre of driving the NDS 1 in order to achieve the Vision 2030. In turn, the PB model becomes the yardstick to establish the working of devolution under the new administration. The need to embrace an effective participatory budget process becomes imperative in this era of devolution and constitutionalised local governance.

Though the Constitution provides for citizen participation in public policy affairs, the environment is still unfavourable to citizen participation in local government due to factors such as resource constraints, communication problems, bureaucratic structures and the dispositions of the implementers (Manduna, Zinyama & Nhema, 2015). The practice of citizen participation in local governance is generally still minimal in Zimbabwe. This is largely attributed to elite domination, among other deep-rooted hindrances (Madzivanyika, 2014). It is against this backdrop that this chapter sought to find milestones made so far as promotion of citizen participation in budget programmes is concerned.

Methodology

The study employed a qualitative research approach, collecting data through in-depth interviews with key informants (Chief Executive Officers, Town Clerks, Councillors, Resident Associations and Traditional leaders), focus group discussions (residents and community members), questionnaires, non-participant observations, desktop study and netnography. Thematic and content data analysis approach was used.

Theoretical Framework

The chapter is underpinned by the ladder of citizen participation theory that was propounded by Sherry Arnstein (Arnstein 1969). Focal essence of the concept of participation is on redistributing power to the *have-not* citizens historically excluded in government programmes, for them to now take part in processes of governance (Arnstein, 1969). To further understand participation, this study presents Arnstein's ladder as a theory of citizen participation. See Figure 11.1

Arnstein's ladder of citizen participation is one of the most referenced and influential models in the discipline of democratic public participation for planners (Gaber, 2019). This ladder illustrates how citizens are denied power and control to influence public policy planning and decision-making processes that include budgeting (Arnstein, 1969).

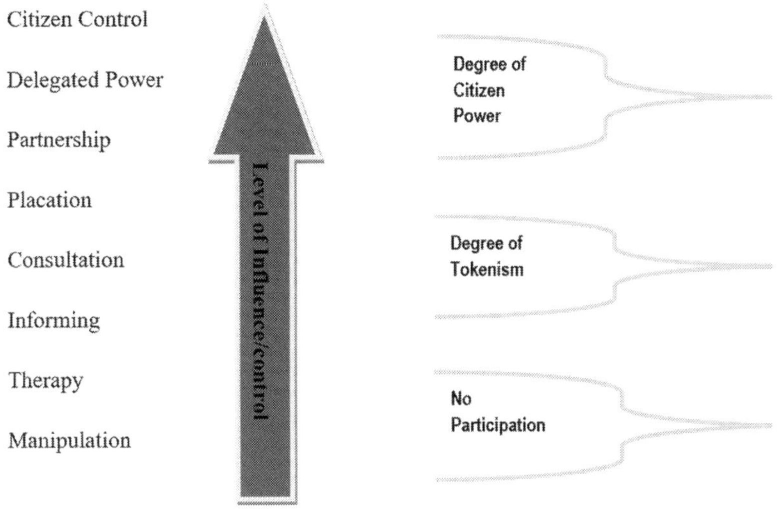

Figure 11.1 Illustration of Arnstein's ladder, a theory of citizen participation.

Source: Arnstein (1969: 217).

There are eight distinct rungs that make up this ladder of citizen participation. The rungs include manipulation, therapy, informing, consultation, placation, partnership, delegated power and citizen control. Manipulation is when the citizens are influenced to support the approval of public officials' decisions through propaganda or being involved in powerless advisory committees (Arnstein, 1969). Practically, the rung of therapy entails educating citizens on government programmes through public meetings or media platforms. Brooks and Harris (2008) explain that the rung of therapy assumes that the local communities are incompetent to make decisions and those in power subject citizens to paternalistic education exercises, or clinical groups, as a form of enlightenment.

In the first tiers (manipulation and therapy), the budget decisions are solely made by the central government officials in their offices and handed down to citizens as mere consumers or informing involves the two flows of information (for example, budget-related information) from public officials to citizens through media platforms, pamphlets and public meetings with no room for feedback or citizens' input (Theyyan, 2016; Arnstein, 1969).

The rung of consultation encompasses the exchange of information between public bureaucrats and citizens through meetings or surveys of which citizens' input is not guaranteed for due consideration. Arnstein (1969) asserts that the rung of placation allows the accommodation of citizens in influential committees or boards that are responsible for making policy decisions, but the public officials still enjoy more decision-making powers. Mapuva and Muyengwa-Mapuva

(2015) claim that participation in the second tier (informing, consultation and placation) only involves informing and consulting local communities without giving them the assurance that their budget input will be taken into consideration in the policy formulation stage.

Rungs such as partnership, delegated power and citizen control have attempted to accord both citizens and public servants the same powers to co-influence the design of policies as well as arriving at budget decisions. In the level of partnership, public office bearers and citizens share the responsibilities to plan and make decisions on government programmes or policies as they wield equal influence and power in planning committees or policy boards (Arnstein, 1969). The rung for delegated power empowers the citizens to hold those in authority accountable so that they deliver on planned development programmes and policies in a transparent manner as they also participate in decision-making committees or boards (Mayanja, 2020; Arnstein, 1969).

The last rung of citizen control is situated at the top of this ladder. Here, when the citizens are empowered with power, they can make budget decisions at planning or formulation stage. For Collins and Ison (2006), the appeal of this model lies in its simplicity and ability to expose, in pictorial form, the power dynamics in many public sector institutions such as subnational authorities. Despite this, the model has been criticised by some scholars (Collins & Ison, 2006) for being insufficient to make sense of participation at a conceptual or practical level. Arnstein (1969) also acknowledges that the model, regarding citizen power, is not distributed neatly as issues of racism, paternalism and resistance of some power holders and ignorance were ignored. Nevertheless, for the purposes of assessing the impact of devolution policy in promoting PB it is very relevant.

Discussion of Findings

Citizen participation in public policy formulation programmes such as budgeting ensures that the policies are grounded on citizen's preferences and that citizens can understand the tough decisions that the government has to make for the public good (Fagence, 2014). To that end, participants were asked the question: Can you explain the major gaps in the budgetary planning process in your local authority?

Participants had mixed opinions and experiences of the gaps in PB programmes. Council officials, representatives of ratepayers and ratepayers' associations, representatives of informal traders and ordinary residents who participated in this study have a general agreement regarding the dissemination of budget information to stakeholders and residents. They revealed that there is poor dissemination of budget information to stakeholders and residents. They noted that this is one of the major gaps negatively affecting subnational governments' budgeting programmes. They sometimes access budget performance and proposed budget documents through social media platforms such as WhatsApp. The following illustrate participants' views and experiences with regard to poor dissemination of information where a representative of the informal traders explained that:

> [I]n my opinion, I think the model of participatory budgeting is not allowing adequate flow of budget information from the local council to ordinary residents. There is a culture of concealing audited, proposed and final budget documents by the council officials and Councilors. We do not know why. In one budget consultation meeting that I attended at Mutapa Hall, the proposed budget was presented from a piece of paper and residents were not given any budget report prior to that Ward budget consultation meeting. Also, the information concerning budget consultation schedules is not well shared with residents and that is why most people fail to attend such meetings.
>
> (Participant 1-FGD-03GR)

Another participant also stated that:

> With my experience in attending these annual ward budget consultation meetings, I have noticed that the biggest gap affecting budget consultation meetings is poor dissemination or sharing of critical budget documents before interviewing stakeholders and after the approval of the council budget. In 2023 and 2024, our city council posted a too technical budget performance and proposed budget statement on the Ward WhatsApp groups but physical copies were not availed. Another lacking issue is that timetable for budget consultation meetings is not shared timely and sometimes we receive the information through rumours which may mean that our council officials and Councilors are sleeping on duty or they are choosing who is supposed to attend the budget meetings. We expect our city council to interface with every resident.
>
> (KI-O14KK)

A visually impaired participant remarked that:

> In my opinion, I think the weakness with budget consultation programs is that our city council is not disclosing budget information such as budget documents or budget schedules to residents. For example, these budget consultation meetings are conducted without our knowledge as the blind community because the information for budget venues and timetable is not packaged to suit our language preferences. I have never seen a budget written in braille language. Furthermore, budget consultation schedules are not dispatched to us.
>
> (K1-17SH)

Furthermore, it was observed that the budget consultation meetings in Gokwe were conducted in the presence of state security personnel from Zimbabwe

Republic Police and Municipal Police Officers. Residents felt uncomfortable to freely air their views. Also observed in Mvuma and Zvishavane was that no municipal official was assigned to interpret the budget presentation for the deaf in case they had attended the budget consultation meetings.

A representative of residents' associations stressed that:

> Though I applaud the Town Councils for sharing the budget performance and proposed budget documents to ratepayers and residents through Ward WhatsApp budget consultation groups, there is a weakness in that budget reports are too technical for illiterate residents to comprehend. The approach excludes other social groups such as the deaf and blind as the budget reports are only presented in one language. Another issue is that not all residents have access to WhatsApp platforms due to the cost of bundles or type of phone gadgets they use.
>
> (KI-019MV)

Complaining about the technical jargon of the council budget reports, one respondent said that:

> Though we are now receiving the budget documents electronically, the budget reports are marred with technical jargons and big figures. Some of us, we are not financially literate to understand some of the budget concepts and figures.
>
> (KI-025GWR)

The foregoing indicates that dissemination of budget information in seven subnational authorities studied is still generally very minimal. Despite these findings, a study done in South Africa has shown that budget openness and transparency play a critical role in ensuring accountability in all levels of governance (Reutener and Fourie, 2015). The failure to effectively disseminate information generates mistrust on the part of the general public which tends to kill their spirit of participation in the future (Cabannes, 2005). Access to detailed and timely budget information by citizens is one of the cardinal tenets to ensure vertical accountability, transparency and credibility in PB programmes at local level (Rainero and Brescia, 2018). Mapuva (2014) acknowledges that ratepayers and residents' associations are critical in ensuring the smooth flow of information between government institutions and the people in order to enhance accountability and transparency at local level. Failure to support these civil society groups may negatively derail the efficient dissemination of information to ratepayers and residents. As shown above, devolution policy has not yet addressed the problem.

It also emerged that lack of inclusivity and transparency is one of the gaps characterising the PB model used in the local councils of Zimbabwe. Participants such as the differently abled and old aged people clearly indicated that the PB practice is lacking inclusivity as the venues and means of shared budget information used by local councils are perpetuating their exclusion. This is contrary to the right of participation in budgetary programmes as espoused in the devolution policy and the United Nations Convention of rights of people with disabilities Article 29, which guarantees people with disabilities the right to participate in political and public life. PB is still affected by a transparency deficit as budget information is ineffectively disclosed to ratepayers and residents.

Failure by subnational authorities to provide public education and awareness is one of the gaps affecting PB planning practices. It came out that representatives of ratepayers and residents' associations mostly train residents who are affiliated to their associations or trusts, and such training meetings are conducted in hotels that are far removed from accessibility of other ordinary residents, thereby jeopardising their rights. Contrary, representatives of ratepayers and residents' associations cited limited funds as the major obstacle that affects rolling out of capacity-building workshops with the general public.

A participant stated that:

> In my view, the major gap that is derailing the participatory budgeting scheme is the lack of civic education and awareness on budgeting issues. Most ordinary residents are generally illiterate in financial matters. Ratepayers and residents' associations operating in Zvishavane only train a very few people while the majority are left untrained.
>
> (Participant 6-FGD-02ZV)

Similar views were highlighted by a senior official of a ratepayers and residents' association who affirmed that:

> I think the ordinary residents are not seeing the importance of a participatory budgeting system because they have not been trained on budgetary planning and its importance to the society.
>
> (KI: 04GWR)

A council official also revealed that:

> There is a lack of budget knowledge in most of the ordinary Vungu residents and other stakeholders due to limited public awareness programmes and training of the local communities in budget expectations and procedures.
>
> (K1-030VG)

A ward member of a residents' trust revealed that:

> Though I had the opportunity to attend a workshop on civic education and awareness on budgeting organised by a local civil group, I noticed

> that such workshops are catering for few residents. The majority are left out.
>
> (KI-041GK)

In a focus group discussion, it was narrated that:

> In my opinion, I think the PB model is good but ordinary residents are not receiving any form of training pertaining to participatory budgeting issues. You find that some people just attend budget consultation meetings without adequate appreciation of what is a budget. Some ordinary residents end up raising irrelevant issues instead of budget related issues which is clear evidence of lacking training and knowledge.
>
> (Participant 1-FGD-02MV)

Results show that most residents are not aware of community issues to raise during ward budget consultation proceedings. During budget consultation proceedings, it was observed that some residents diverted from the budget agenda during their contributions to discuss political issues or raise service delivery complaints. This seems to reflect that the residents are not aware what they are supposed to contribute during ward budget consultation meetings. Matovu (2007) confirms that there is a gap of public education and awareness programmes on PB practices in African countries that are inclusive of Zimbabwe.

Results in this study have also found that incentives to motivate citizens' desire to participate in budgeting by local councils are missing. Participants believed that they feel motivated to take part in local authorities' governance processes when their contributions are considered, service delivery is improved, and when they also receive T-shirts or transport money. Some participants cited ignorance on the part of residents, poor service delivery, loss of trust and confidence in their local authorities, work commitments and corruption allegations as factors that demotivate them from participating.

This is in agreement with Lilleker and Koc-Michalska (2016) who found that several forms of citizen participatory practices, including PB, are failing due to lack of motivation. Lack of motivation for the general citizens and other stakeholders was a big gap crippling the implementation of PB at local level in some Asian countries (Mills, 2017). On the other hand, this study contradicts Sobanjo (2016) who concludes that the success story of Brazil's PB is attributed to community-based organisations' role in motivating the local communities to participate at local level.

Unlike in Zimbabwe, Brazil's delegates are provided with transport to attend budget meetings which is one of the key factors to motivate citizenry participation. In light of this, Airong and Xiang (2008) suggest that local government sectors should develop mechanisms that motivate citizens to have interest to take part in budgetary participatory processes. A number of scholars share the same view that PB practice flourishes when the electorate are sufficiently motivated to participate in decision-making on issues that affect their daily lives (Bashir and Muhammed, 2012).

Failure of council budgets to reflect citizens' development and service delivery needs and priorities is one of the gaps identified in this study. Participants believe that city budgets are not reflecting their inputs. While council officials argued that the final budgets actually reflect every stakeholder's interest as it is one of the key requirements considered by the parent ministry whenever they are approving local authority budgets.

One participant revealed that:

> With my experience of attending budget consultation meetings, I noticed that what attendees say is not what is announced by our municipality. It seems our municipality is merely consulting us to rubber stamp their pre-municipal budget document because the budget draft always sails through at local authority level despite our strong objections. The problem is that we only comment on the draft budget rather than contributing to its formulation.
>
> (KI-015VG)

Similarly, Marumahoko, Chigwata and Nhede (2018) found that in Kwekwe, Zimbabwe, residents' inputs are not being considered in the final budget and this is attributed to the fact that council officials have the final say. Marumahoko et al. (2018) further reveal that the citizens' inputs during ward budget consultation meetings are largely taken as mere recommendations and there is no guarantee that their input will be incorporated into the final budget because this is regarded as a consultation process.

Mansuri and Vijayendra (2013) and Abraham and Platteau (2004) suggest that elite domination in budgeting may reinforce existing inequalities especially when the voices of local elites, the rich and interest groups have greater influence in the budget process than those of the poor community. As demonstrated in the second rung of Arnstein's Ladder of Citizen Participation, this means local authorities are implementing a tokenistic approach of consultation which is characterised by a high level of manipulation and elite domination where residents' input has no guarantee for consideration in the final budget (Arnstein, 1969). The interpretation may mean that residents have no power to influence final budget decisions.

The other gap that emerged from this study is that the PB process and practice is mainly dominated by elected local political elites and appointed administrative officials. However, ordinary residents play a very limited role in the budgetary planning processes. Respondents indicated that the proposed budget drafts are formulated without them and imposed to merely make comments on adjustments of rates, user and license fees. Researchers observed that the cities of Gweru, Shurugwi and Kwekwe presented a prepared budget proposal during the ward budget consultative meetings. Another observation was that the ward consultation proceedings were dominated by the appointed council officials who led the proceedings, and the elected Chairperson of the Finance Committee assisted in explaining the budget contents. This practice gives citizens little leverage to hold the government accountable and enter into a 'social contract', on the one hand, and turn the state into a network of actors who aim to rule through new patrimonial and prebendalism (Verkoren & Kamphuis, 2013).

The implication of the top-down and elite-dominated approaches is that there is exclusion of citizens from full participation and their governance and service delivery needs will not be captured in the consolidated budget (Juma, Rotich and Mulongo, 2014).

Adopting a bottom-up implementation structure in PB helps the budget document to mirror the interests of citizens rather than the elite only. Using Arnstein's Ladder of Citizen Participation Theory, this form of citizen involvement in budgeting epitomises the category of tokenism as residents are merely consulted without guarantee that their inputs will be considered in the consolidated budgets (Arnstein, 1969).

The study reveals that political polarisation and the current economic downturn are negatively affecting the effective and meaningful participation of citizens in local authorities' ward-based PB meetings in Zimbabwe. Most participants reveal that ward Councillors mobilise residents who are affiliated to their political party organisations. Some ordinary residents are not attending ward budget consultation meetings because of the economic crisis prevailing in the country which demotivates them. This is regardless of devolution policy provisions which call for rights to participation in budgetary programmes.

It is evident that weak transparent systems and corruption are major factors impeding full participation of citizens in local councils' budgetary planning processes in Zimbabwe. Participants revealed that deliberate failure by council officials to make budget decisions more accessible to the general public and rampant allegations of corruption kill the spirit of citizens' participation. Corruption thrives in weak accountability and transparency systems. Corruption of all forms generates and perpetuates distributional inequality, enriching the minority and impoverishing the majority. Corrupt practices result in non-delivery of essential services as money meant for these services ends up in private hands, thus denying the community of a better life and non-adherence to the principles of rule of law, accountability, transparency, inclusion and participation.

The foregoing has dampened citizens' confidence and faith in local councils. These results are also corroborated by Dube (2011) who observes that perceived systemic corruption and weak governance systems adversely affect the performance of all public enterprises, including urban local authorities' PB systems. There is also evidence in Brazil and South Africa that shows that corruption impedes citizen participation in local governance processes due to trust deficit in local government sectors (Mantzaris and Pillay, 2017).

Conclusion

The chapter brings home critical issues on the nexus between PB and the human rights economy. From the ensuing discussion, it is highly probable that PB can significantly enhance the human rights economy in Zimbabwe's devolved subnational structures, provided its tenets are religiously observed. PB is a critical mechanism that promotes the local human rights economy as these two share the same principles such as community engagement, transparency, accountability, distributional equality, inclusivity and participation. The research, however, reveals gaps in PB, such as lack of government will, poor dissemination of information, lack of inclusivity and transparency, lack of public education and awareness, lack of incentives to motivate citizens' desire to participate, lack of consideration of public inputs and the participatory model being elite-controlled, top-down and lacking in accountability. The promotion of the human rights economy is consequently compromised in such an environment where local authorities are implementing a tokenistic approach of consultation which is characterised by high levels of manipulation and elite domination. The chapter further notes that Zimbabwe's devolution agenda since 2018 has failed to facilitate the right to participation in subnational governments. In order to improve the situation, there is a need to convert all barriers into positive influencing factors. This can be done through integrating the principles of human rights into the PB process such as inclusivity, participation, transparency, accountability, equality and non-discrimination.

Bibliography

Abraham, A. and J. P. Platteau. 2004. 'Participatory development: where culture creeps.' In Rao, V. and Walton, M. (eds.) *Culture and public action*. (pp. 210–233). Standford, CA: Standford University Press.

Agere, S. 1998. *Zimbabwe Post-Independence Public Administration: Management Policy and Issues and Constraints*. Dakar: Codesria.

Airong, A., and G. Xiang. 2008. "Study on Motivation of Citizens' Participation Under the Conditions of e-Government." In *Proc. International Conference on Management of e-Commerce and e-Government*. Los Alamitos: IEEE Press.

Arnstein, S. R. 1969. "A Ladder of Citizen Participation." *Journal of the American Planning Association* 35 (4): 216–224. http://www.tandfonline.com. doi:10.1080/01944366908977225.

Bashir, A., and A. B. Muhammed. 2012. "Challenges of Democratisation at the Grassroots in Nigeria: A Case of Taraba State." *Research on Humanities and Social Sciences* 2 (7): 98–108.

Brooks, R. W. S. and Harris. G. R. 2008. "Citizen Participation, NEPA, and Land-Use Planning in Northern New York, USA." *Environmental Practice* 10 (4): 140–151.

Brown, G. 2016. '*The Universal Declaration of Human Rights in the 21st Century: A living document in a changing world. A report by the global citizenship commission.*' Global Institute for Advanced Study: Open Book Publishers.

Cabannes, Y. 2005. "Children and Young People Build Participatory Democracy in Latin American Cities." *Children, Youth and Environments* 15 (2): 185–210.

Chakaipa, S. 2010. "Local Government Institutions and Elections." In J. de Vesser, N. Steytler, and N. Machingauta (eds.), *Local Government Reform in Zimbabwe: A Policy Dialogue*. Cape Town: Community Law Centre, University of the Western Cape.
Chigudu, D. 2014. "Implementing New Public Management in Zimbabwe: Challenges and Obstacles." *Journal of Governance and Regulation* 3 (2): 42–49.
Chigwata, T. C., S. Marumahoko, and A. Madhekeni. 2019. "Supervision of Local Government in Zimbabwe: The Travail of Mayors." *Law, Democracy and Development* 23: 44–67.
Collins, K., and R. Ison. 2006. "Dare We Jump Off Arnstein's Ladder? Social Learning as a New Policy Paradigm." In *Proceedings of Participatory Approaches in Science and Technology Conference*, 4–7. Edinburgh.
Constitution of Zimbabwe. 2013. Harare: Government Printers.
Dube, T. 2011. "Systematic Corruption in Public Enterprises in the Harare Metropolitan Area: A Case Study." Master's Thesis, University of South Africa.
Fagence, M. 2014. *Citizen Participation in Planning*. 1sted. United States: Pergamon Publishers.
Gaber, J. 2019. "Building 'A Ladder of Citizen Participation'." *Journal of the American Planning Association* 85 (3): 188–201. doi:10.1080/01944363.2019.1612267.
Goldfrank, D. 2012. "The World Bank and the Globalization of Participatory Budgeting." *Journal of Public Deliberation* 8 (2): 1–20.
Jonga, W. 2014. "Local Government Systems in Zimbabwe and Associated Challenges: Synthesis and Antithesis." *Archives of Business Research* 2 (1): 75–98.
Juma, T. O., J. K. Rotich, and L. S. Mulongo. 2014. "Devolution and Governance Conflicts in Africa: Kenyan Scenario." *SSRN Electronic Journal* 4 (6). doi:10.2139/ssrn.2461292.
Kurebwa, J. 2015. "A Review of Rural Local Government System in Zimbabwe from 1980 to 2014." *IOSR Journal of Humanities and Social Science* 20 (2): 94–108. doi: 10.9790/0837-202594108.
Lilleker, D., and K. Koc-Michalska. 2016. "What Drives Political Participation? Motivations and Mobilization in a Digital Age." In *Paper presented at the 66th ICA Annual Conference: Communicating with Power*, 9–13 June. Fukuoka, Japan.
Madhekeni, A., and G. Zhou. 2012. "Legal and institutional Framework: The 'Achilles Heel' of Local Authorities and Raison D'etre of Ministerial Intervention in Zimbabwe." *Journal of Public Administration and Governance* 2 (3): 20–32.
Madzivanyika, L. 2014. "Local government, Participatory Processes and Citizen Engagement." Dissertation, University of Western Cape, South Africa.
Makumbe, J. 1996. *Participatory Development*. Harare: University of Zimbabwe Publications.
Manduna, K., T. Zinyama, and A. G. Nhema. 2015. "Local Government Participatory Budget System in Zimbabwe: The Case of Harare City Council, 1995–2013." *Public Policy and Administration Research* 5 (11): 38–60.
Mansuri, G., and R. Vijayendra. 2013. *Localising Development: Does Participation Work?* Policy Research Report. Washington, DC: World Bank.
Mantzaris, E., and P. Pillay. 2017. "Legal and Institutional Measures Against Corruption in Southern Africa: Case Studies." In M. Powell, D. Wafa, T. Mau, and M. De Vries (eds.), *Corruption in a Global Context*. IASIA.
Mapuva, J. 2014. "Local Governance, Democratisation and Constitutionalism in Zimbabwe." *International Journal of Politics and Good Governance* 5 (4): 1–25.
Mapuva, J., and L. Muyengwa-Mapuva. 2015. "Arnstein's Ladder of Citizen Participation and Citizen Participation in Zimbabwe." *International Journal of African and Asian Studies* 11: 1–14.

Marango, T., M. Magaya, J. Francis, and J. Kamuzhanje. 2020. "Budget Formulation: An Insight into Zimbabwean Local Government Citizen Participation." *African Journal of Democracy and Governance* 5 (4): 169–188.
Marumahoko, S., T. C. Chigwata, and N. T. Nhede. 2018. "Participatory Budgeting in the City of Kwekwe (Zimbabwe): A Perspectives on the Issues, Trends and Options." *African Journal of Public Affairs* 10 (4): 196–211.
Matovu, G. 2007. "The Challenges and Constraints of Introducing Participatory Budgeting as a Tool for Resource Mobilization and Allocation and Realizing Good Governance in Africa." In *Paper presented at the 7th Edition of the Africa Local Government Action Forum (ALGAF)*, February 2. http://siteresources.worldbank.org/CMUDLP/Resources/Challenge-and-constraints-Paper.pdf. Accessed 16 February 2024.
Mayanja, C. S. 2020. "Ladder of Citizen Participation: Insights into Female Student Representatives on Public University Councils of Uganda." *International Journal of Education and Policy Studies* 12 (2): 121–132.
Mills, L. 2017. *Decentralisation of budgeting processes.* London and Birmingham: Department for International Development and University of Birmingham.
Moyo, J. N. 1993. *Politics of the National Purse: Public Budgeting as Public Policy in Zimbabwe.* Harare: Southern African Research and Documentation Centre.
Muchanyuka, P., and P. Jeranyama. 2016. "An interrogation of Civic Participation in Promoting Social Accountability." *International Journal of Humanities and Social Science*, 6 (9): 1–11.
Munyede, P., and V. P. Machengete. 2020. "Rethinking Citizen Participation and Local Governance in Post-Corona Virus Pandemic in Zimbabwe." *Transatlantic Journal of Multidisciplinary Research* 2 (1–2): 1–16.
Munzwa, K., and W. Jonga. 2010. "Urban Development in Zimbabwe: A Human Settlement Perspective." *Theoretical and Empirical Researches in Urban Management* 5: 120–146.
Office of the High Commissioner for Human Rights. 2024. *The Human Rights Economy – from Concept to Practical Application.* United Nations Human Rights Office of the High Commissioner. United Nations. https://www.ohchr.org/en/statements-and-speeches/2024/06/human-rights-economy-concept-practical-application. Accessed 8 February 2025
Paradza, G. 2010. "Reflections on Zimbabwe's Past as Building Blocks for its Future." *Centre for Policy Studies* 23 (1): 1–11.
Ranger, T. O. 2007. "City Versus State in Zimbabwe: Colonial Antecedents of the Current Crisis." *Journal of Eastern African Studies* 1 (2): 161–192. doi:10.1080/17531050701452390.
Rainero, C., and V. Brescia. 2018. "The Participatory Budgeting Towards a New Governance and Accountability." *International Journal of Management Sciences and Business Research* 7: 1–67.
Reutener, M., and D. Fourie. 2015. "The Role of Civil Participation in the South African Budgeting Process." *Journal of Public and Municipal Finance* 4 (3): 7–15.
Sachikonye, L. 2017. "The Protracted Democratic Transition in Zimbabwe." *Taiwan Journal of Democracy* 13 (1): 117–136.
Sobanjo, B. A. 2016. "Strengthening Participatory Democracy through Participatory Budgeting." DPhil Thesis, Walden University.
Theyyan, B. M. 2016. "Arnstein's Ladder of Citizen Participation: A Critical Discussion." *Asian Academic Journal of Multidisciplinary* 2 (7): 241–247
Verkoren, W and Kamphuis, B. 2013. State Building in the Rentier State: How Development Policies Fail to Promote Democracy in Afghanistan. *Development and Change.* 44 (3): 501–526.

Walby, S. 1990. *Theorising Patriarchy*. Oxford: Blackwell Publishers.
Wekwete, K. 1991. "Growth Center Policy in Zimbabwe with Special Reference to District Service Centers." In N. D. Mutizwa-Mangiza and A. Helmsing (eds.), *Rural Development in Zimbabwe*, 187–221. Aldershot: Averbury.
Yoshikuni, T. 2006. *African Urban Experiences in Colonial Zimbabwe: A Social History of Harare before 1925*. Harare: Weaver Press.
Zhou, G. 2012. "Public Administration in Zimbabwe: A Framework Approach." *Journal of Public Administration and Governance* 2 (2): 132–150.
Zhou, G., R. M. Mukonza, and H. Zvoushe. 2016. "Public Budgeting: Trends, Processes, and Practices." In *Public Budgeting in African Nations: Fiscal Analysis in Development Management*, 134–156.

12 The Role of Local Governments in Upholding Human Rights and Promoting Economic Justice

Addressing Corruption and Illicit Financial Flows

Pradeep Wagle and Maria José Veramendi Villa

Introduction: The Negative Impact of Corruption on the Enjoyment of Human Rights[1]

There is no international legally agreed definition of corruption. The United Nations Convention Against Corruption (UNCAC) lists the conducts that may constitute corruption and urges State parties to criminalize those conducts in their domestic legislation: bribery in the public and private sectors (articles 15, 16, and 21), embezzlement in the public and private sectors (articles 17 and 22), trading in influence (article 18), abuse of functions (article 19), illicit enrichment (article 20), money-laundering (article 23), concealment (article 24), and obstruction of justice (article 25) related to the conducts above (UNODC 2004, 17–25). For the purposes of this chapter, we follow the commonly used definition of corruption provided by Transparency International on its website as of 13 February 2025: "abuse of entrusted power for private gain", with a focus on publicly entrusted power (Transparency International n.d.-a). In practice, as well as in academic literature, corruption is generally divided into two sub-categories, reflecting its two main manifestations: grand and petty.[2] Grand corruption generally refers to abuses of high-level power, while the latter encompasses daily acts of corruption in the administration and distribution of public services. It is important to note that often a particular scheme of corruption involves various levels of public administration and officials and thus involves both "types" of corruption (Peters 2018).

A group of experts convened by Transparency International in 2019 defined grand corruption as "the commission of any of the offences in UNCAC Articles 15–25[3] as part of a scheme that: (1) involves a high-level public official; and (2) results in or is intended to result in a gross misappropriation of public funds or resources; or grave or systematic violations or abuses of the human rights of a substantial part of the population or of a vulnerable group" (Dell 2023).

This type of corruption is detrimental to human rights in itself; however, it is important to note that combatting it presents a variety of potential pitfalls with regard to the protection and promotion of human rights. Particularly,

DOI: 10.4324/9781003474845-16

many anti-corruption reforms are not holistic and are aimed primarily to facilitate investments and create a business-friendly environment. Therefore, they are not designed to address the specific problems and effects of acts of corruption, nor their effects on the most marginalized.[4]

Petty corruption, on the other hand, occurs at a lower level of civil service personnel engaging directly with citizens daily, compromising access to public services and, therefore, the fulfilment of human rights. When public servants demand or take money or favours in exchange for services, this affects the ability of all citizens to freely access available services without discrimination. A person living in poverty who needs access to healthcare, for example, would be disproportionately affected by this type of corruption, which also ensures that poverty continues to perpetuate.

The International Covenant on Economic, Social, and Cultural Rights (ICESCR) is breached when healthcare systems are corrupt. The COVID-19 pandemic has provided ample evidence of this fact with "frontline personnel caring for the sick [unable to] get the required number of facemasks, other basic equipment, or life-saving medicine due to severe overpricing or diversion of funds or goods" (Kjaerum 2021, 298). The availability of high-quality healthcare services is jeopardized by grand corruption, such as the illicit use of public health money, particularly in environments with low resources. For instance, money meant for building hospitals or buying vaccines can be misappropriated, depriving communities of vital facilities or treatments that could save lives. People living in conditions of poverty who cannot afford bribes are disproportionately affected by petty corruption, which denies them access to necessary medical care. One example of this is the requirement for unofficial payments for medical care.

Corruption in the education system regularly results in violations of the right to education, guaranteed by Article 13 of the ICESCR. For example, poor regions are left with understaffed or ill-equipped schools when instructors bribe officials to get jobs in wealthy urban areas. This prevents underprivileged pupils from receiving quality education and maintains educational inequities. Corruption can sometimes reach the admissions process, where families are forced to pay bribes to get their children enrolled in public schools. These actions exacerbate inequality by obstructing the fair allocation of opportunities and resources. Local governments in particular have the responsibility to minimize and root out this form of corruption.

Corruption is often consolidated in and by local governments through favouritism and nepotism. One obvious reason is the proximity of elected officials to their constituency and their knowledge of each other. In smaller communities, social and professional networks often overlap, making the proximity even more obvious and thus raising the chances of favouritism and corruption. Arbitrary discretion is used on who is chosen to fulfil a public contract or join a political committee. Oftentimes, unqualified people gain these opportunities or positions at the expense of the community. For example, an unqualified and/or personally connected construction business may bid for the contract to build a public hospital, siphoning money from the cost of construction, leading to a faulty building that is dangerous and more costly for the government to maintain and repair overtime.

Multidimensional Links between Corruption and Human Rights

The links between corruption, anti-corruption responses, and human rights are multidimensional, and the negative impact of corruption on human rights is widely acknowledged, both in academic literature and in practice (HRC Resolution A/HRC/28/73 2015; Juwita 2023; U4 n.d.). This section will draw out the general connections between corruption and human rights, before moving on to discussing the specific links between corruption and economic, social, and cultural rights. Human rights are universal, indivisible, and interdependent and because corruption's effects on human rights are multidimensional, the negative impacts are felt on all rights. The UN common position to address global corruption recognizes that "corruption, political instability, economic development and human rights are interconnected" (UN Secretary General 2020, 7).

Efforts to explicitly link corruption to human rights within the international system have been ongoing for over 30 years. In its 1991 session, the Sub-Commission on the Prevention of Discrimination and Protection of Minorities, while considering agenda item 7 on "The New International Economic Order and the Promotion of Human Rights" and item 8 on the "Realization of Economic, Social and Cultural Rights", discussed the problem of capital flight and fraudulent enrichment of high-ranking State officials. During the discussions, Member States emphasized the problem caused by illicit financial flows to developing countries, including foreign debt and debt servicing, unemployment, and underdevelopment. The Sub-Commission considered this matter and adopted a draft resolution on the topic, which then became a resolution of the Commission on Human Rights (Sub-Commission on Prevention of Discrimination and Protection of Minorities 1991).

United Nations Resolution 1992/50 linking corruption and human rights, entitled "Fraudulent enrichment of top State officials prejudicial to the public interest, the factors responsible for it, and the agents involved in all countries in such fraudulent enrichment", was adopted by the Commission on Human Rights on 3 March 1992. This resolution established a link between corruption and the realization of economic, social, and cultural rights. The Commission emphasized the need to combat corruption and the transfer abroad of stolen assets and the need to restitute to despoiled peoples the funds stolen by their leaders. Not only did the Commission consider that these transfers damaged the economic interests of peoples who have been victims of institutionalized corruption, but it was also convinced that developed countries had a "special responsibility to contribute diligently" to the return of these funds. It also emphasized the need for mutual legal assistance and regretted the obstacles to extradition of persons guilty of misappropriation of funds (UN Commission on Human Rights Resolution E/CN.4/RES/1992/50 2021).

In 2003, the United Nations Sub-Commission established a mandate for a Special Rapporteur on corruption and its impact on the full enjoyment of human rights, in particular economic, social, and cultural rights, with the Rapporteur preparing multiple reports on the topic until the end of the mandate in 2006.[5] In 2013, the Office of the High Commissioner for Human Rights (OHCHR 2013) clearly outlined these links in an official pamphlet, "The Human Rights Case Against Corruption", following up with a report from the Human Rights Council (HRC) Advisory Committee in 2015 (OHCHR 2013; HRC Advisory Committee 2015). The Council has addressed corruption in several biennial resolutions, including on *the negative impact of corruption on the enjoyment of human rights*, on *the role of good governance in the promotion and protection of human rights*, and on the two resolutions on *promoting human rights and the Sustainable Development Goals through transparent, accountable, and efficient public services delivery*.

The report highlighted corruption as a "key hindrance to transparency, accountability and efficiency in public service delivery". It stressed that when public service delivery is compromised by corrupt practices, the effects go above and beyond the entrenchment of inefficiency; rather, peoples' human rights are often directly affected, including the right to health, education, and an adequate standard of living. The report stated that "corruption in the health and education sectors disproportionately affects women, girls and other groups at risk of discrimination" (HRC 2024, para 53).

Corruption undermines States' ability to meet their pre-existing legal obligations to maximize all available resources to progressively realize economic, social, and cultural rights and other human rights. By eroding the tax base and discouraging public and private investments, corruption and associated illicit financial flows strip societies of vital and scarce resources, which are indispensable for the structural transformation, economic growth, and sustainable development of all countries. Corruption further heavily erodes public confidence in State institutions, the rule of law, as well as States' efforts to uphold human rights.

Obligations of States under international human rights law cover all levels, branches, and institutions, and include local governments.[6] Through the provision of public services, local governments address needs and priorities related to the realization of humanity and develop and enact policies that affect people's rights (HRC 2024, para 30). As a result, local governments are in contact with people in the most direct way. They receive demands, claims, and complaints from residents and are uniquely placed to understand public service delivery challenges and needs.

Many local governments face obstacles when fulfilling their role of duty bearers for the realization of human rights and achievement of sustainable development. Particularly in low-income countries, these challenges include "a lack of awareness of human rights obligations, limited capacity and resources, inadequate institutional structures within local or regional administrations and, in many cases, corruption" (HRC 2024, para 31).

A critical link between corruption and human rights is the siphoning of resources and public funds from the State, and often from those who need them the most. Human Rights Treaty Bodies (2016) have "identified mismanagement of resources and corruption as obstacles to the allocation of resources to promote equal rights". Moreover, corruption acts as an obstacle to sustainable development across all 17 Sustainable Development Goals (Tabatadze 2024). While anti-corruption is directly addressed in SDG 16 (Peace, Justice, and Effective Institutions), it is itself a pre-condition, seen as an enabler and accelerator of the entire 2030 Agenda (UN Secretary General 2020, 5). Indeed, "there can be no sustainable development where corruption thrives" (Jenkins 2019).

Beyond public spending, corruption spreads within public service delivery, the judiciary, and law enforcement. When pervasive, corruption significantly undermines public trust in the independence of the judiciary, while at the same time allowing corrupt law enforcement officials to act with impunity. Corruption impeding the investigation of high-profile cases, such as killings of anti-corruption activists, has a significant negative effect on the trust that citizens place in public institutions as well as local and national governments (Mijatović, 2021). This directly impacts the right to liberty and security of persons, the right to equality before the law, the right to effective remedy, the right to not be subjected to arbitrary arrest, and the right to be presumed innocent. Moreover, when the public believes that the government and its employees are self-interested and corrupt, it can result in civil disengagement and social unrest. Additionally, anti-corruption measures, improperly designed and implemented, provide further risks and potential for human rights violations.

Intersections between Corruption and the Human Rights Economy (HRE)

Vulnerable and Marginalized Populations and the Impact of Corruption at the Local Level

Habibov, Fan, and Auchynnikava (2019) found that higher levels of corruption lead to lower levels of public trust and satisfaction with both national and local governments. This section further explores the negative impacts of corruption on the most vulnerable and marginalized groups at the local level.

The well-being of all people should be the primary goal of economies. Equity and inclusivity should take precedence over exclusive profit-oriented interests, which are currently the dominant economic incentives. The HRE calls for an approach that requires economies to refocus on meeting the needs of all people, especially the poor, vulnerable, and marginalized groups that experience poverty and inequality and align economic policies and fiscal decision-making with international human rights norms and standards and obligations. Structural challenges, such as corruption and illegal financial flows, add another layer of challenges and impede the ability to create greater fiscal space to address poverty, inequality, and other structural challenges. States are required by international law to use all available resources to the maximum level possible to progressively realize the rights of the people to economic, social, and cultural advancement. This obligation is often deprioritized due to fiscal policies, poor governance, and corruption.

One of the everyday tragedies in a local society affected by corruption is that economically disadvantaged populations often rely on public services for themselves and their families. These include, but are not limited to, health, education, medicines, social welfare, water supply, and public transportation. Even if these services are available, corruption often compromises their availability, adequacy, quality, and accessibility. Economically disadvantaged persons have been found to "bear the brunt" of corruption within local government administrations in the Bonthe District of Sierra Leone, for instance, across many sectors. Access to basic healthcare services is obstructed due to rampant bribery, access to education is obstructed due to misallocation of funds intended to provide education to children of low-income families, while the right to development is obstructed due to the siphoning of funds intended for infrastructure projects like roads and bridges (Koroma et al. 2024, 141–142).

Furthermore, corruption undermines democratic structures and procedures which are crucial for defending the rights of underrepresented groups. In many contexts, elections are reportedly tainted by corruption, such as vote-buying and fraud. Money is mobilized without formal banking channels as gifts and donations to private individuals or groups. The elected officials who win elections because of corrupt practice serve the interests of those who gave them money or helped them in the electoral malpractices. These voices of marginalized groups are muffled, and their issues are not considered when election systems are tainted by vote-buying or manipulation. For instance, claims of electoral fraud and corruption have prevented rural and minority people from actively participating in political decision-making in nations like Zimbabwe (European Union Electoral Observation Mission, 2023, UNECA, 2013). The most vulnerable people in Venezuela (Transparency International, n.d.-b), who lack the resources to question the system, have been disproportionately affected by corruption, which has also contributed to the breakdown of public services there.

Ethnic minorities, especially those predominantly inhabiting rural areas that may be poorly accessible from urban centres, are particularly vulnerable to corrupt local officials. These areas tend to be first victims of corrupt officials adjusting budgets when embezzling public funds. The Indonesian West Lombok district is one example of the exploitation of this vulnerability, with local officials spending 350,000 USD on luxury vehicles in 2002, while "forgetting" to allocate development funds for minority-dominated villages (Duncan 2007, 725). Such brazen instances of corruption led researchers to call corruption in West Lombok "perpetual", as numerous high-level officials have been accused, investigated, and found guilty for corruption since the end of the 1990s (Sutarna et al. 2021).

Because of resources and other constraints discussed above, vulnerable people are less able to influence policy decisions and legislative change. These groups are more susceptible to exploitation and are not included in decision-making processes; they frequently include indigenous populations, ethnic minorities, and those living in poverty. Because authorities put their interests over the welfare of the people and resources are diverted from programmes intended to help them, corruption exacerbates their lack of political clout. Corrupt local government officials, whether engaging in petty daily corruption, blocking access to services, or participating in grand corruption through illicit sale of land, have a greater effect on marginalized groups. The latter are rendered powerless and abandoned by local officials wielding instruments with the most direct and immediate capacity to improve economic and social conditions.

Strong anti-corruption measures must be put in place to end this cycle. To ensure fair development and protect everyone's human rights, especially those of the most disadvantaged, transparent governance, robust accountability systems, and inclusive policies are essential (Minkova, 2018).

Corruption and Economic Development

The fact that countries with a more equitable redistribution of wealth enjoy sustainable growth and longer periods of economic development is well established. It follows that countries suffering from corruption are less able to implement sound redistribution policies and are thus not able to benefit fully from sustainable economic development. These countries are also less attractive for foreign direct investment and are more prone to resource misallocation, directly and negatively affecting the enjoyment of all rights, particularly economic, social, and cultural rights, as well as the right to development.

Levels of economic prosperity have also been widely shown to negatively correlate with levels of corruption in the economic literature at the macro level (Blackburn, Bose, and Haque 2006; Chêne 2014; Ugur and Dasgupta 2011).

This highlights the important fact that many of the world's poorest countries are the most corrupt and could benefit from foreign investment the most (Ambraseys and Bilham 2011). Beyond the lower levels of investment, corruption acts as a cost of doing business, which reduces the profitability of investment projects, thus also reducing any taxes or other levies that the State can leverage for the benefit of its population. In countries with high levels of corruption, officials may prioritize public projects that provide more opportunities to extract rents from foreign investors. This affects the right to education, for instance, as government spending on education has been found to negatively correlate with corruption levels (Chêne 2014). Given that the State can play an active and leading role in the redistribution of wealth, corruption can have negative effects not only on existing public projects, but also on future projects that may aim to contribute to a fairer wealth redistribution.

The Right to Health: Corruption and the HRE

This section highlights the intersectional effects of corruption on the HRE through the right to health and demonstrates that corruption is not a victimless crime. Corruption affects the most marginalized persons within a society disproportionately. This includes persons living in conditions of poverty, women, racial and ethnic minorities, persons of diverse sexual orientations and gender identities, persons with disabilities, indigenous groups, and other persons in situations of political, economic, and social disadvantage and marginalization. The effects of corruption are disproportionate partly because these groups are often the most dependent on public services, and at the same time least able to influence State policies and corrupt officials.

The effects are disproportionate because persons already in situations of marginalization are less likely to be protected from human rights violations, making them easy targets for corrupt officials, whether in local or national government, law enforcement, or judiciary. As such, corruption has a profound and compounding negative impact on their ability to enjoy their human rights, but also on development, as corruption increases the likelihood that politically and socially marginalized communities are not able to participate fully in, and reap the full benefits of, economic development. With regard to the right to health, research has been clear: individuals in poor health or at high socioeconomic risk are more likely to make informal payments (Habibov and Cheung 2017; Williams and Horodnic 2017).

Research has shown that the health sector is particularly vulnerable to corruption due to its complexity, the large number of different stakeholders, and the highly complex interactions between them. It is also particularly vulnerable to the insidiousness of corruption as a culture, here meaning not only a relatively high number of illegal acts, whether part of grand or petty corruption practices, but also the pervasiveness of unethical behaviour. As a result of this complexity, vulnerability, and the heterogeneity of health systems, holistic and systems thinking approaches are required to tackle corruption in the health sector.[7]

The right to health showcases the complex intersectional effects of corruption on the HRE, as it is particularly vulnerable in the context of corruption. First, by depriving the State of resources that otherwise could have been used on, for example, expanding access to health care to ensure universal health coverage, leading to violations of the right to health. The World Health Organization (WHO) estimates that 7.3 per cent of all annual spending on health globally is diverted due to corruption, a total annual amount that even at pre-COVID-19 levels was significantly higher than the USD 370 billion required to achieve universal health coverage (WHO 2023, 1).

Furthermore, human rights violations through the right to access to healthcare can be demonstrated by both "grand" and "petty" corruption. In terms of the former, securing universal access to quality healthcare is crucial for fostering sustainable development and advancing the goal of ensuring healthy lives for individuals, as outlined in SDG 3. When corruption is systemic, the right to health is dramatically affected. According to the WHO, up to 80 per cent of non-salary funding for health can be diverted from intended use in some countries. In countries where a culture of corruption is allowed to fester within broader society leading to high rates of bribery, rates of maternal and child mortality are also high (WHO 2023). The production of medical products and equipment, regulation of medical value chains, public health procurement, and even antimicrobial resistance can all be negatively affected and disrupted by corruption (WHO 2023).

Local governments are key stakeholders in healthcare, and rampant local corruption has the potential of severely restricting access to healthcare services. A quantitative study analysing data from 80 municipalities in the Philippines, for example, showed that corruption clearly undermined the delivery of health services. Moreover, this analysis showed that corruption has a greater negative effect on households' use of public healthcare facilities in rural areas when compared to urban areas, where alternative options were more readily available (Azfar and Gurgur 2006, 37–38).

Petty corruption similarly is a significant barrier to achieving the right to health, especially in contexts when government workers request additional payments for public services. In this way the impact of corruption is particularly harsh on marginalized and vulnerable communities, who lack the means to pay bribes for accessing essential public services (Tabatadze 2024). When they are forced to make the extra payments, this further entrenches their economic marginalization, delaying sustainable development by denying universal health coverage.

In a recent publication, Transparency International and the Equal Rights Trust presented case studies on how corruption and discrimination can impact a person's access to quality education and health care services (Barnes and Bergin, 2025). The case studies highlight the key role of local authorities and officials from local schools, universities, hospitals, and medical facilities in being sources of corruption. For example, in the case of Rwanda's fortified blended foods (FBF) programme, involving the distribution of nutrient-rich flour designed to meet the daily dietary requirements of recent and expectant mothers and young children, broad discretionary powers given to local leaders in designating the beneficiaries, who are meant to be selected from among the poorest households in Rwanda after a basic medical assessment carried out by community health workers, have led to corruption. Lack of financial resources by families to meet the demands of corrupt officials and fear to file complaints against them due to potential exclusion from the programme have severe physical and mental impacts for families (Barnes and Bergin, 2025).

The gendered effects of corruption, in particular sexual corruption, negatively affect women health care workers and patients, blocking access to health services, thereby eroding the right to health. Corruption in the health sector in general affects women disproportionately due to their higher and differentiated needs for health services – as well as due to traditionally enforced gender roles of women as primary care providers within the home, which place further and disproportionate burden on them if public healthcare systems are rife with corruption. This entrenches gender inequality and hinders sustainable development by not allowing women to reap the full benefits of the healthcare system, enjoy their right to health, and as a result reduces their capacity to fully enjoy the right to education and the right to work, thus not allowing them to participate fully in economic development.[8] In the same case study of Rwanda, an interviewee "shared a belief that some doctors may engage in acts of sexual corruption in exchange for enabling women's access to the FBF programme" (Barnes and Bergin, 2025).

Conclusion: Local Governments' Role in Combatting Corruption and Promoting Economic Growth

In February 2024, *The Guardian* reported that "[a]cross the UK, 36 local authorities have had councillors and staff accused of economic crimes including fraud and the misuse of public funds, with dozens arrested and convicted" (Murray, 2024). The article further highlights that a report on the role of monitoring officers – the person responsible for legal governance in each council – found that

> monitoring officers feel that the lack of clout in the available sanctions has fed a culture of disrespect and contempt for the rules and the institutional frameworks that govern them. [Interviewed] monitoring officers [indicated] that some councillors see it as a badge of honour to have been through a grievance process as it demonstrates some sort of rebellious or anti-establishment behaviour. It also undermines trust among the public, especially those who have made complaints.
>
> (Stride and Walker 2023, 16)

Some circumstances that favour the occurrence of corruption in local governments are the lack of oversight which allows public officials to behave without accountability and public pressure; this includes also the lack of adequate sanctioning regime. In these situations, misconduct is not only possible but also incentivized as there is an ostensible link between personal connection, private interest, nepotism, and lack of accountability. In these contexts, corruption becomes not just an infrequent phenomenon but rather a systematic feature of local governance. Local governments are often in charge of some of the most important and direct public services, and without adequate frameworks promoting transparency and accountability, they may unjustifiably inflate the cost of essential public services and increase taxes without explanation.

Some key recommendations for addressing corruption in local government are to: (i) empower local governance structures with the necessary tools and resources, such as the ones described in the following paragraph, to create a corruption-free environment, uphold human rights, and promote sustainable economic growth; and (ii) implement effective anti-corruption measures, such as education and awareness campaigns, transparent and participatory spending, adequate legislative frameworks that ensure a system of accountability for local officials, access to justice and remedies for victims, reporting and whistleblowing mechanisms at the subnational level to promote economic justice and the well-being of people. Addressing illicit financial flows that deprive people of their fair share of national resources will only be possible if local governments promote the human rights framework of anti-corruption by fostering more transparent, accountable, and participatory governance. (iii) Due to the size and proximity of local governments to their people, local governments should be best situated for providing public services with transparency and fiscal discipline and should ensure social audit mechanisms. Furthermore, successful implementation of anti-corruption policies at the local level can create more success and begin a domino effect on other municipalities and levels of government who implement these policies.

The UNDP Guide to corruption-free local government proposes a series of tools/methodologies which can be adapted by local governments to prevent corruption such as: committing to an integrity policy and a code of ethics; allocating roles and responsibilities; conducting a thorough risk assessment; developing and implementing an integrity plan, ensuring competent staff, communication, transparency, and partnership; implementing integrity controls; ensuring safe reporting; conducting effective investigation; implementing disciplinary procedures; monitoring, implementing, and conducting internal audits and treating adequately non-compliances and improving through review and integration of results from monitoring and implementation into decision-making (Minkova, 2018). Other tools such as the simplification of administrative processes and enhancing mechanisms for citizen participation such as public hearings, disaggregated and accessible data (data that can be easily found, used, and understood by people), and the establishment of auditing commissions can support combatting corruption at the local level.

Improving transparency is key to countering corruption, particularly implementing measures such as maintaining digital and accessible records for the public and implementing routine financial auditing from a third party. Other measures can include encouraging democratic participation by surveying people who rely on public services the most to gauge their satisfaction and receive their feedback, holding public hearings about budget programmes and planning, and implementing meaningful public participation in budget creation and the monitoring of spending. In this context, meaningful public participation in budget creation and the monitoring of spending allows for public scrutiny and promotes efficient spending and effective prevention of corruption.

Local governments are often in charge of some of the most important and direct public services, and as a result, improving the transparency of their budget planning is essential for efficient and fair use of monies towards public programmes and responsibilities. To prevent favouritism, nepotism, shortcuts, and inflated prices in contract bidding, some cities (such as New York City) require bidders to complete a comprehensive questionnaire that looks at measures such as financial assets, capability, experience, and the key people associated with and at the head of the company (Gonzales de Asis 2000).

Corruption undermines the realization of human rights, increases inequality, and contributes to economic injustice. The impact of corruption remains disproportionate to marginalized populations while it erodes confidence in democratic institutions. It is a systematic challenge to society which must be addressed by promoting robust anti-corruption measures rooted in transparency, accountability, and participatory governance. The local government's role is significant in promoting transparency and accountability at the local level; they can significantly reduce corruption and malpractices in governance. Only through strong, coordinated, rights-based, and inclusive efforts can the cycle of corruption be broken, communities can thrive, and human rights can be universally realized.

Notes

1 The authors would like to thank Dr Vsevolod Kritskiy for his support in the research and elaboration of this chapter.
2 As there is no agreed definition of corruption, similarly grand and petty corruption are not fully defined but operational enough for use by practitioners and academics. For a practitioner perspective, see U4 Anti-Corruption Resource Centre. n.d. "Glossary". Accessed April 11, 2025, for definitions of petty and grand corruption. https://www.u4.no/terms. For academic discussions of the distinctions and relationships between the two, see, for instance, Mashali, Behzad. 2012. "Analyzing the relationship between perceived grand corruption and petty corruption in developing countries: case study of Iran." *International Review of Administrative Sciences* 78(4): 775–787. https://doi.org/10.1177/0020852312455991 or Nystrand, Malin J. 2014. "Petty and Grand Corruption and the Conflict Dynamics in Northern Uganda." *Third World Quarterly* 35(5): 821–35. https://doi.org/10.1080/01436597.2014.921432.
3 Bribery of national public officials; bribery of foreign public officials and officials of public international organizations; embezzlement, misappropriation, or other diversion of property by a public official; trading in influence; abuse of functions; illicit enrichment; bribery in the private sector; embezzlement of property in the private sector; laundering of proceeds of crime; concealment; obstruction of justice.
4 See, for instance, Gathii, James Thuo. 2009. "Defining the Relationship between Human Rights and Corruption." *University of Pennsylvania Journal of International Law* 31(1): 125–202. https://scholarship.law.upenn.edu/jil/vol31/iss1/3.
5 See reports of the Special Rapporteur on corruption and its impact on the full enjoyment of human rights, in particular economic, social, and cultural rights: E/CN.4/Sub.2/2003/18, E/CN.4/Sub.2/2004/23, E/CN.4/Sub.2/2005/18 and A/HRC/11/CRP.1 available here: https://digitallibrary.un.org/search?ln=en&p=subjectheading%3A%5BMbonu%2C%20Christy%20Ezim%5D&f&rm&sf&so=d&rg=50&c=United%20Nations%20Digital%20Library%20System&of=hb&fti=0&fct__1=Reports&fti=0.
6 See, for instance, International Law Commission, Article 4 of the Articles on Responsibility of States for Internationally Wrongful Acts, https://legal.un.org/ilc/texts/instruments/english/draft_articles/9_6_2001.pdf.
7 See Glynn, Emily H. 2024. "Corruption in the health sector: A problem in need of a systems-thinking approach." *Frontiers in Public Health* 10. https://doi.org/10.3389/fpubh.2022.910073.
8 See U4 Anti-Corruption Centre. n.d.. "Gender, corruption and health." U4 Expert Answer. https://www.u4.no/publications/gender-corruption-and-health.pdf.

Bibliography

Ambraseys, Nicholas and Roger Bilham. 2011. "Corruption Kills." *Nature* 469: 153–155. https://doi.org/10.1038/469153a

Azfar, Omar and Tugrul Gurgur. 2006. "Local-level Corruption Hits Health Service Delivery in the Philippines." In Jana Kotalik and Diana Rodriguez (eds.), *Grand Corruption Report 2006*. Transparency International. Pluto Press.

Barnes, Sam and Jamie Bergin. 2025. *Barriers to Basics: Corruption and Discrimination in Education and Health Services*. Transparency International and the Equal Rights Trust. https://www.transparency.org/en/publications/barriers-to-basics-corruption-discrimination-in-education-health-services

Blackburn, Keith, Niloy Bose and M. Emranul Haque. 2006. "The Incidence and Persistence of Corruption in Economic Development." *Journal of Economic Dynamics and Control* 30 (12): 2447–2467. https://doi.org/10.1016/j.jedc.2005.07.007

Chêne, Marie. 2014. *The Impact of Corruption on Growth and Inequality*. Report. Transparency International Anti-Corruption Helpdesk. https://knowledgehub.transparency.org/assets/uploads/helpdesk/Impact_of_corruption_on_growth_and_inequality_2014.pdf

Dell, Gillian. 2023. "Tackling Grand Corruption Impunity. Proposals for a Definition and Special Measures." *Working Paper, Transparency International*. https://images.transparencycdn.org/images/2023-Working-paper-Tackling-grand-corruption-impunity.pdf

Duncan, Christopher R. 2007. "Mixed Outcomes: The Impact of Regional Autonomy and Decentralization on Indigenous Ethnic Minorities in Indonesia." *Development and Change* (38) 4: 711–733.

European Union Election Observation Mission ZIMBABWE. 2023. Final Report. https://www.europarl.europa.eu/cmsdata/279784/Zimbabwe-General-elections-Final-report.pdf

Gathii, James Thuo. 2009. "Defining the Relationship between Human Rights and Corruption." *University of Pennsylvania Journal of International Law* 31 (1): 125−202. https://scholarship.law.upenn.edu/jil/vol31/iss1/3

Gonzales de Asis, Maria. 2000. *Reducing Corruption at the Local Level*. Report 34793. World Bank Institute. https://documents1.worldbank.org/curated/ar/724801468327614172/pdf/347930municipal1eng.pdf

Habibov, Nazim and Alex Cheung. 2017. "Revisiting Informal Payments in 29 Transitional Countries: The Scale and Socio-Economic Correlates." *Social Science & Medicine* 178: 28–37. https://doi.org/10.1016/j.socscimed.2017.02.003

Habibov, Nazim, Lida Fan, and Alena Auchynnikava. 2019. "The Effects of Corruption on Satisfaction with Local and National Governments. Does Corruption 'Grease the Wheels'?" *Europe-Asia Studies*, 71 (5): 736–752. https://doi.org/10.1080/09668136.2018.1562044

Human Rights Council Advisory Committee. 2015. *Final Report of the Human Rights Council Advisory Committee on the Issue of the Negative Impact of Corruption on the Enjoyment of Human Rights*. Report A/HRC/28/73. https://documents.un.org/doc/undoc/gen/g15/000/55/pdf/g1500055.pdf

Human Rights Council. 2024. *Role of Public Service Delivery in The Promotion and Protection of Human Rights and in the Achievement of the Sustainable Development Goals*. Report A/HRC/56/34. https://documents.un.org/doc/undoc/gen/g24/073/26/pdf/g2407326.pdf

Human Rights Treaty Bodies. 2016. *Contributions to the 2030 Agenda for Sustainable Development*. https://www.ohchr.org/sites/default/files/Documents/Issues/MDGs/Post2015/HRTB_Contribution_26May2016.pdf

Jenkins, Matthew. 2019. "The Many-Headed Hydra: How Grand Corruption Robs us of a Sustainable Future." *Transparency International Blog*, December 16, https://www.transparency.org/en/blog/the-many-headed-hydra-how-grand-corruption-robs-us-of-a-sustainable-future

Juwita, Ratna. 2023. "Exploring Corruption as a Violation of Human Rights in the Practices of International Human Rights Institutions." *Journal of Human Rights Practice* 15 (1): 302–321. https://doi.org/10.1093/jhuman/huac048

Kjaerum, Morten. 2021. "The Post-Crisis Human Rights Agenda." In Morten Kjaerum, Martha F. Davis and Amanda Lyons (eds.), *COVID-19 and Human Rights*. Routledge.

Koroma, Steven Mohamed, Mohamed Yusuf, Emmanuel Dauda, and Joseph Gbondo Theophilus Gando. 2024. "The Effects of Corruption on Local Government Service Delivery in Sierra Leone: The Case of Bonthe District Council." *IJSDR* 9 (9): 135–146.

Mijatović, Dunja. EU Commissioner for Human Rights. 2021. "Corruption Undermines Human Rights and The Rule of Law." *The Commissioner's Human Rights Comment*, January 19. https://www.coe.int/en/web/commissioner/blog/2021/-/asset_publisher/aa3hyyf8wKBn/content/corruption-undermines-human-rights-and-the-rule-of-law

Minkova, Milena. 2018. *Guide To Corruption-Free Local Government*. Report, United Nations Development Programme. https://www.local2030.org/library/486/Guide-To-Corruption-Free-Local-Government.pdf

Murray, Jessica. 2024. "Lawyers Raise Alarm at Struggle to Tackle UK Local Government Corruption." *The Guardian*, February 2. https://www.theguardian.com/uk-news/2024/feb/02/lawyers-raise-alarm-at-struggle-to-tackle-uk-local-government-corruption

OHCHR. 2013. *The Human Rights Case Against Corruption*. https://www.ohchr.org/sites/default/files/HRCaseAgainstCorruption.pdf

Peters, Anne. 2018. "Corruption as a Violation of International Human Rights." *European Journal of International Law* 29 (4): 1251–1287. https://doi.org/10.1093/ejil/chy070

Stride, Greg and Andrew Walker. 2023. *The Changing Role of the Monitoring Officer*. Report, Local Government Information Unit. https://lgiu.org/wp-content/uploads/2023/11/The-Changing-Role-of-the-Monitoring-Officer.pdf

Sub-Commission on Prevention of Discrimination and Protection of Minorities. 1991. *Report on its Forty-Third Session*. Report E/CN.4/Sub.2/1991/6. https://digitallibrary.un.org/record/132407?ln=en&v=pdf

Sutarna, Iwan Tanjung, Subando Agus Margono, and Agus Heruanto Hadna. 2021. "Post Decentralization Corruption: A Study on Perpetual Corruption at The Local Level in West Lombok." *Policy & Governance Review* 5 (3): 274–289. https://doi.org/10.30589/pgr.v5i3.461

Tabatadze, Tamari. 2024. "Corruption as a Barrier to Sustainable Development." *MEIG Highlights*, May 10. https://www.meig.ch/highlight-18-2024-corruption-as-a-barrier-to-sustainable-development/#:~:text=Nowadays%2C%20there%20is%20widespread%20consensus,%2C%20national%2C%20and%20international%20scales.

Transparency International. n.d.-a "What is Corruption?" Accessed February 13, 2025. https://www.transparency.org/en/what-is-corruption.

Transparency International. n.d.-b "Corruption and Human Rights Violations in Venezuela" Accessed February 14, 2025. https://www.transparency.org/en/news/corruption-and-human-rights-violations-in-venezuela.

U4 Anti-Corruption Resource Centre. n.d. "Basic Guide to Corruption and Human Rights". Accessed February 13, 2025. https://www.u4.no/topics/human-rights/basics.

Ugur, Mehmet and Nandini Dasgupta. 2011. *Evidence on the Economic Growth Impacts of Corruption in Low-Income Countries and Beyond.* Report 1914. EPPI-Centre, University of London. https://eppi.ioe.ac.uk/cms/Portals/0/PDF%20reviews%20and%20summaries/Corruption%20impact%202011%20Ugur%20report.pdf?ver=2011-08-25-153146-490
UN Economic Commission for Africa. 2013. "African Governance Report III, Elections & the Management of Diversity." ISBN UNECA 978–92–1–125120–3. ISBN Oxford University Press 978–0–19–964505–3. https://www.undp.org/sites/g/files/zskgke326/files/migration/africa/Africa-Governance-Report-3.pdf
UN Office on Drugs and Crime. 2004. *United Nations Convention Against Corruption.* https://www.unodc.org/documents/brussels/UN_Convention_Against_Corruption.pdf
UN Secretary General. 2020. *The UN Common Position to Address Global Corruption – Towards UNGASS 2021.* https://digitallibrary.un.org/record/4016590?ln=en&v=pdf
Williams, Colin C. and Adrian V. Horodnic. 2017. "Rethinking Informal Payments by Patients in Europe: An Institutional Approach". *Health Policy* 121(10): 1053–1062. https://doi.org/10.1016/j.healthpol.2017.08.007
World Health Organization. 2023. *Tackling Corruption to Move Towards Universal Health Coverage and Health Security.* WHO Technical Brief. https://cdn.who.int/media/docs/default-source/universal-health-coverage/who-uhl-technical-brief-anti-corruption.pdf?sfvrsn=a9a746f2_3

13 Municipal Monies as Policy Tools to Advance Human Rights Economies

Ester Barinaga

Introduction

On the bustling streets of Maricá, Brazil, a new form of currency is quietly reshaping the economic landscape, empowering vulnerable communities, and challenging traditional notions of money. Stickers on storefronts and merchants' cash registers inform that "we accept mumbucas", with customers swiftly swiping the Mumbuca card or opening the Mumbuca phone app to pay at local grocery stores and restaurants, clothing shops and pharmacies, and for construction materials and services. But mumbuca isn't just about money and commerce; it is also about resilience and human rights. In 2021, in the midst of the pandemic lockdown, over 42% of the city's population received a monthly welfare payment in mumbucas (Freitas 2022). Although across the country citizens lost their jobs, commerce had to close, and hunger increased, in Maricá, trade in mumbucas thrived, sustaining local businesses, preventing the loss of jobs, and maintaining citizens' access to food (Balakrishnan et al. 2024).

Meanwhile, on the other side of the Atlantic in the city of Viladecans, Spain, the mayor has similarly introduced a local currency to "act as an incentive for energy efficiency and as a mechanism to increase the economic capacity of vulnerable economic groups" (Implementation plan of the vilawatt currency, 4). In Viladecans, the currency is implemented to address energy-related challenges and strengthen the local economy (Vilawatt Statutes; see also Corrons 2018). Vulnerable families apply for subsidies, which are disbursed in vilawatts and spent in affiliated local businesses to buy tighter windows and doors, more efficient heating systems, better insulation, or solar panels. As a result, more than 55 households have been retrofitted and the three pilot buildings have achieved an average energy savings of 56% (Viader Bosch 2022). As in Maricá, in Viladecans, the municipal currency is helping to improve access to basic services for vulnerable citizens, this time by reducing energy poverty.

It will surprise many to learn that, all around the world, local public actors – from municipalities to city districts – are issuing their own currencies. Whether implemented to promote a greener economy (such as Makkie in Amsterdam, The Netherlands; Lixo in Lisbon, Portugal; or Vilawatt in Viladecans, Spain), a society that cares for the elder (such as Fireau Kippu in Japan or Zeitvorsorge

DOI: 10.4324/9781003474845-17

in St Gallen, Switzerland), a more inclusive city (such as the Torekes in Ghent, Belgium, and Mumbuca in Maricá, Brazil), or to increase local economic activity (such as Grama in Sta. Coloma, Spain; Lvga in Lugano, Switzerland; and Sengzen in Sint-Niklaas, Belgium), local public actors are re-appropriating, re-designing, and re-organising money to make it work for their territory and its citizens.

For all their multiplicity, diversity of purposes, and variety of designs, these local monies share an understanding of their relationship with conventional currency as *complementary*. They aim not to compete with and eventually substitute the national currency in a given territory – an ambition often heard in the cryptocurrency world – but rather to complement the national monetary system by addressing some of its shortcomings. By limiting their use to a well-defined locality, and by being designed to be a poor medium for saving, these local forms of money take aim at characteristics of national money that are major problems for many regions and people today: (1) capital flows to strong economic and financial centres, leaving peripheral regions with a shortage of money; and (2) capital flows to financial markets and accumulates with a very small number of people, entrenching economic inequality. Both phenomena drain conventional money from circulation in the local real economy, depriving the average citizen of a medium of exchange with which to conduct everyday trade and satisfy everyday needs (van Arkel et al. 2024). Because local currencies are not accepted outside the locality, and because their savings value is therefore limited, residents readily spend them in casual transactions. And, as they are spent and re-spent locally, these local monies continue to circulate and serve the local economy.

What we can learn from these forms of money goes beyond the many localised examples. Municipal currencies teach us to rethink money from a thing neutral to the inner workings of the economy – a view common in mainstream economics – to see it as a socio-political instrument to infrastructure the economy and organise society. They question the single currency dogma, showing us the advantages of having multiple currencies circulating in one territory. They teach us that money can be designed and re-designed according to the needs and priorities of the community it is meant to serve. Further, by bringing their design and governance closer to the polity, they demonstrate that money can be made into a tool for deepening democracy. As such, local currencies in general, and municipal currencies in particular, serve as living laboratories for the development of knowledge and practices for new ways of organising life together.

Key Ideas Guiding Local Complementary Currencies

Today's local currency experiments, like local currencies in previous historical periods (Amato and Fantacci 2018), enshrine the *circulation* of money – its *velocity*, to be precise – as the key to a currency that works for the people. It is a position far removed from the focus on the quantity of money – or its supply, to be technical – that pervades today's monetary policy; it suffices to recall the quantitative easing and tightening policies that have dominated the first decades of the 21st century.

The argument for focusing on circulation is the direct relationship between the flow of money through a territory and the level of economic activity in that territory, representing the level of employment. A virtuous cycle of sorts: The more money circulates, the more economic activity there is; the more economic activity there is, the more jobs are created. And since workers are also consumers, more employed people spend more money, moving it through the economy and in turn creating more jobs and even more spending. Economists refer to this as *the multiplier effect*. A simple picture illustrates this insight (see Figure 13.1):

If money needs to circulate in order to work for the real economy, then the methodological advice is to follow the money in order to observe where its circulation is hindered. Local complementary currency practitioners, activists, and municipal policy-makers identify two main reasons for the low circulation of money in an economy. The first is suggested in Figure 13.1. A free market approach to capital mobility results in money *leaking out* of regions with lower rates of return and low value-added industries in the periphery (satellite cities, rural areas, the global south). The money flows into centres with higher rates of return and advanced high value-added industries and services (urban financial centres and the global north) (Sacks 2002; Ward and Lewis 2002; Palley 2011). Within a nation and between nations, peripheral cities and regions struggle to retain the very capital they need to build productive capacity for a human rights economy.

The second reason for the low velocity of money was emphasised by John Maynard Keynes, one of the most renowned economists of the 21st century. Reflecting on the causes and consequences of the Great Depression, Keynes found the problem was neither the lack of talent among workers nor the reduced productive capacity of the economy, "[f]or the resources of Nature and men's devices are just as fertile and productive" as they were before the crash (Keynes 1933a, 140). Unemployment had risen, but workers were just as fit, factories just as ready, and resources just as available. The trouble lay in a lack of understanding of how money works, on "hav[ing] involved ourselves in

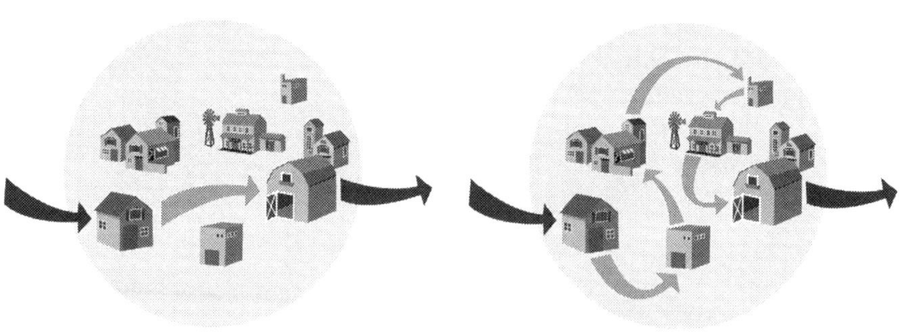

Figure 13.1 Illustration of the multiplier effect.

Source: Created by Social Trade Organization (STRO) 2016.

a colossal muddle, having blundered in the control of a delicate machine, the working of which we do not understand" (Keynes 1933b, 136). More specifically, the problem lay in the way in which saving and spending – two of the main uses of money – articulated to depress demand.

As a universal medium of exchange, people use money to buy and consume, to meet needs of their own and of their households. This spending behaviour hinges on money amply circulating in the economy, which results in money staying in circulation. In a simple formulation often heard among currency practitioners, "my spending is your income, and your spending is my income." In other words, the more and faster money is spent, the more economic activity there is, and the further spending there is. Yet, spending also depends on the value ascribed to money. Perceived as a safe – "liquid" in the economists' jargon – store of value, people also use money to save for the proverbial rainy day. But saving takes money out of circulation in the real economy. And while saving may be a rational individual behaviour, when this behaviour is generalised due to sudden uncertainty about the economic situation the future will bring – due, for example, to the outbreak of a crisis, war, a pandemic, etc. –

> then the effect of saving is merely [...] to increase the number of the unemployed. Moreover, when a man is thrown out of work in this or any other way, his diminished spending power causes further unemployment amongst those who should have produced what he no longer can afford to buy. And so the position gets worse and worse in a vicious circle .
>
> (Keynes, 1931/1933b, 151–152)

In other words, the individual interest to save is misaligned to the collective interest of having money widely circulating in the economy. "After all", Keynes reasoned, "this is only the plainest common sense". Keynes continued:

> For if you buy goods, someone will have to make them. And if you do not buy goods, the shops will not clear their stocks, they will not give repeat orders, and someone will be thrown out of work.
>
> (Keynes, 1931/1933, 152)

If citizens and the private sector were not spending, then the solution Keynes suggested to "the problem of poverty in the midst of potential plenty" (Keynes 1963/1935) – and what he is most known for – was to increase public spending so as to increase economic activity.

> The patient does not need rest. He needs exercise. You cannot set men to work by holding back, by refusing to place orders, by inactivity. On the contrary, activity of one kind or another is the only possible means of making the wheels of economic progress and of the production of wealth go round again. Nationally, too, I should like to see schemes of greatness and magnificence designed and carried through.
>
> (Keynes, 1931/1933, 153)

While the prescription may seem clear – increase public spending to increase the amount of money in circulation and therefore economic activity and the possibility of investing in building capacity for advancing a human rights economy – its implementation at the local level is less clear. This constitutes a third challenge to the circulation of money in the local economy. John Maynard Keynes may have exhorted local authorities to spend – "Now is the time for municipalities to be busy and active with all kinds of sensible improvements" (Keynes, 1933, 153) – but in a single currency regime, municipalities are often assigned budgets that cannot meet their needs for economic, social, and cultural investment. Moreover, as we saw above, in a context of free capital movements, those scarce budgets quickly leak out of the municipality, further deepening monetary scarcity, and further diminishing the capacity of municipalities to implement human rights policies.

Municipal currencies offer a solution to all three challenges. By giving municipalities the power to issue their own currency, they solve the lack of local monetary sovereignty that condemns them to tight budgets in the first place. By restricting the use of the currency to the municipality, they reduce the outflow of money from their territory. And by constraining its use to the consumption of local goods and services, they remove any desire to save in that currency. After all, whenever the municipal and the national currencies can be used equally, the holder of money would prefer to spend a currency that cannot be used elsewhere and save the national currency which has a much wider range of uses – a monetary behaviour described by *Gresham Law*: bad money drives good money out of circulation.

In addition to re-appropriating and reclaiming money, the actors behind municipal currencies also bring a clear focus on local needs to the design of these currencies. This focus shapes the design of the circuits through which municipal currencies are introduced, circulated, and withdrawn from the economy. If, as in Maricá, Brazil, the ultimate purpose behind the introduction of the local currency is to promote a more caring, more inclusive economy, then the needs of the most vulnerable are placed at the heart of the monetary circuits. If, as in Viladecans, Spain, the primary objective is to promote a greener economy and reduce energy poverty, then the design and implementation of the currency link the needs of the environment and vulnerable populations with the resources to attend those needs. In this way, by addressing the needs and priorities of the local economy, municipal currencies act as tools to advance local policy goals. This means that the potential of municipal currencies to support the development of human rights economies ultimately depends on the policy goals they are designed and implemented for.

Let's now turn to the cases of Maricá and Viladecans to analyse what a needs-focused monetary design can teach us about how money can be *made to work* to promote human rights-based local economies.

Mumbuca

Located some 40 km north of Rio de Janeiro, along the Brazilian Atlantic coast, Maricá is home to some 200,000 inhabitants. A satellite city to Rio, and with no industrial or productive capacity within its territory, about 40% of Maricá's working population commutes to Rio and other neighbouring cities to earn a living (Instituto Darcy Ribeiro 2023). They, too, often spend their income outside of Maricá. The city's economy is further characterised by a large number of families living under the poverty line, an extensive informal economy, and youth with little hope for the future.

The city of Maricá receives a large sum of royalties from the oil fields in Bacia de Santos. In an effort to support the most vulnerable families, in 2011, the mayor decided to distribute part of these royalties as a social benefit added to the federal government's welfare programme "Bolsa Família" – a national cash transfer programme conditioned on keeping children vaccinated and in school. The mayor was, however, aware that the royalties transferred as welfare to citizens in the form of Brazilian reais soon leaked out of Maricá as residents and merchants used it to buy from outside the city or to pay debts owed elsewhere. That is, paid in Brazilian reais, the extended welfare programme was strengthening Maricá's economy and its vulnerable families only to a very limited extent.

With the intent "to promote inclusive local development, generating work and income for the population" (Rodrigues and Neumann 2021, 11), in December 2013, Maricá introduced a municipal currency, Mumbuca, through the Mumbuca Community Bank (Cernev and Proença 2016). Oil royalties backed the new currency on a one-to-one basis. Mumbucas were injected into the city's economy as extended welfare benefits – on top of the regular benefits in the national currency – to the city's low-income families. Though merchants had no obligation to accept the currency as payment for their goods, they were given the possibility to convert their earned mumbucas into Brazilian reais coming from the royalties backing the currency. This served to ensure that beneficiaries could access basic goods and services in mumbucas. To keep it local and constrain money leaking out of the municipality, convertibility was restricted to merchants registered in the municipality. Conversion was also charged 2%, which went to fund operations of the Mumbuca Community Bank (for a depiction of the Mumbuca system, see Figure 13.2).

The Mumbuca monetary system developed organically, following a trial-and-error process through which the local public authority and the community bank learned together. Though it was initially a smaller venture, the city gradually increased the size of welfare benefits paid in mumbucas, enlarged the range of beneficiaries, and developed the underlying technology. In late 2014, one year after its inception, 14,000 families received a complementary family benefit of 85 mumbucas per month – equal to 85 reais – which eventually grew to 130 mumbucas per month, and later transformed into 530 mumbucas per month. A family of four thus saw its total allowance increased from 130 to 520

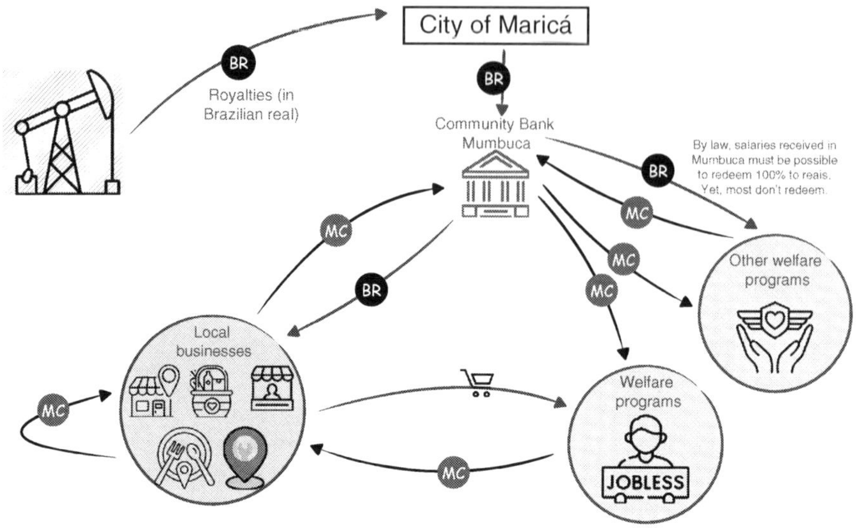

Figure 13.2 Illustration of the Mumbuca monetary system.

Source: Created by the author.

mumbucas. New welfare programmes catering to other precarious citizens were added in 2015: a "youth solidarity minimum income" – 100 mumbucas monthly for young persons aged 14–29 – and a "pregnancy minimum income" – 85 mumbucas per month paid to mothers during pregnancy up to the child's first birthday.

Distrusting yet "another political initiative," merchants were initially reluctant to accept mumbucas; in 2014, the first registration saw the number of merchants in the mumbuca network barely growing beyond 100. To promote acceptance, the city cancelled the 2% redemption fee for merchants converting mumbucas into Brazilian reais before the fifth of the month. Another key development during these initial years was the city's decision to support the digitalisation of the infrastructure. In 2018, Mumbuca went from a card-based currency to a digital phone-app currency supported by the e-Dinheiro payment platform[1] alongside the Mumbuca card. The e-Dinheiro platform allowed beneficiaries not only to receive and spend their mumbucas, but also gave them access to regular banking services, such as a savings account, a checking account, or the possibility to get a smaller credit. A previously unbanked and vulnerable population could now pay their bills, make P2P transfers, or buy a phone on credit. In this way, the expansion enabled by a monetary technology driven by a community bank embedded mumbuca deeper into Maricá's economy.

The continuous tinkering with Mumbuca's monetary system – from its rules and beneficiaries to its technology and partners – meant that by the time the Covid-19 pandemic hit Maricá, the city was well prepared to quickly roll out an encompassing unconditional basic income (UBI) programme. First, it enlarged, simplified, and unified its various welfare benefits under two programmes: a "renda básica e cidadania", literally "citizen's basic income", handing 300 mumbucas per person and month to all registered citizens unconditional of their means, and a "renda minima" or "minimum income" of about 1,000 mumbucas handed to precarious micro-entrepreneurs in the gig economy as well as to employees that companies retained despite the economic downturn brought by the lockdowns. Second, the fact that the technology was already in place and citizens were versed in its use enabled the immediate implementation of the UBI-like emergency benefit programmes (De Wispelaere et al. 2024). In this way, the distribution of the welfare benefit through a municipal currency contributed to strengthening the realisation of economic and social rights.

While implementation of the emergency basic income approved by the Brazilian Congress on the onset of the pandemic was riddled with challenges, in April 2022, the Mumbuca-based UBI successfully reached out to 42% of Maricá's population (Freitas 2022). With a large informal economy, many Brazilian citizens are not registered in the federal government's registry, and even if registered, many of them do not have a bank account. During a time of increased health risk, agglomerations formed at the entries of government agencies and bank offices across the country as citizens queued to register, renew their national identity cards, and start a bank account through which to receive the emergency basic income they were eligible for. In Maricá, instead, citizens eagerly downloaded the Mumbuca app to register and claim their rightful basic income, the city easily transferring the Mumbuca basic income to its citizens (Gonzalez et al. 2021). The number of Mumbuca bank accounts grew from 37,550 in December 2019 to 65,374 in September 2021 – a 74% increase. Most tellingly, the volume of trade in mumbucas in local businesses grew from 36,172,646.47 in 2019 to 254,403,346.66 in 2021 – a 603% growth in local trade. As a result, between March 2020 and April 2021, the city experienced a 7% increase in formal employment, compared to the decline in other municipalities of the state of Rio de Janeiro and Brazil at large (Rodrigues 2021). Designed to circulate locally, mumbuca served the local economy by guaranteeing merchants survived the pandemic lockdowns, thus maintaining local jobs and guaranteeing that Maricá's vulnerable residents could access food and other basic goods and services.

A monetary system anchored in local government allows the infrastructural capacities of money to empower public development policies at the city level. A welfare policy that benefits the population at large directly addresses the concerns for inequality, precarity, and poverty. When delivered in a currency organised to work for the region a little longer – by constraining its use to the local territory – the public welfare policy not only supports low-income citizens but has the potential to further strengthen local businesses and the local economy. As money remains circulating in the territory, it remains working for the territory. The local nature of the monetary infrastructure and its articulation through local welfare policies are both key features to understand the rapid change the currency effected on the economic dynamics of Maricá.

The Mumbuca municipal currency includes, however, a design feature that weakens its ability to work for the territory, its economy, and its people. The possibility for local businesses to redeem mumbucas into Brazil's national currency opens up a gate for money to leak out of Maricá. What's more, convertibility risks the long-term sustainability of any local currency. Such dynamics were readily observable in the complementary-currency-based UBI-like programme implemented in Barcelona between 2018 and 2019. After 13 months, once the backing in euros was exhausted, the programme necessarily ceased (Martín Belmonte et al. 2021). In Maricá, in 2018, businesses redeemed 80.65% of the mumbucas injected into the economy, big businesses redeeming to a much larger extent than small businesses (Diniz et al. 2024). Had Maricá not had a stable and secured source of national money in oil royalties, the possibility to redeem would have consumed the backing of the local currency and, with it, mumbucas would have ceased to exist. Such a high conversion rate was a sign of the, then, limited trust – or use, or both – local businesses had for the local currency.

Yet, as local businesses gained trust in the commitment of public authorities and as the mumbuca economy developed, conversion ratios went down. 71.78% of mumbucas were converted into Brazilian reais in 2019, 74.98% in 2020, 73.82% in 2021 (Prefeitura de Maricá and E-dinheiro 2021). Over 12,600 businesses accept the local currency in payment for their goods and services, 67% of which trade at least once a month in the local currency, and 26% of which pay for all their supplies exclusively in mumbucas (Freitas 2022). As the number of merchants using mumbucas for all their purchases grows, the more the municipal currency circulates in the economy, and thus the more and more varied the local businesses accepting and spending in mumbucas. This means not only a more resilient local economy but also more possibility for vulnerable citizens to cover their basic needs. The so-called "network effect" as it plays out in monetary systems – the more and more varied the merchants associated with the local money, the more valuable the monetary tokens. For the value of a currency for an economy rests on the community of users behind it.

Vilawatt

A city of some 67,000 inhabitants in just 20.4 km^2, Viladecans grew in the 1960s and 1970s to become a service city to the Catalan capital. Some of its most densely populated neighbourhoods were constructed with poor building techniques before the Spanish legislation on building insulation of 1976 and consume, as a result, above the average levels of energy. Those neighbourhoods are home to low-income residents, likely to suffer from energy poverty and unable to afford the retrofitting of their residential buildings for energy efficiency. Viladecans City Council conceived Vilawatt to usher citizens, merchants, and public institutions into collaborating "to promote and ensure a secure, clean and efficient use of energy" in the city. The four key instruments used to ignite the transition to "a new energy model at the local level" are "energy supply, energy culture, retrofitting of buildings and a local currency linked to energy savings."[2]

Issuance of vilawatts is firmly entwined with the energy savings goal that guides the initiative. As in Maricá, public spending is focused on the territory; yet different from the Brazilian city, the municipal currency is accepted for payment of certain municipal taxes and municipal services. That is, the origin and direction of circulation of vilawatts goes from public investment to private spending to tax payments (see Figure 13.3). As businesses can always find use for the municipal currency in the payment of local taxes, such a monetary design makes the money more readily acceptable by a variety of businesses.

In Viladecans, the initial public investment was largely funded by the EU programme *Urban Initiative Actions* (UIA) and focused on reducing the energy consumption and in developing the energy production capacity of buildings. Windows, doors, fences, and blinds were changed; internal and external insulation was installed; and solar panels were placed on roofs. Citizen communities were created with the capacity to share energy with other neighbourhoods even if these are not directly connected to the Vilawatt network. An information office was set up to advise citizens on their contracts and bills, and bulk-buying of renewable energy was coordinated by the Vilawatt Consortium. Half of the energy savings thus accrued are then issued in vilawatts and automatically transferred to citizens in the Consortium. The other half is reinvested in retrofitting other buildings through direct public investment or through subsidies to citizens. On a voluntary basis and in the near future, civil servants will be able to apply for a minor portion of their salary to be paid in vilawatts. The more than 3,500 citizens who take part in the initiative find use for their vilawatts in

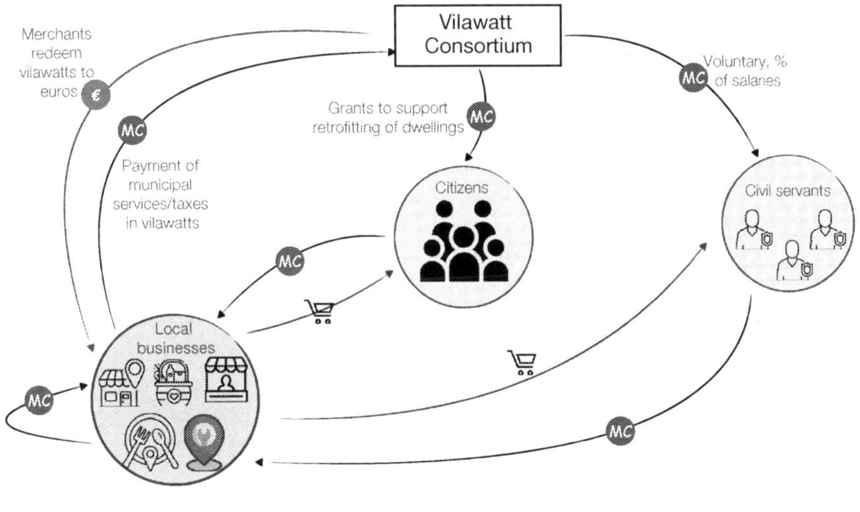

Figure 13.3 Illustration of the Vilawatts currency system

Source: Created by the author.

the more than 400 local merchants associated with the network who, in turn, can spend the local complementary money in goods and services among themselves and, as of 2022, to pay municipal taxes and services. In other words, in the design of its monetary rules, Vilawatt entangles the city's fight for climate neutrality and against energy poverty into the city's local economy.

Anchoring the issuance of vilawatts on accomplished reduction in energy consumption and introducing them into circulation through rewards for, and further investment on, energy saving measures, the Vilawatt monetary circuits are decisively articulated to the energy needs of the people. The municipal currency thus aligns the interests of individual citizens with the interests of nature. Beyond aligning interests, Vilawatts monetary tokens visualise energy savings. At the intersection of government bureaucracy and scientific objectivity, numbers – more so when they constitute rewards for the behaviour they visualise – act as vehicles for igniting democratic debate;[3] in this case, a broad discussion among citizens and local businesses of everyone's role in the energy transition and the recognition of the need to update one's know-how and skills for advancing a climate neutral future – a re-skilling that the Vilawatt Consortium has facilitated through the creation of learning communities, the offering of training programmes to small businesses, and active labour market interventions that prioritise the most vulnerable citizens – thus approaching the green transition from a human rights-based perspective. In this way Vilawatt not only aligns the interests of residents in Viladecans with those of the planet. Most importantly, in underscoring every single one's energy use, Vilawatt heightens self-reflection on one's energy practices in relation to those of one's neighbours – personal meditations that nudge the individual motive of action from monetary gain to care for the environment. To put it clearly: Money articulated around energy savings cultivates, by design, awareness of our collective responsibility for the Earth that we all share.

The impact of Vilawatt is visible in the number of dwellings retrofitted – 55 – the aggregate energy savings in the city – 56% – the ubiquity of energy debate, which has become part of citizens' everyday life, the expansion of the project from the initial district to include the whole city, and the persistence of the initiative beyond the initial EU funding. The optimism generated is such that the year targeted for the city to achieve climate neutrality has moved from 2050 to 2030.

The Vilawatt Consortium, which governs the Vilawatt municipal currency, upholds the human right to participation by involving local merchants, citizen associations, and public entities like the City Council in decision-making. Since the currency's issuance and circulation are based on energy savings by residents and businesses, these groups play a critical role and are therefore included in the governance of the currency. Consortium members regularly engage with residents and businesses to understand their concerns, practices, and knowledge around energy consumption and production. This inclusive, public-private-citizen partnership ensures that the community's voices shape Vilawatt's development, guiding both the currency and shaping the policy goals for which it has been designed.

Conclusion: Remaking Money to Advance Human Right Economies

While the Universal Declaration of Human Rights formulates a compelling vision and a powerful language to guide national and international economic, social, cultural, and civil policies, and while its recognition by the United Nations General Assembly has facilitated the advance of human rights in a majority of countries (Hannum 1996), the declaration contains little on the way of practical guidance and effective instruments to address global and macro-economic barriers – like global capital flows and unequal capital accumulation – that hinder the advancement of human rights economies. Efforts have focused on the making of human-based policies at the national level that have proved difficult to implement partly because such policies presume generous budgets at the local level where those policies are to be implemented (Global Citizenship Commission 2016, 65–69).

And yet, the implications of human rights deficiencies are most felt at the local level. Intent to address the many challenges their citizens face, municipalities around the world are quietly re-appropriating the power to issue their own money, thereby crafting a profound shift in how local economies function and are governed. This re-appropriation is not merely a technical scheme. Rather, taking the power to issue their own municipal currencies constitutes a significant political and social act that empowers local governments to address specific needs prioritised within their territories. In Maricá, Brazil, and Viladecans, Spain, we saw how these municipal currencies – Mumbuca and Vilawatt – are tailored to meet the unique socio-economic and socio-environmental conditions that limit the improvement of human rights in their communities.

The cases of Mumbuca and Vilawatt underscore the adaptability of municipal currencies to local contexts. Unlike national currencies, which, by definition and design, fail to address localised issues, municipal monies can be precisely designed and governed to advance particular objectives. Whether the goal is to boost local commerce, enhance social welfare, or achieve environmental targets, municipal currencies offer a versatile tool for local governments. This malleability in design enables municipalities to tailor their monetary systems to the specific socio-economic and socio-environmental circumstances they face.

Moreover, the emergence of municipal currencies challenges traditional notions of money as a neutral medium of exchange. Instead, it positions money as a socio-technical infrastructure that can be re-designed to serve public purposes – a shift in perspective that allows for a re-organisation of the economy based on local priorities, needs, and values. As such, municipal currencies become instruments for economic democracy, allowing citizens and local governments to collaboratively shape their economic futures.

In re-thinking money through the lens of municipal currencies, we are invited to imagine a more decentralised and participatory economic system. By reclaiming monetary sovereignty at the local level, municipalities are not only addressing immediate economic and social issues but also pioneering new ways of organising economic life, ways that prioritise community well-being, environmental sustainability, and human rights. Serving as small-scale living laboratories, these municipal experiments are paving the way to a better-informed, more monetary-conscious public (Barinaga 2024; Feinig 2022). They are, too, quietly advancing more just ways of organising life together.

Notes

1 The payment platform e-Dinheiro was developed by Instituto e-Dinheiro – formerly Instituto Palmas – a non-profit organisation that supports the development of community development banks across Brazil. See Cernev and Diniz (2020) and Ansonera et al. (2021). For the history of Instituto Palmas itself, see Melò (2023).

2 Vilawatt Consortium Statutes, p. 3. And in Ajuntament de Viladecans. 2019. *Protocol de Funcionament Moneda Local Vilawatt*, p. 4. Empirical details for Vilawatt come from Vilawatt's webpage, the Statutes of the Vilawatt Consortia, Vilawatt currency design, operational protocols, and official impact reports, the description of the project in the UIA (Urban Innovative Actions) website, the UIA Case Study Viladecans, the final Journal UIA Vilawatt project, as well as a variety of pages hosted under the European Union European Regional Development Fund.

3 On the politics of visibility and trust performed through numbers, see Porter (1995, 2020).

Bibliography

Amato, M., and L. Fantacci. 2018. "Complementary Currencies." In S. Battilossi, Y. Cassis, and K. Yago (eds.), *Handbook of the History of Money and Currency*. Singapore: Springer.

Ansonera, A., E. H. Diniz, E. S. Siqueira, and M. Pozzebon. 2021. "From Community Bank to Solidarity Fintech: The Case of Palmas e-Dinheiro in Brazil." In T. Walker, J. McGaughey, S. Goubran, and N. Wagdy (eds.), *Innovations in Social Finance*, 251–268.

Balakrishnan, S., R. Costa, J. Haushofer, and F. Waltenberg. 2024. *Welfare Effects of a Permanent Unconditional Cash Transfer Program: Evidence from Maricá, Brazil*. National Bureau of Economic Research, Working Paper 33089.

Barinaga, E. 2024. *Remaking Money for a Sustainable Future: Money Commons*. Bristol University Press.

Cernev, A., and E. Diniz. 2020. "Palmas para o e-Dinheiro! A evolução digital de uma moeda social local." *Revista de Administração Contemporânea* 24(5): 487–506.

Cernev, A., and B. Proença. 2016. "Mumbuca: a primeira moeda social digital do Brasil." *Revista Brasileira de Casos – Gvcasos* 6(2).

Corrons, A. 2018. *Monedes Complementàries com a Eina de Desenvolupament Local (Complementary Currencies as a Local Development Tool)*. AMB (Àrea Metropolitana de Barcelona).

De Wispelaere, J., L. Morales, and F. Waltenberg. 2024. "Basic Income as a Pandemic Social Protection Instrument: Lessons from Maricá, Brazil." *International Social Security Review* 77(1–2).

Diniz, E., J. Porto de Albuquerque, J. Campos, B. Andrade de Figueiredo, J. A. Ribeiro Yamaguchi, and M. Fazito. 2024. *Assessing Implications of Cash Transfer Programmes with Local Currency to Intra Urban Development: The Case of Maricá*. Available at http://dx.doi.org/10.2139/ssrn.4943442

Feinig, J. 2022. *Moral Economies of Money: Politics and the Monetary Constitution of Society*. Stanford University Press.

Freitas, F. 2022. "Transferência de renda com moeda social em Cabo Frio, Itaboraí, Niterói e Maricá: alívio da pobreza ou renda básica?" *Gestão, Política e Sociedade.* https://www.estadao.com.br/politica/gestao-politica-e-sociedade/transferencia-de-renda-com-moeda-social-em-cabo-frio-itaborai-niteroi-e-marica-alivio-da-pobreza-ou-renda-basica/

Global Citizenship Commission. 2016. *The Universal Declaration of Human Rights in the 21st Century, a Living Document in a Changing World.* United Kingdom: Open Book Publishers.

Gonzalez, L., A. K. Cernev, M. H. de Araujo, and E. H. Diniz. 2021. "Digital Complementary Currencies and Public Policies during the COVID-19 Pandemic." *Brazilian Journal of Public Administration* 54(4): 1146–1160.

Hannum, H. 1996. "The Status of the Universal Declaration of Human Rights in National and International Law." *Georgia Journal of International and Comparative Law* 25: 287.

Instituto Darcy Ribeiro. 2023. *Maricá. Panorama Socioeconômico.* Prefeitura de Maricá.

Keynes, J. M. 1933a/1930. "The Great Slump of 1930." In *Essays in Persuasion.* London: Macmillan and Co.

Keynes, J. M. 1933b/1931. "Saving and Spending, a BBC Address." In *Essays in Persuasion.* London: Macmillan and Co.

Keynes, J. M. 1963/1935. "A Self-Adjusting Economic System." *Nebraska Journal of Economics and Business* 2(2): 11–15.

Martín Belmonte, S., J. Puig, and M. Roca. 2021. "Crisis Mitigation through Cash Assistance to Increase Local Consumption Levels: A Case Study of a Bimonetary System in Barcelona, Spain." *Journal of Risk and Financial Management* 14(9): 430–447.

Melò, J. 2023. *As Moedas Sociais do Brasil: Do Palmacard ao e-dinheiro.* Arte Visual.

Palley, T. I. 2011. *The Contradictions of Export-Led Growth: Public Policy Brief.* Jerome Levy Economics Institute of Bard College, 119.

Prefeitura de Maricá, and E-dinheiro. 2021. *Métrica e Volumetria dos Programas Sociais da Prefeitura de Maricá: RBC, PAT, PAE e Aluguel Social. Balanço 2018–2021.* Instituto E-dinheiro Brasil.

Porter, T. M. 1995. *Trust in Numbers: The Pursuit of Objectivity in Science and Public Life.* Princeton University Press.

Porter, T. M. 2020. *Democracy Counts: On Sacred and Debased Numbers.* Princeton University Press Ideas.

Rodrigues, D. P. 2021. *Inclusão Financeira e o Uso de Fintechs como Instrumentos de Políticas Públicas.* Master's Thesis. Fundação Getulio Vargas.

Rodrigues, D. P., and D. M. Neumann. 2021. "Moeda Social e Desenvolvimiento Local em Maricá (RJ)." *Fundação Getulio Vargas.*

Sacks, J. 2002. *The Money Trail: Measuring Your Impact on the Local Economy Using LM3.* New Economics Foundation.

Van Arkel, H., L. Muns Terrats, and J. Alenda-Demoutiez. 2024. *Boosting Your Economy by Making Money Virtuous.* Social Trade Organisation (STRO).

Viader Bosch, R. 2022. "Presentation Given by Ramón Vader Bosch – Director of General Services, Mayor's Office of Viladecans – during the Visit Deep Dive Partner Cities Vilawatt UTM Project." July 22, 2022.

Ward, B., and J. Lewis. 2002. *Plugging the Leaks: Making the Most of Every Pound That Enters Your Local Economy.* New Economics Foundation.

14 The Racial Wealth Gap

Local Solutions for Equality and Justice

David Radcliffe

Introduction

The racial wealth gap in the United States represents one of the most enduring and visible consequences of systemic racism and historical inequality. Wealth—as opposed to income—captures the accumulated economic advantages and disadvantages that individuals and groups experience over generations. The disparity in wealth between racial groups highlights not only historical injustices, such as slavery and redlining, but also contemporary policies and practices that perpetuate inequality. This chapter explores the dimensions of the racial wealth gap, its causes, and potential policy solutions, with a focus on Baby Bonds as a transformative initiative. It highlights the efforts of Connecticut leaders, who passed and funded the first State baby bond effort in the United States. Connecticut's success has led to more than a dozen States introducing baby bond legislation. By examining local and State policy momentum and the economic, political, and social factors underlying wealth inequality, this chapter aims to demonstrate that intentional, equity-driven policies are essential to promoting justice and inclusion.

The Wealth Gap and Why Wealth Matters

Historically, policies such as the Homestead Act and the G.I. Bill disproportionately benefited White Americans, creating a foundation for wealth accumulation that excluded Black and Indigenous populations. These policies reflect how discrimination is institutionalized through economic systems, shaping access to wealth and mobility. Recognizing these structural barriers is essential for developing policies that address their root causes and promote equity (Rothstein, 2017).

In addition to an understanding of the roles of systemic discrimination in resource allocation vis-à-vis specific communities and which investments will have the most impact, it is important to consider a fundamental measure of stability and opportunity: wealth. Wealth enables people to plan their futures and live self-determined lives. When examining racial economic disparities in the United States, wealth is where the largest gaps emerge. For people who lack

DOI: 10.4324/9781003474845-18

adequate income and housing, quality and affordable healthcare, and/or decent jobs, their life choices are severely constrained. To change this, public policy must go far beyond income redistribution; it must help people build wealth—a key buffer against economic uncertainty and an engine of generational progress.

According to the Survey of Consumer Finances, conducted by the United States Federal Reserve (2019), as of 2022, the median White family held over $285,000 in wealth, while the median Black family wealth was around $44,900—just 15 percent as much. The median Latino family fared slightly better at about 20 percent of the median White family wealth (Cunningham and Paul, 2024). A focus on income inequality overlooks the broader and more entrenched issue of wealth inequality. Wealth disparities are far more pronounced than income disparities and play a central role in perpetuating systemic inequality, particularly along racial lines (Shapiro, 2004).

For example:

- Two households may have the same income, but if one has inherited wealth, they are far better positioned to invest in education, buy property, and weather financial crises.
- Policies addressing income (e.g., raising wages) won't necessarily close the racial wealth gap, which requires structural changes like reparations or targeted asset-building programs.

This distinction underscores the need for policies aimed at building wealth, not just increasing income, to achieve true economic equity (Hamilton and Darity, 2010a).

Racial Wealth Gap—Historical Trajectory

In the United States, the wealth gap is not due to personal deficiencies, individual failures, or lack of hard work on the part of Black Americans and other groups that have little to no wealth (or even negative wealth), but rather due to public policies and practices over generations that have intentionally excluded certain groups (Hamilton, 2016). The 20th century in America was a period where Black Americans experienced segregation through rules, laws, and customs in housing, education, employment, and more. Within this context and against the backdrop of the realities and legacy of slavery from less than 100 years earlier, here are some key examples from the mid-20th century that have helped set the stage for today's wealth gap:

Social Security—1930s

In 1935, Social Security was created to address the problem of economic security for older persons by creating a system in which workers would provide for their own future economic security through taxes paid while employed. It's important to note that the original Social Security program excluded domestic and agricultural workers, about half of whom were Black men and 90 percent women.

This exclusion wasn't incidental—it was a political compromise to appease Southern lawmakers who sought to maintain racial and economic hierarchies by denying Black workers access to these benefits. As historian Vanessa May details, these Southern legislators found allies elsewhere, including among White middle-class women in the North (May, 2011).

The G.I. Bill—1940s

In 1944, the same year President Franklin Roosevelt introduced the idea of an economic bill of rights, the G.I. Bill helped millions of Americans to get a college education and buy a first home. While the G.I. Bill's language did not specifically exclude African-American veterans, it was structured in a way that excluded 1.2 million Black veterans who had served their country during World War II. On one hand, the G.I. Bill helped create a "middle class" of (primarily) White homeowners, with a generational impact on wealth. On the other hand, for Black veterans, the benefits were modest at best, due to discrimination and segregation in education and housing. An estimated one in three students at historically Black colleges and universities after the war were Black veterans, but the schools largely did not have the capacity to fulfil the demand and were compelled to turn away many applicants. Concurrently, redlining put home loans for Black Americans largely out of reach. Despite its mixed legacy, the history of the G.I. Bill demonstrates that the government can foster broad-based wealth creation (Cunningham and Paul, 2024).

Federal Highway Construction—1950s

The federal highway construction and urban renewal of the mid-20th century initiatives disproportionately displaced Black communities by demolishing thriving neighborhoods to make way for highways or redevelopment projects. For example, in Saint Paul, Minnesota, the historically Black Rondo neighborhood was virtually destroyed when the federal government built Interstate 94 through the community. Similar stories occurred across the country, including the destruction of the Hayti district in Durham, North Carolina.

These so-called "urban renewal" efforts uprooted families, eradicated local businesses, and erased entire communities. In doing so, they stripped Black families of their primary wealth-building assets—homes and businesses—hindering their ability to achieve economic security across generations. The effects of these projects are still felt today, as many displaced families were unable to recover financially, again contributing to the widening racial wealth gap (Cunningham and Paul, 2024).

Additionally, starting in the early 1970s, political sentiment regarding social mobility shifted radically from government mandates to promote economic security toward a neoliberal approach in which the market is presumed to be the solution for all our problems, economic or otherwise. As a result, the onus of social mobility shifted further onto the individual, while the market became more inadequate at addressing rising inequality (Piketty, 2013). The accumulation of disadvantages as a result of the above and other policies, practices, resource flows, and perspectives has led to and cemented a severe wealth gap. Recent policy responses have not met the moment, much of which focus on helping families survive rather than thrive. The US tax code favors those who already have more wealth (Piketty, 2013).

To address the wealth gap and achieve prosperity and equality will require not just political and civil rights but also the economic rights necessary to ensure that everyone has the opportunity and resources to succeed. Human rights-enhancing economic policies can repair and address root causes of, and structural barriers to, the enjoyment of human rights by groups experiencing racial discrimination from a point of view that considers aspects of a person's identity—like race, gender, class, sexuality, disability, and age (Hamilton and Bisnath, 2024).

Toward Inclusive Economic Rights: Baby Bonds

In the United States, much of the framing of the wealth gap argues that it is due to the poor choices and decision-making of certain people (Shapiro, 2004). This framing is wrong, as has been demonstrated by carefully conducted studies (Pew Research Center, n.d.). The intergenerational wealth gap is structurally created and has virtually nothing to do with individual choices or behavior (McGhee, 2021). Instead, wealth transfers within families better position some young adults with capital to purchase wealth-generating assets.

Whether a young adult has access to this seed money is not based on individual action or inaction, but rather on the economic position in which an individual is born. Young adults from households without wealth or with very limited wealth receive very little capital from their families. Without initial seed capital, these young adults begin their lives far behind those of their more economically advantaged counterparts in building wealth over their lifetimes (Oliver and Shapiro, 1995).

Baby Bonds are specifically intended to meaningfully close the wealth gap by providing the most resources to children whose households have the lowest amount of wealth. Baby Bonds is public seed funding that establishes, in perpetuity, a guarantee to "start-up" capital for young adults to use for activities that build wealth, like home ownership or entrepreneurship.

How did Baby Bonds in America come to be? While providing capital to young people may seem new or radical, the concept of economic rights is neither of these. In his 1797 pamphlet, *Agrarian Justice*, philosopher and political activist Thomas Paine proposed a "public system of economic security" funded through a tax on inherited property that would provide seed capital to young adults when they turned 21, as well as "age old pension" in the form of annual income support to adults over the age of 50. He argued that all people reaching adulthood should receive a capital grant to help them "begin the world". In Paine's proposal, we find the seeds for what later became foundational elements for a lifetime of economic security, including Social Security and Baby Bonds. "It is a right, and not a charity, that I am pleading for" (Paine, 1797).

In the 200 years since Paine's proposal, there have been other key US policy moments that set the stage for today's Baby Bonds:

- In 1862, an early federal social security-type pension system to provide steady income was set up for Civil War Union soldiers (later, former Confederate states created and funded their own pension system). Black Union veterans were eligible for pensions, as were women—either as widows or veterans, primarily nurses.
- That same year, Congress passed an asset-building program known as the Homestead Act which opened land ownership to male citizens, widows, single women, and immigrants pledging to become citizens. At the time, this opportunity was not open to most Black people, who were still enslaved. Unfortunately, much of the land made available through the Homestead Act was formerly inhabited by Native Americans, who were further displaced by this new act. Researchers estimate that 20 percent of the US population (mostly White people) can trace their family history of building wealth to land acquired through this one piece of legislation (Rothstein, 2017).
- On January 16, 1865, near the end of the American Civil War, General William Tecumseh Sherman issued Special Field Orders, No. 15. This order provided for the confiscation of 400,000 acres of land along the Atlantic coast of South Carolina, Georgia, and Florida and dividing it into 40-acre parcels for the benefit of approximately 18,000 formerly enslaved families and other Black people then living in the area. Four months later, after the assassination of President Lincoln, the orders had little concrete effect because President Andrew Johnson issued a proclamation that returned the lands to southern owners who took a loyalty oath. Although mules are not mentioned in the orders, this order and eventual rescission were a main source for the expression "forty acres and a mule" (Du Bois, 1935).

The mixed results of these and other policy interventions led scholars to consider new ways to think about and address poverty and wealth inequality.

In 1989, UK economist Julian Le Grand may have been the first in modern policy discourse to propose 'baby bonds', or in his words, a "universal grant of basic capital (UBC)". Le Grand proposed that a grant of £10,000 should be awarded to every citizen on his or her attaining the age of majority, funded by inheritance tax.

The idea of providing financial resources to children as a means of reducing economic inequality gained additional momentum in a 1991 book by Michael Sherraden called *Assets and the Poor* (Sherraden, 1991). Sherraden, Shapiro, and others opened the conversation of economic well-being and poverty beyond income and subsistence and contributed to an understanding of the roles of assets in forging justice, mobility, and economic inclusion (Shapiro, 2004). Their work inspired policy proposals in the early 2000s, including child savings accounts, the United Kingdom's Child Trust Fund as envisioned by Le Grand and others, as well as the American Savings for Personal Investment Retirement and Education effort.

US Baby Bonds was introduced in an article "Can 'Baby Bonds' Eliminate the Racial Wealth Gap in Putative Post-Racial America?" (Hamilton and Darity, 2010b). This seminal work energized the consideration of Baby Bonds. These accounts would help create a more equal starting point for children born into poverty regardless of their family background and focus on wealth, rather than income. The program is affectionately known as 'Baby Bonds' but is more accurately labeled a 'Baby Trust', since it is actually a trust account program, not a bond account program.

The concept of Baby Bonds is focused on the initial endowment itself—rather than savings alone—as a necessary ingredient to put families on a pathway to wealth accumulation. In doing so, these substantially endowed accounts will lead to significant wealth building. To that end, Baby Bond accounts will provide all children—but especially those from families with little to no wealth—with the necessary capital to have financial agency and economic security to take risks and shield against losses (Markoff, Hamilton, and Radcliffe, 2024).

In the past ten years, the idea of Baby Bonds has gained traction in academic circles, think tanks, and government policy discussions. Various economists and researchers have discussed the potential benefits of such a policy, including reducing wealth inequality and improving economic mobility. Baby bonds came to wider public attention in the United States in 2019, when United States Senator Cory Booker (D-New Jersey) ran for president on a platform that featured a federal baby bonds program. At the federal level, the first substantive attempt to introduce legislation in support of Baby Bonds was made by Senator Booker in 2018 with the introduction of the American Opportunity Accounts Act. Since then, Sen. Booker has worked with Rep. Ayanna Pressley (D-Massachusetts) to develop and promote the legislation. Sen. Booker and Rep. Pressley reintroduced the bill in the 118th Congress in February 2023.

In many ways, baby bonds are a modern manifestation of Roosevelt's vision of "freedom from want". Baby Bonds is a means for achieving economic security and attainment of economic rights. It is a foundational financial resource that ensures no child is born into an economic system that prevents them from fully participating in society. Just as Roosevelt envisioned a future where no American would face poverty, hunger, or insecurity, baby bonds offer a way to help achieve that promise by providing the financial tools necessary to overcome systemic barriers to wealth and opportunity (Cunningham and Paul, 2024).

In addition to federal Baby Bonds legislation, there has been important progress at the state and local level. In 2021, both Connecticut and Washington, D.C., passed local Baby Bond programs, followed by California in 2022. As of July 2024, 20 states had introduced or seriously considered baby bond legislation. There are also smaller scale baby bond pilot projects underway or under construction in ten places at the local level.

The First Baby Bond Baby: A Connecticut Case Study

On July 1, 2023, Nolan Ramirez was born in the small city of New Britain, Connecticut (population 74,000), a former manufacturing powerhouse and now struggling to recover from generations of deindustrialization. Nolan's birth was more than a personal milestone; he was the nation's first "Baby Bonds" baby. Nolan's future will be built on a unique financial foundation that children born before that day in Connecticut lack. Through Connecticut's Baby Bonds program, Nolan and more than 16,000 other children whose births are covered by Medicaid (public health insurance for those with lower incomes) received $3,200 in the fiscal year 2024. With investment growth, each account will be worth between $11,000 and $24,000 by the time the children make a claim for their share of the Baby Bonds trust, between the ages of 18 and 30. These funds can be used to attend college, buy a home, or start a business—all activities that are critical to building wealth (Cunningham and Radcliffe, 2024).

The interest in the idea began in earnest after the murder of George Floyd by police in May 2020, sparking a reckoning that saw lawmakers scrambling for policies that might address the striking disparities between Black and White Americans (Bloomberg News, 2022). Connecticut State Treasurer Shawn Wooden's response was to find a solution that would meaningfully counter the severe disinvestment experienced by communities like the neighborhood where he grew up. In line with his goals to seed reinvestment in largely disinvested communities, Senator Booker's proposed federal legislation was adapted for application at the state level. In 2023, Treasurer Wooden's successor, Erick Russell, identified a funding source for Baby Bonds that allowed the program to go forward (CT Mirror, 2023).

The Connecticut Baby Bonds Trust wields a powerful feature of the Baby Bonds policy concept: The program is race neutral in design and implementation, as *all* babies born into poverty will benefit. But the *impact* will be race conscious, in that, with a greater percentage of Black and brown babies born into poverty, those communities will receive a proportionally greater benefit from Baby Bonds.

Why States and State Treasurers Matter

The impact of the Baby Bonds will be most fully realized as a progressively funded federal policy, as it is the federal government that has the right-sized level of resources and administrative capability. Until then, progress on Baby Bonds at the state level is providing important inspiration and learning for eventual federal policy. There is precedent for federal policy to follow state innovation—Social Security, the Affordable Care Act, and marriage equality all had their start as state-level efforts.

State progress on Baby Bonds has been led largely by state treasurers, starting with Connecticut State Treasurer Erick Russell and his predecessor Shawn Wooden. Beyond Connecticut, treasurers in California, Massachusetts, Nevada, New Mexico, Rhode Island, Vermont, and Washington have also been advocates for baby bonds over the past two years.

The state treasurer's offices manage all state banking and credit relationships, ensure bills are paid on time; oversee the state's public pension funds; safeguard the assets of state employees, teachers, and retirees; and manage the state's debt, bonding programs, and cash flow—overseeing investments in transportation, infrastructure, housing, childcare facilities, and more.

What's unique about the role of treasurer is that state investments made today often won't bear fruit for five, seven, or ten years down the line—far longer than an election cycle. State treasurers have an obligation to consider the long-term future. Baby bonds are an investment whose economic value will only be realized 18–30 years later (Russell, 2024). As more states like Connecticut pass Baby Bonds legislation and implement the program well, it is more likely that the federal government will follow the lead of states.

Opportunities and Challenges

Balancing Immediate Needs and Long-Term Solutions

Baby Bonds highlight a fundamental tension in social policy: addressing immediate needs versus investing in long-term solutions. It's hard to ignore the prevalence of poverty, near poverty, and inequality in the United States, with many households living paycheck to paycheck, forced to make choices like paying rent or buying food—or covering medical expenses and childcare. While these immediate financial pressures are real and severe, they require short-term support. However, they do not address the root causes of the racial wealth gap (Meiksins and Dubb, 2019).

Some Baby Bonds critics question the value of Baby Bonds because they do not meet the immediate needs of people (Bruenig, 2023). However, it is important to note that addressing immediate needs alone will never break the cycle of intergenerational poverty and increasing inequalities. Proponents note that there should not be a choice between funding basic needs and Baby Bonds; both are essential.

Program Challenges

The targeted nature of State Baby Bonds addresses a critical gap in current social and economic policies in the United States. By focusing on children born into low-income families, these programs directly tackle a root of intergenerational poverty and wealth disparities. While means testing at birth isn't perfect, it's an administratively efficient way to reach those most likely to lack family wealth. The program's universal application within this target group also avoids stigmatization, ensures broad coverage, and is consistent with a human rights approach.

While state-specific baby bond programs and proposals vary, they face several shared challenges (Cunningham and Radcliffe, 2024):

Funding Sustainability: Ensuring long-term funding is one of the biggest hurdles for Baby Bonds programs. While states like Connecticut have guaranteed funding for at least 12 years, future administrations who may have different political views or priorities or experience economic downturns could jeopardize the financial, political, and administrative support for these programs.

To address these risks, Connecticut illustrates one effective approach. By establishing a dedicated trust fund, Connecticut helps ensure that funds are insulated from future political changes and budget reallocations. This model provides a framework for other jurisdictions to secure and protect a dedicated long-term funding source that can avoid program disruptions.

Eligibility Criteria: States typically use Medicaid eligibility or income thresholds to identify families for baby bond programs. However, these criteria could exclude certain groups who still face significant financial hardship, such as children of immigrants, families slightly above the income threshold, and those eligible for, but not enrolled in, Medicaid. Moreover, historically universal programs (like Social Security) have proven to be more efficient and more politically sustainable than means-tested programs.

Account Structure: States must design Baby Bonds accounts to maximize growth potential while maintaining flexibility and ease of administration by using diversified investment strategies, minimizing administrative costs, implementing automatic enrollment, providing substantial initial endowments, and balancing restrictions with flexibility for wealth-building purposes.

Use Restrictions: Most baby bond programs limit the use of funds to specific wealth-building activities. There's an ongoing debate about whether recipients should have more flexibility in how they use their Baby Bonds once they reach adulthood.

Financial Education: Several States require recipients to complete a financial literacy course before accessing funds. However, there is mixed evidence on the long-term effectiveness of financial education programs. Proponents prefer 'financial coaching' or 'financial advising' to financial education, support that many wealthy people use to protect and grow their wealth.

Long-Term Impact: The full economic benefits of Baby Bonds programs won't be realized for many years, so it will be decades before we have evidence-based data on effectiveness. Nearer term, it may be useful to consider earlier impacts of baby bonds as discussed below.

Anticipated Impacts of Baby Bonds on Wealth, Health, and Economic Rights

The potential impacts of Baby Bonds are profound. By targeting wealth inequality at its root, the policy could significantly improve economic outcomes for communities that have been prevented from being full participants in the economy, with multiplier effects on the economy and society. A 2019 study by Naomi Zewde estimates that a nationwide Baby Bonds program could reduce the wealth gap between young White and Black Americans by up to 80 percent. For example, the median wealth of young Black Americans could increase from just $2,900 to $57,845, offering a significant step toward closing the racial wealth gap (Zewde 2019).

A 2024 Urban Institute report which models the impact of a federal Baby Bonds program on family wealth, student debt, home equity, and retirement savings across gender, race, and ethnicity projects that:

- **All American families with children born between 2024 and 2048 would experience an increase in wealth**. The average account balance at age 18 would be $26,000 for Black people, $27,000 for Hispanic people, and $18,000 for White people.
- **There would be a reduction in the racial wealth gap**. *Without* Baby Bonds, the researchers project that in 2042–2046, the median White family would have 2.4 times the wealth of the median Black and Hispanic families. *With* Baby Bonds, White families were projected to have 2.1 times the median wealth of Black families and 1.9 times the median wealth of Hispanic families, a narrower racial wealth divide.
- **There would be a reduction in the total amount of debt held by student loan borrowers** at age 45 and would decrease the share of people that take on student loans, with greater impacts on loans for Black and Hispanic people.
- **There would be an increase in home equity accumulation** among those that use the funds to buy a home, with greater impacts on Black and Hispanic people, especially for Black women.

Beyond wealth creation, the policy could have broader social and economic impacts. Increased access to education and homeownership could improve health outcomes and reduce economic disparities, and at state and federal levels, additional tax revenue will be generated.

The psychological and health impacts of Baby Bonds should not be underestimated. Knowing that a child has access to a substantial capital endowment can positively influence family planning and aspirations from birth. It changes the narrative around what's possible for low-income families, potentially affecting health, educational, and career goals from an early age. This shift can have ripple effects throughout a child's development well before the funds become available (Cunningham and Radcliffe, 2024).

The Connection between Health and Wealth

The pandemic brought to light the harm to physical, emotional, and social well-being that a lack of wealth can inflict on American families. Historically, families who are more likely to experience the fallout from economic or health crises are disproportionately non-White families with low levels of wealth. Those with less resources are exposed to greater health, environmental, and financial risks—and already face higher rates of uninsurance and underinsurance, residential and occupational segregation, housing vulnerability, and job loss (Federal Reserve Board, 2023).

There is evidence that wealth is the strongest indicator of financial well-being and predictor of subsequent health. There is also increasing evidence of an association between health and lower debt and higher credit scores (Ettman, et al., 2020). According to Himmelstein and others, research suggests that wealth inequality in the United States is associated with significant inequities in survival; thus, policies that build wealth for those without may be an effective strategy to decrease inequities and improve population longevity (Himmelstein, 2024). Furthermore, Himmelstein's research suggests that a federal Baby Bonds proposal could *lead to longer life*:

> Consistent with prior research, we found that Black households have less wealth than other households. This pattern reflects structural racism in capital markets (e.g., compromised access to mortgages and business loans) and in labor markets (e.g., limiting Black workers' access to jobs with robust retirement benefits). These findings suggest that Black households might experience particularly large health benefits from society-wide wealth redistribution. Indeed, even the simulation of the most modest (baby bonds) proposal suggested that the longevity of Black adults could increase by 4.0 years.
>
> (Himmelstein, 2024a)

Additionally, having wealth:

- improves physical and mental health across all age groups throughout the life cycle (Marmot, 2015);
- allows people to not only cover ongoing expenses but also manage unexpected expenses, to plan for and invest in their futures, and to pass an inheritance on to their children (Shapiro, 2004); and
- protects health by enabling people to avoid unmanageable debt, to afford health-promoting goods, to spend more time on health-promoting activities, and to feel less anxious and in control of their lives (Marmot, 2015).

Building for the Future by Investing in All Families

Baby Bonds are just one example of the kind of bold, transformative policy the nation needs to address centuries of structural racism and economic exclusion and the resulting wealth divide in America. But they are not a silver bullet that will reverse generations of racial and economic injustice. A comprehensive, multifaceted approach must incorporate other key policies including (Cunningham and Paul, 2024):

- **Health Equity and Housing Policy**: To truly address inequality, public policy must ensure that people's basic needs, such as quality healthcare and adequate and affordable housing, are met. Policies that support healthcare for everyone and safe housing can provide the stability people need to thrive and accumulate wealth over time.
- **A Job Guarantee and Guaranteed Income**: Every individual should have the right to meaningful work and a baseline of income to meet their own needs. A job guarantee would provide secure employment for all, while a guaranteed income would ensure that no one is left behind in an increasingly precarious labor market. These policies work together to stabilize household incomes, reducing poverty and providing the foundation for wealth building.
- **Public Goods and Place-Based Policies**: Public goods such as public transit, quality education, and community infrastructure are powerful tools for closing racialized wealth gaps. Access to reliable transportation and well-resourced schools can significantly expand economic opportunities for marginalized communities. Place-based policies that invest in underdeveloped and historically excluded areas provide the foundation for equitable economic development at the local level, ensuring that growth benefits everyone, not just a select few.

Conclusion

As this chapter has shown, economics, politics, and intentional policies embedded in economic and social rights are essential for the construction of inclusive economies at the local and national levels. In the United States, relationship between economic policies, racialized politics, and systemic discrimination is exemplified in the racial wealth gap, which has persisted and worsened over generations. The racial wealth gap in the United States represents one of the most enduring and visible consequences of systemic racism and historical inequality. The disparity in wealth between racial groups highlights not only historical injustices, such as slavery and redlining, but also contemporary policies and practices that perpetuate inequality.

Yet these wealth disparities present today are not inevitable. They are the result of policy choices. Policies that are intentional about addressing racial and other types of discrimination are essential components of economic rights. One notable policy innovation that is gaining momentum in the United States is baby bonds, a powerful solution that invests seed capital in young adults who are born into poor economic circumstances so that they can pursue wealth-building activities like home ownership and entrepreneurship. Since Connecticut became the first state in the country to pass and fund Baby Bonds, another 20 States have either introduced or are seriously considering Baby Bonds legislation. Additionally, at the time of this writing, there are Baby Bonds pilot programs under construction or underway in 11 cities and States. Given the critical need to address wealth inequality and the impressive momentum at the State level, scaling up and embracing innovative solutions like Baby

Bonds in the United States and beyond can begin to build an economy that truly serves the needs of all people and generates economic inclusion and mobility. When we invest in people as the central resource of our economic system, we create the conditions for more just, healthy, and prosperous societies.

Bibliography

Bruenig, Matt. 2023. "Why the Connecticut Baby Bond Program Is Bad." *People's Policy Project*, June 30. Accessed January 24, 2025. https://www.peoplespolicyproject.org/2023/06/30/why-the-connecticut-baby-bond-program-is-bad/

Connecticut Office of the State Treasurer. 2021. *Connecticut Baby Bonds Initiative*. CT: Hartford.

Cunningham, Gary L., and David Radcliffe. 2024. "A Fair Shot for Every Child: The Nuts and Bolts of Baby Bonds." *Nonprofit Quarterly, December* 11, 2024.

Cunningham, Gary, and L. Paul. 2024. "Building an Economy With Purpose." *Nonprofit Quarterly*.

Du Bois, W. E. B. 1935. *Black Reconstruction in America, 1860–1880*. New York: Harcourt, Brace & Company.

Ettman, C. K., S. Galea, G. H. Cohen, and D. U. Himmelstein. 2020. "Association Between Wealth and Psychological Resilience in the US During the COVID-19 Pandemic." *JAMA Network Open* 3(10).

Federal Reserve. 2019. *Survey of Consumer Finances*.

Federal Reserve. 2023. "Report on the Economic Well-Being of U.S. Households." Accessed January 24, 2025. https://www.fedsearch.org/board_public/search?source=board_pub&text=Report+on+the+Economic+Well-Being+of+U.S.+Households%3A&submit=Search

Hamilton, Darrick. 2016. "The Racial Wealth Gap: Why Policy Matters." *Review of Black Political Economy* 43(1–2): 75–79.

Hamilton, Darrick, and S. Bisnath. 2024. "Racial and Gender Inclusion through Economic Policies Informed by Economic and Social Rights." *G 20 Paper*. https://t20brasil.org/en/pbs?nucleo_id=1%2F&page=4

Hamilton, Darrick, and W. A. Darity Jr. 2010a. "Can 'Baby Bonds' Eliminate the Racial Wealth Gap in the United States?" *Review of Black Political Economy* 37(3–4): 207–216.

Hamilton, Darrick, and W. A. Darity Jr. 2010b. "Can 'Baby Bonds' Eliminate the Racial Wealth Gap in Putative Post-Racial America?" *Review of Black Political Economy* 37(3–4): 207–216.

Himmelstein, D. U. 2024. "Medical Debt and Its Impact on Health and Well-Being in America." *JAMA Internal Medicine*. Accessed January 24, 2025. https://jamanetwork.com/journals/jamainternalmedicine/fullarticle/2814487

Markoff, Shira, David Radcliffe, and Darrick Hamilton. 2024. *A Brighter Future with Baby Bonds: How States and Cities Should Invest in Our Kids*. Washington, DC: Institute on Race, Power and Political Economy and Prosperity Now.

Marmot, Michael. 2015. *The Health Gap: The Challenge of an Unequal World*. New York: Bloomsbury Publishing.

May. 2011. "Excluded from Labor Protections." *dWhere Stories*. Accessed January 24, 2025. https://www.dwherstories.com/timeline/excluded-from-labor-protections

McGhee, Heather. 2021. *The Sum of Us: What Racism Costs Everyone and How We Can Prosper Together*. New York: One World.

Meiksins, Rob, and Steve Dubb. 2019. "How the New Deal Hardened Racial Wealth and Homeownership Inequities." *Nonprofit Quarterly, February* 26, 2019.

Oliver, M. L., and T. M. Shapiro. 1995. *Black Wealth/White Wealth: A New Perspective on Racial Inequality*. New York: Routledge.

Paine, Thomas. 1797. *Agrarian Justice*. Philadelphia: Printed by R. Folwell, for Benjamin Franklin Bache.

Pew Research Center. n.d. "Trends in Income and Wealth Inequality." Accessed January 24, 2025. https://www.pewresearch.org

Piketty, Thomas. 2013. *Capital in the Twenty-First Century*. Translated by Arthur Goldhammer. Cambridge, MA: Belknap Press of Harvard University Press.

Rothstein, Richard. 2017. *The Color of Law: A Forgotten History of How Our Government Segregated America*. New York: Liveright Publishing.

Russell, Erick. 2024. "Building Wealth for All: The Power of Baby Bonds in Connecticut." *Oliver*. Accessed January 24, 2025. https://nonprofitquarterly.org/building-wealth-for-all-the-power-of-baby-bonds-in-connecticut/

Shapiro, Thomas. 2004. *The Hidden Cost of Being African American: How Wealth Perpetuates Inequality*. New York: Oxford University Press.

Sherraden, Michael. 1991. *Assets and the Poor: A New American Welfare Policy*. Armonk, NY: M.E. Sharpe.

Urban Institute. 2024. "Modeling the Impact of a Federal Baby Bonds Program." Accessed January 24, 2025. https://www.urban.org/research/publication/modeling-impact-federal-baby-bonds-program

Zewde, Naomi. 2019. "Universal Baby Bonds Reduce Black-White Wealth Inequality, Progressively Raise Net Worth of All Young Adults." *Review of Black Political Economy* 46 (2): 123–141.

Index

Pages in *italics* refer to figures, pages in **bold** refer to tables, and pages followed by "n" refer to notes.

Made in the USA
Monee, IL
12 November 2026

0b4c9c1a-3ed4-4ad5-b95e-b1dde3df5974R02